Vernacular Rights Cultures

Vernacular Rights Cultures offers a bold challenge to the dominant epistemologies and political practices of global human rights. It argues that decolonising global human rights calls for a serious epistemic accounting of the historically and politically specific encounters with human rights, and of the forms of world-making that underpin the stakes and struggles for rights and human rights around the globe. Through combining ethnographic investigations with political theory and philosophy, it goes beyond critiquing the Eurocentrism of global human rights, in order to document and examine the different political imaginaries, critical conceptual vocabularies, and gendered political struggles for rights and justice that animate subaltern mobilisations in 'most of the world'. *Vernacular Rights Cultures* demonstrates that these subaltern struggles call into being different and radical ideas of justice, politics and citizenship, and open up different possibilities and futures for human rights.

Sumi Madhok is Professor of Political Theory and Gender Studies at the London School of Economics and Political Science. She is the author of *Rethinking Agency: Gender, Developmentalism and Rights* (2013) and co-editor of *Gender, Agency and Coercion* (2013) and *The SAGE Handbook of Feminist Theory* (2014).

Vernacular Rights Cultures

The Politics of Origins, Human Rights and Gendered Struggles for Justice

Sumi Madhok

Shaftesbury Road, Cambridge CB2 8EA, United Kingdom

One Liberty Plaza, 20th Floor, New York, NY 10006, USA

477 Williamstown Road, Port Melbourne, VIC 3207, Australia

314–321, 3rd Floor, Plot 3, Splendor Forum, Jasola District Centre, New Delhi – 110025, India

103 Penang Road, #05–06/07, Visioncrest Commercial, Singapore 238467

Cambridge University Press is part of Cambridge University Press & Assessment, a department of the University of Cambridge.

We share the University's mission to contribute to society through the pursuit of education, learning and research at the highest international levels of excellence.

www.cambridge.org
Information on this title: www.cambridge.org/9781009423939

First published 2021
First paperback edition 2024

A catalogue record for this publication is available from the British Library

Library of Congress Cataloging-in-Publication data
Names: Madhok, Sumi, author.
Title: Vernacular rights cultures : the politics of origins, human rights, and gendered struggles for justice / Sumi Madhok.
Description: New York : Cambridge University Press, 2021. | Includes bibliographical references and index.
Identifiers: LCCN 2020050762 (print) | LCCN 2020050763 (ebook) | ISBN 9781108832625 (hardback) | ISBN 9781108961844 (ebook)
Subjects: LCSH: Human rights--Government policy. | Ontology--History. | Social justice.
Classification: LCC JC571 .M3244 2021 (print) | LCC JC571 (ebook) | DDC 323--dc23
LC record available at https://lccn.loc.gov/2020050762
LC ebook record available at https://lccn.loc.gov/2020050763

ISBN   978-1-108-83262-5   Hardback
ISBN   978-1-009-42393-9   Paperback

For Alaka Madhok, Ireel Jasmin and Tara Leichil

three extraordinary women

Contents

Acknowledgements

I write my acknowledgements at a time that moves in rhythm with the anxieties and urgencies of the pandemic. In this radically rearranged time, life, living and work, I am even more deeply appreciative of the innumerable acts of thoughtfulness, kindness, encouragement, generosity and care that has enabled me to stay with the book over the many years it has taken to write it. And it is with particular joy and pleasure that I acknowledge my debts, and not least those that have been accumulated during the most recent time of writing this book, a time that has coincided with that of the pandemic

I must begin with a grateful acknowledgement of an Andrew W. Mellon Postdoctoral fellowship in 2005, as that is when it all began. A couple of years later, a small grant from the British Academy enabled fieldwork in India and Pakistan, and this fieldwork was allowed to deepen through a grant from the LSE Annual Fund. And, finally, a Leverhulme Research Fellowship during 2015–16, together with some sabbatical leave from my teaching responsibilities allowed me to go back to the field, and to also weave the different strands of the research together. The book's insistence on bringing ethnographic sensibilities to bear on theoretical and conceptual work could only become possible through the attentiveness and generosity of so many people. Over two decades, the indomitable, inspirational and courageous Kavita Srivastava has unfailingly provided insightful and important insights into my fieldwork, and also piercingly intelligent and astute conversations on rights movements. For many other such thoughtful conversations both in and off the field in India and Pakistan, I am also grateful to Aasim Sajjad Akhtar, Hamseera Bano, Amitabh Behar, Bharat Bhati and Marudhar Ganga Society Jodhpur, Kiran Dubey, Mohini Devi, Bhanwari Devi, Harmi Bai, Napi Bai, Chandan Jain, Piyush Javeria, Dharam Chand Kher, P. L. Mimroth, Aparna Sahay, Sunny Sebastian, Sujit Sarkar, Bharat Vishakha, Kotra Adivasi Vikas Manch, Sister Alveena and Sasvika Society in Ajmer, and *sarpanch* Tej Singh and *sarpanch* Narayan Singh. I am particularly grateful to the Centre for Dalit Human Rights in Jaipur for making their publications and resource materials available to me.

I have been very privileged to have very generous and close readers of my work, and, for this I am indebted to Robin Dunford, Mary Evans, Clare Hemmings, Marsha Henry, Niraja Gopal Jayal, Kimberly Hutchings, Engin F. Isin, Shail

Mayaram, Kate Nash, Diane Perrons, Anne Phillips, Shirin M. Rai, Leticia Sabsay, Wendy Sigle, Kalpana Wilson and Sadie Wearing. As the book was nearing completion, I had the wonderful honour of having two book chapters read at two research workshops at the LSE in 2018 and 2019, one led by Sherene H. Razack and another by Isabella Bakker. I am very grateful to both for their careful engagements with the book, and also to the workshop participants, especially, Emma Spruce, Ece Kobaciak, Jenny Chanfreau, Kate Millar and Georgina Waylen. Some of the book's arguments were also presented at the universities of Nottingham, Edinburgh, Warwick, Delhi, Frankfurt, LSE, Lund, Uppsala, Tampere, Helsinki, Oxford and Loughborough, and the book is richer for these engagements. I have also been fortunate to receive research assistance from Azmat Bashir, Billy Holzberg, Julia Hartviksen and Nazish Zahoor, all brilliant and careful researchers. Billy Holzberg read the first full draft, and his insights and careful reading made a real difference to the subsequent ones. Hazel Johnstone, Sarah Quraishi, Olga Nunez Miret, Ania Plomien, Lindsay Simmonds, Priya Raghavan, Nour Almazidi and Nazanin Shahrokni gave generous advice and encouragement at many crucial moments.

The intense phase of writing the book coincided with a new MSc course on 'Gender and Human Rights' that I introduced at the LSE in 2017. And teaching the course has been a real joy and a privilege, mostly because of the wonderful students the course attracts every year. And this year, the extraordinary acts of care, kindness, generosity and critical thinking of my students left me quite undone, and I acknowledge all their generosity, and especially the music playlists they collectively curated for me during the pandemic, and which became the soundtracks for the last stages of writing this book. In particular, I want to thank Bemnet Agata, Cecilia Cordova-Liendo, Tama Knight, Armand Azra bin Azlira, Ajoke Bodunde, Paromita Bathija, Isabel Medem, Kylie Andrews, Corina Rueda, Erica Vigano, Sofia Ercolessi, Philip Edge, Emma Hossein and Valentina Contreras.

Qudsiya Ahmed and her team at Cambridge University Press have been a gift, and I am grateful to them for their many efforts in bringing this book into the world.

My family in Delhi, Jaipur and Sheffield have been wonderful pillars of strength. My mother Alaka Madhok's generosity of spirit, and unwavering insistence on individual and collective action towards making a concrete and material difference in the world, is an inspiration. Rajat Madhok and Deeva Singh are the best friends and fellow travellers one could hope for. And, Jayanta, Jasmin and Tara show me generous possibilities for living and loving in a kinder, equal and a more just world every day.

Sumi Madhok
Sheffield, October 2020

1 An Introduction

Vernacular Rights Cultures and Decolonising Human Rights

Haq is the Arabic word for a right. It is also the word for a right in Urdu, Persian, Turkish and Hindustani. The first recorded existence of *haq* can be traced to classical Hebrew and it is also found in the older Semitic languages such as Aramaic and Mendian. Over the centuries, the word has travelled across the globe to become the principal word to signify a right in South Asia, the Middle East and North Africa. *Haq* or *hukk* appears in Hindustani and Urdu lexicon through the influence of Persian in the Indian subcontinent where it cuts across geographical, religious and linguistic boundaries to become the principal word deployed to claim rights by subaltern groups in northwestern India and Pakistan. Not surprisingly, in the course of its travels, it has gathered complex meanings and iterations that inform political imaginaries, subjectivities and political cultures of rights and rights claim-making. What can the presence of *haq* in the vernacular and its use tell us about contemporary articulations, practices and discourses of rights and human rights in 'most of the world'? What can it tell us about the different contexts of rights, meanings of rights, and about the conceptual languages of rights in 'other' parts of the globe? What does an attention to *haq* tell us about the forms of rights politics, subjectivities and the processes of political subjectivation these engender? And, furthermore, what can it tell us about the 'other' political cultures, imaginaries, contestations and struggles for rights? How can scholarly investigations of contemporary struggles for *haq* inform global human rights scholarship? And how useful is the global human rights framework for conceptually capturing political struggles for *haq*?

In South Asia, *haq* is a key literal and conceptual term used to signify a right or an entitlement in contemporary subaltern political struggles. Many at the forefront of these multitudinous subaltern rights mobilisations in the Indian subcontinent are engaged in struggles for their 'life rights'. While some are resisting precarity and dispossession heralded in by neoliberal developmentalism and its championing of privatisation of natural resources, others are struggling to redefine the substantive content of existing formal constitutional guarantees and are mobilising to put in place new and expanded entitlements. What different stories of human rights would we tell if we produced human rights scholarship from the standpoint of the stakes and the struggles of these subaltern groups at the frontline of human rights mobilisations demanding *haq* in 'most of the world'?[1] What difference would such a standpoint make to the stories of human rights that we are accustomed to telling and hearing? What would human rights scholarship look like? What kinds of disciplinary and scholarly labours would it involve? And what kinds of epistemic erasures of human rights politics would this disrupt and what kinds of new possibilities for imagining and expanding rights and human rights would it bring into view?

By asking these questions, this book produces a perspectival shift in the study of human rights—a shift in standpoint that is explicitly oriented towards the study of vernacular rights cultures. The vernacular political cultures of rights documented in this book are neither 'modes of literary' (Pollock 2000: 593), nor are they 'print cultures' (Mir 2011) or indeed, involved in 'ways of doing things with texts' (Pollock 2000: 594). They are active sites of subaltern politics, struggles and contestations over rights and human rights. And, although, there is some literary production at these sites,[2] this book predominantly tracks and documents the oral narratives of subaltern groups engaged in contemporary struggles for rights entitlements in order to provide an epistemic accounting of the political imaginaries, gendered subjectivities and critical vocabularies of rights and political agency that inform these struggles. By all accounts, these are non-elite, particular and unprivileged sites of rights articulation and politics. They are therefore, not the 'universal', the 'cosmopolitan' and the 'global' but rather signal the unequal epistemic power relations between global human rights and the politics of vernacular rights cultures, and this is why the latter are 'the vernacular' and not 'the global'. Vernacular rights cultures do not 'emerge' 'but are "made"'[3] through subaltern political struggles that are intersectional, gendered and intensely conflictual. In the book, I refer to the subaltern as a specifically material, gendered and epistemic location in historically specific power relations that are 'relational', 'intersectional' and 'dynamic' (Nilsen and Roy 2015).[4] As historically specific, gendered and material locations and relations, the subaltern, as a group and as a politics, have increasingly registered their presence as resistors, activists and also as grassroots mobilisations[5] but rarely as epistemic sites with their specific political imaginaries, critical vocabularies of world-making and conceptual languages of rights and entitlements. And therefore, even while subaltern historical and political presence is increasingly noted, their epistemic presence is often actively ignored or wilfully refused and erased.

A focus on vernacular rights cultures enables the following: First, to attend to the urgent problem of the lack of conceptual diversity by facilitating the production of conceptual work from and in different geographical and 'non-standard' background contexts and conditions, that is, contexts outside those in which concepts are standardly produced, described and visualised. If anything, building conceptual diversity is *the* key intellectual project of vernacular rights cultures. Second, to shift dominant epistemic and methodological perspectives, from telling mainly state-centric stories about histories of institutional and legal progress of human rights and about the conduct of nation states and large organisations in the international arena to examining the multiple and differential circuits of geopolitical power within which global human rights operate. Third, it allows a focus on the different conceptual languages invoked by subaltern groups to articulate entitlements. Fourth, it facilitates assessments of how rights operate politically and the political cultures they produce at different geographical locations. And, finally, it allows to put in place serious epistemic, conceptual and methodological attention to the different political imaginaries, gendered relations and citizenship practices and subjectivities that come into being as a result of subaltern rights politics. This book orients this shift in perspective from exclusively institutionally focused studies on human rights to the actual work that rights and human rights politics does in subaltern settings in 'most of the world': a shift in perspective towards the study of vernacular rights cultures.

The word *haq* provides me with my cue for studying vernacular rights cultures. For nearly two decades, I have been tracking the deployment of *haq* through the deserts of Rajasthan in northwest India where different subaltern groups have been mobilising to demand rights to food, public information, gender and caste equality and employment from the state, and Adivasi[6] groups are demanding rights to sacred and ancestral forests, streams and lands. The word *haq*, however, does not recognise national borders and formations; if anything, it undermines them. Consequently, I have been ethnographically tracking the deployment of *haq* within subaltern mobilisations in India and in Pakistan; from Rajasthan's eastern regions, which are mostly rocky, thorn scrub forested and sand filled terrains to the Aravalli hills in its south, where the dry tropical forests burst into thick lush undergrowth in the monsoons.

And, tracking it further across the border and into the green fertile plains of the Punjab in Pakistan, a land fed by South Asia's five large rivers, where the word *haq* is mobilised by very poor marginal peasants, who are taking on the great might of Pakistan's military over their struggle for land ownership to emerge as the most significant working class struggle against the military in postcolonial Pakistan.

Through such an ethnographic tracking of *haq* across different subaltern mobilisations in India and Pakistan, this book puts together a conceptual account of *haq* and tells a different story of human rights. This different story of human rights documents the different political imaginaries of *haq* that animate rights struggles of subaltern groups in the region, and the ways in which these disrupt, speak back, expand and also help decolonise global human rights talk. In particular, it documents the political imaginaries of *haq* that underpin the claims for rights or *haq* articulated by subaltern and very poor women, including Dalit[7] and Adivasi women, within grassroots mobilisations demanding rights to food, employment, public information, accountability and land rights in rural movements in India and Pakistan. Tracking *haq* across India and Pakistan allows us to view the dispossession, exclusion and privilege that uphold contemporary power relations in the region and also the nature of resistance mounted by subaltern groups against these. The deployment of rights and human rights by these subaltern groups show up the legal and political promise of rights but also their fraught, conflictual, gendered and precarious nature to reveal the specific configurations of power within which rights and human rights operate, and the particular work they do in different historical contexts. A gender lens in studying vernacular rights cultures is vital, not least because demands for gender equality or *haq* for women and for those identifying outside the binary gender divide is a question that almost invariably needs to be begged separately and seldom occurs organically within citizen mobilisations. Moreover, bringing a gendered perspective is to demonstrate not only an awareness of the power relations that govern political struggles but also of the intersectional and conflictual nature of rights politics—a politics that for marginalised groups is always a matter of political struggle.

Decolonising Human Rights

In the last two decades, human rights have captured the scholarly imagination. In some critical strands of this contemporary human rights discourse, however, one is able to discern an unmistakable strain of wariness and reflexivity. The wariness owes in large part to the paradoxical, alienating, exclusionary and politically conservative effects of global human rights, and the growing reflexivity can be traced to increasing calls for more empirical research on human rights and for studying the different normative meanings and practices of rights in different contexts. In some sections, this reflexivity has also led to calls to decolonise human rights (Gilroy 2010; Suárez-Krabbe 2016; Dunford 2016; Maldonado-Torres 2017). The question of decolonising human rights is part of a larger project to decolonise academia and academic scholarship. There are different views on what decolonising might mean and involve. For some scholars, decolonisation is a noun and is not a 'metaphor' for 'social justice projects' (Tuck and Yang 2012: 1). Here, decolonisation is very clearly associated with the question of Indigenous sovereignty and involves the 'repatriation of Indigenous land and life.' Others understand decolonisation as challenging the racialist and hetero-capitalist imperialist formations underpinning academia. In this regard, their intervention is to produce ethical, epistemic and structural transformations in the production of knowledge (Smith 1999; Wynter 2003; de Sousa Santos 2007; Maldonado-Torres 2007, 2017; Gilroy 2010; Lugones 2010; Mignolo 2012; Connell 2014; Mbembe 2016; Mignolo and Walsh 2018; Cusicanqui 2012). In recent years, the location of knowledge production has emerged as an important question in debates that seek to decolonise knowledge production with some scholars explicitly bringing their location in the 'colonial present' under epistemic and ethical scrutiny to ask: 'how do we understand our locations in the colonial present, as we contemplate and work towards the imperative of decolonization?' (Vimalassery et al. 2016: 1). Others call for a re-location of theory building to and from the Global South (Comaroff and Comaroff 2012; Connell 2014) and the 'third world' (Mignolo 2018). I acknowledge these important and critically significant interventions towards 'doing theory from the global south' but also suggest that the problem, however, lies not so much at the level of theory production, for that simply reflects on the patterns that one looks at and assumes, but at the level of concepts. In other words, it is not so much the lack of diversity in theory production that is the problem but the lack of diversity of conceptual production in different parts of the globe which constitutes the difficulty at hand. There is a need for different and a wide-ranging set of concepts that are able to describe different worlds, practices and ethics and, therefore, different concepts need to be in hand before the work of theory can proceed to describe the different patterns of thinking that emerge from 'most of the world'. For quite simply, there are not enough concepts in place to produce theorised accounts of phenomena and of different and historically specific encounters with the world.

But what does it mean to decolonise human rights? In this book, I argue that the work of decolonising human rights, which is mostly engaged in tracking different genealogies and historical trajectories of rights, must be supplemented by conceptual work aimed at capturing the gendered stakes and struggles over rights and human rights in 'most of the world', without losing sight of the global fields of power in which they operate and the power relations they put in place and reproduce. This attention to conceptual work on rights and human rights is crucial if we are to shift the epistemic centre of human rights talk and politics. Now, of course, to produce alternative genealogies of human rights is to produce a critique of the Eurocentered nature of historiography and of philosophical discourses of human rights and their reflection within human rights politics, laws and institutions (Gilroy 2010; Maldonado-Torres 2017). These interventions are very important and significant in drawing attention to the epistemic, institutional and normative power of global human rights. However, we also require a theoretical framework that is able to capture the generative and productive nature of rights and human rights discourses: to produce not only political struggles on the ground but also particular political imaginaries, subjectivities and gendered relations that contest and challenge oppressive practices and relations and importantly, generate new visions of justice. To insist on the conceptual descriptions of human rights in 'most of the world' is to insist on the productivity of rights; the two are hardly separate projects, even if they might have a slightly different focus.

But how to conceptually capture the politics of rights and human rights in 'most of the world'? And how to undertake such a task and why does it matter? Engaging these questions seriously is to commit oneself to telling those *other* stories of rights and human rights; stories that fall outside of the hegemonic institutionally focused accounts of global human rights. The feminist theorist Clare Hemmings insightfully reminds us of the 'importance of telling stories differently'. Stories matter, she writes, 'in part because of the ways in which they intersect with wider institutionalizations ...' (Hemmings 2011: 1). This book commits itself to telling different stories of rights and human rights differently. The *other* stories of rights and human rights that appear in this book are neither uncritically celebratory nor are they outrightly dismissive of rights and human rights, but seek to excavate instead the power structures and epistemic relations that produce such binary responses. These other stories refuse originary frameworks and premises with their ascription of epistemic and political agency to nation states and global human rights organisations mostly based in the Global North. While recognising that nation states are vital to meeting human rights obligations, they also contend that scholarly judgements and narratives of rights and human rights do not begin and end with accounts detailing with minute precision the myriad ways in which nation states perform realpolitik over human rights. Instead, these stories insist on holding nation states to account for their doing of human rights. These are stories that refuse Eurocentric and originary discourses of human rights to establish a different starting point: they bring into view subaltern mobilisations that demand rights and human rights taking place in 'most of the world'. Through this epistemic standpoint, they engage in a serious and sustained critique of Eurocentrism of global human rights discourse while insisting on the productivity and creative dynamism of human rights struggles and politics in 'most of the world'. Finally, these other stories do not focus on the 'translations of global human rights' alone but insist on documenting the particular political imaginaries, gendered subjectivities and political cultures of rights that come into being as a result of struggles over rights and human rights. In short, these are the stories of vernacular rights cultures—and, are also the stories that this book sets out to tell.

In particular, stories of vernacular rights cultures eschew three hegemonic stories of human rights. Consider, for instance, how we have become accustomed to speaking and hearing about human rights in terms of three dominant visions: a particular temporality linked to their 'origin'; of a particular rights bearing subjectivity and legal personhood; and finally of particular institutional structures and forms of institutional activity. That human rights originate in the West and that human rights belong to, operate from and perform for the West are a standard preoccupation of both celebratory and critical human rights accounts. In effect, this politics of origins is the key framework for thinking of human rights—shared by not only its celebrators and detractors but also by critical and progressive scholarship on human rights. The politics of origins is not without effects: it puts in place particular forms of racial, epistemic and political erasures. The story of the politics of origins is first and foremost a racial story. As scholars have noted, institutional histories of racism haunt historical, philosophical and legal accounts of human rights.[8] In more recent times, the politics of origins contributes to eclipsing the role of anticolonial movements against imperial power, preferring to focus on the role of Western lawmakers and peacemakers,[9] but also in epistemically silencing the scale and momentum of contemporary rights mobilisations and claim-making across the globe. Its other epistemic effects include the production of theoretical foreclosures and binary 'cultural' rights talk. These are exemplified by the binary distinctions and hermetically sealed epistemic borders that are readily sketched between what are seen as 'Asian cultural values' and Western human rights, between universalist ideas of human rights and culturally particularist preferences that do not rate human rights, between choosing either economic development or human rights, and so forth. The binarism of rights talk has led to a spectacular failure to pay attention to the forms of rights politics, the political cultures and the modes of activism engaged in by subaltern groups in 'most of the world'—not least by nation states who have deployed the binarisms of rights talk to silence democratic aspirations to great effect. The lack of epistemic agency and authority accorded to rights mobilisations in the Global South has led to a widespread time–space provincialism in human rights scholarship with its predominant focus on post–World War II Anglo-Euro-American stories of the growth and spread of global governance, international law and international institutions and of the 'global' histories and politics of globalisation, neoliberalism and global non-governmental organisations (NGOs), and, more recently, of accounts explicitly focused on the pursuit of global justice and the growth of Western sponsored international humanitarianism. These dominant stories of human rights that populate conservative and liberal accounts but are also rehearsed by radical democratic theorists (Balibar 2002; Rancière 2004; Brown 2015) have led to a widespread acceptance of a depoliticisation thesis that not only silences and eclipses accounts of the ongoing mobilisations for rights in 'most of the world' but has also resulted in the absence of at least two kinds of enquiries. First, it has meant that (human) rights mobilisations in 'most of the world' have yet to centrally preoccupy scholarship on human rights within radical democratic theory and political philosophy, which continue to be predominantly focused on the Euro-American experience of the 'right to have rights' and on the paradoxes and aporias resulting from the founding or originary moments of republicanism (that is, on the abstract theoretical and philosophical problems set off by the French and the American revolutions). Second, despite the growing awareness for a need for scholarly work on human rights and rights in different parts of the globe, there exists a striking lack of scholarship that is explicitly aimed at not only tracking alternative genealogies of human rights but also producing conceptual work that captures the stakes and struggles over rights and human rights besides being able to critically engage, challenge and speak back to the scholarly field of global human rights. For instance, it is certainly the case that, in recent years, there have been powerful critiques of teleological and originary histories of human rights. However, these have not opened the door to an acknowledgement of 'other' human rights stories and struggles and, importantly, to how these other stories might expand theoretical conceptual and empirical thinking on the meanings and work that human rights do in different parts of the world.

Vernacular Rights Cultures sidesteps the politics of origins. As a conceptual intervention, the lens of vernacular rights cultures refuses the theoretical foreclosures and binary deadlock of mainstream discussions on human rights to argue that vernacular rights cultures are not wholly derivative from or entirely oppositional to Western notions and conventions of human rights or, indeed, entirely discrete in form. This is not an argument of there being hermetically sealed or 'pure', authentic and orginary rights traditions. In fact, quite the contrary. These stories of vernacular rights cultures are made and remade through interlocking relations that are historically, productively, intimately, and coercively produced and experienced. They come into being within specific historical encounters through which their contemporary meanings are forged, including encounters with the forms of anticolonial nationalism and legal settlements of the postcolonial state, with developmentalism, bureaucratisation, neoliberalism, and the proliferation of the non-state organisations advocating 'human rights'. Therefore, the claims of vernacular rights cultures are not claims to purity or authenticity.

If anything, the ubiquitous use of *haq*, an Arabic, Persian and Urdu word, invoked by subaltern groups who speak a range of different languages— Punjabi, Rajasthani, Hindi, Bhili and Bhilodi—renders this claim to purity and authenticity somewhat weak. I must however, make clear here that although, the work on vernacular rights cultures draws on important insights of critical Indigenous scholarship, there are crucial differences between them, not least because they respond to very different historical relations of coloniality. Consequently, the critique of the politics of origins advanced in this book is directed specifically at the stories that global human rights likes telling about itself, and is, therefore, a different argument from those of 'origin' and 'prior' theorised by theorists of Indigeneity and from their critiques of the settler colonial state (Bruyneel 2007; Povinelli 2011; Simpson 2014).

Alongside the question of origins and temporality of human rights, a second dominant strand of human rights storytelling focuses on a particular rights bearing subjectivity and a sovereign legal and moral personhood that is meant to embody the subject of human rights. But who are the subjects of human rights?

Are the subjects of human rights individuals or are they nation states? Scholars point out that while human rights offer protections for individual rights, it is also the case that human rights have been '*made* empty words by the relentless focus on the nation state as the only conceivable form of political community' (Phillips 2015: 67, emphasis added). And, who is this individual or human of human rights? The 'human' of human rights is often seen to correspond to an eighteenth century idea of an unencumbered legal person who is a world citizen and who owes allegiance not to parochial identities, attachments and feelings but rather to cosmopolitan ideals of world citizenship. But as influential feminist, postcolonial, anticolonial, Black, queer, and Indigenous scholarship has shown, the concrete human of human rights is a binary and cisgendered, heterosexual, unencumbered, possessive, propertied, able bodied, white male abstracted from all relations and commitments, and predominantly located in the Global North.[10] Scholars have drawn links between this exclusive figure of the human and the exclusionary histories and politics of human rights. Powerfully noting that the history of human rights is a history of exclusions, they point out that the routinely invoked self-evidence of human rights is, in effect, a fraught, exclusivist and a contested claim, one that is supported by neither historical evidence (James 1989; Trouillot 1995) nor philosophical argument (Wynter 2003). And, furthermore, that the history and philosophy of human rights has neither been universally applicable to all humans and, nor has it actually ever been applied without qualifications (James 1939; Trouillot 1995; Wynter 2003; Phillips 2015; Suárez-Krabbe 2016). Indeed, ideas of human rights flourished alongside colonialism, empires bankrolled by slavery, indentured labour and unspeakable violence on slaves and colonial subjects. And, they continue to flourish today amidst existing forms of coloniality, settler colonialism and modern forms of slavery, imperialism and racism. If anything, where human rights have been won, it has hardly been as a result of the persuasive strength of their ideals alone or as a result of inevitable historical progress set in motion by human rights but rather as the outcome of long histories of struggles—histories that have been forced into silence (Trouillot 1995).

Quite unlike the subjects of human rights, the subjects of vernacular rights cultures are not 'world citizens', nor are they only nation states. They are neither privileged nor propertied but are precarious, very poor, racialised, bureaucratically marked and surveilled subjects many of whom are Dalit and Adivasi groups. While the book documents the rights encounters and experiences of these subjects mostly with the nation state, the latter is neither the chief protagonist in this story nor are nation states the only subjects of human rights here. By not centring the nation state as the only subject of human rights is however, not to be led by a form of 'state phobia' (Dhawan 2015: 51) but rather to recognise those 'other' subjects of rights who have been marginalised by the nation state and global human rights scholarship, and who encounter and experience the state in myriad intimate, coercive and agential ways.[11]

Finally, the stories in this book are not stories of humanitarian actors who animate contemporary stories of human rights by enacting the rights of the 'victims' of human rights (Rancière 2004: 307). Humanitarianism, as a 'moral and political project' (Ticktin 2014: 273), encompasses a range of actors, events, spaces, violence, ethics and politics. Although a fragmented and a heterogenous enterprise, the last 30 years have witnessed humanitarianism's moral project of care and rescue increasingly underwritten by military support and intervention, leading scholars to describe the contemporary global context as one of the 'humanitarian present' (Weizman 2011: 1), where human rights, humanitarianism, international human rights law and military interventions share aims and objectives for 'calculating and managing' contemporary violence (Weizman 2011: 4). Together they constitute an 'integrated' humanitarian–political–legal approach favoured by the United Nations (UN) and other international NGOs (INGOs) which converts refugees from indistinguishable 'victims' and 'objects of compassion' into an indistinguishable mass of 'unwanted and undesirable' 'migrants' to be confined, managed and administered in the refugee camps that keep them at a safe distance from the West. A striking consequence of these camps being set up and managed 'outside' Europe has been the steady disappearance of the 'refugee' from Europe's borders and from its political discourse, and of the appearance of the figure of the 'migrant' in its place. This figure of the 'migrant' performs important symbolic, legal and political work for Europe—of releasing Europe from structural and political accountability for the humanitarian emergencies brought on and worsened by its military interventions while at the same time also temporarily discharging Europe from its responsibility under the refugee conventions. These contemporary humanitarian assemblages are hardly critique-free zones, and scholarly arguments rage on over the politics of humanitarianism that refuses difficult questions to do with structural inequalities and injustices (de Waal 1997; Ticktin 2014), preferring to engage instead in a politics of 'moral sentiments' focused on suffering and misfortune (Fassin 2011: 1). Many of these critiques of humanitarianism mostly focus on the 'antipolitics'

(Ferguson 1994; Ticktin 2014: 277) of humanitarian interventions, and on the operations of international aid and refugee administrations across different sites. There are also however, other critical and politically generative accounts of humanitarianism, which emphasise the 'politics of the displaced' (Weizman 2011: 61) and provide important insights into humanitarianism as a 'condition', where refugees 'enact the politics of living' (Feldman 2012: 155), and negotiate competing demands of humanitarianism and development (Gabiam 2012).

This book does not travel in the direction of either of these three dominant narratives but rather shifts our theoretical, conceptual and empirical focus to subaltern mobilisations on the ground that produce vernacular rights cultures. These political cultures of rights arise as subaltern mobilisations and movements make demands for rights that are inflected by their particular literal and conceptual languages, cultures, histories and political contexts of struggles. Vernacular rights cultures produce rights claims directed at the state and through different modes of 'acts of citizenship' (Isin and Nielsen 2008: 2) change not only the forms of citizenship through which rights are enacted but also the content of rights themselves.

To summarise, viewing rights politics in 'most of the world' through the framework of vernacular rights cultures offers a lens through which the complexity and dynamism of rights-based mobilisations might be analytically captured—not simply as those which are mimetic and engaged in the translation, enactment and localisation of global human rights but rather as those which have their specific languages of rights and entitlements grounded in specific political imaginaries, justificatory premises and subjectivities. In other words, vernacular rights cultures are productive and generative: they generate both a distinct set of rights and distinct practices through which rights are delivered, but also transform the rights that are inscribed in constitutions and political imaginaries.

Accordingly, the study of vernacular rights cultures is the study of the forms that rights politics takes in 'most of the world' and of the ways it disrupts hegemonic global human rights talk. It is a conceptual, epistemic and empirical project, which refuses the binary deadlock between triumphant universalism and a regressive cultural relativism produced by the pervasive politics of origins and the time–space provincialism that governs global human rights.

Instead, it enables a conceptual optic into the 'active' empirical, epistemic and political life of rights and into the specific politics that drives struggles for rights in different locations. At stake therefore, in displacing the politics of origins and its time- space provincialism are questions of epistemic authority, agency and democratic politics. Thinking in terms of vernacular rights cultures enables us to do the following: first, to refuse originary discourses of human rights and to insist on theoretical and empirical specificity—both of rights subjectivities and of the political stakes and struggles over rights. Second, to disrupt the binarism of nomenclatural politics of West and non-West without missing either historical or political specificity and geopolitical location or indeed mischaracterising their relationship to hegemonic human rights discourses. Third, to underscore the importance of attending to forms of meaning-making including 'strategies' of utilisation of rights, the precise usage and meaning of which is linked not only to the historical and cultural identity of the group making a rights claim but also to the particular kinds of politics and institutional settings that they inhabit and strive towards. Finally, it allows us to resignify rights politics, subjectivities and discourses as not simply local variants of 'global human rights cultures' but as historically, socially and politically located practices whose spatial, temporal and epistemic specificities require careful theorisation.

The Vernacular of Human Rights and Human Rights in the Vernacular

As would be evident by now, vernacular rights cultures put in place a multi-perspectival shift in thinking about human rights that are temporal, scalar and spatial on the one hand, and ethical, methodological and conceptual on the other. First, they enable a focus on a different temporality of human rights. Recent scholarship on human rights has engaged in producing a different timeline for the emergence of human rights (Hunt 2007; Moyn 2010). However, this shift in the temporality of human rights remains mired in a time-space provincialism, that is, even though the temporality of human rights discussions shifts, the geopolitical location of human rights enquiry remains firmly located in the West. Second, this framework allows a shift in the scale of analysis from a dominant nation-centric and institutionalist-statist one to a transnational one. A transnational scale as opposed to an international one enables an analysis of the different circuits and sites of power within which human rights operate but also allows the examination of the different articulations and critical engagements with rights and human rights by differently positioned subjects of rights. Consequently, by refusing to accord privilege to only nation states and/ or international organisations as the principal actors in contemporary human rights, deploying the framework of vernacular rights cultures brings into focus different actors as knowledge producers and stakeholders of human rights. This scalar shift is essential as much of the progressive and critical scholarship of human rights, even where it engages in producing temporal shifts (Hunt 2007; Bourke 2011; Moyn 2010; Jensen 2015), mainly concerns itself with retracing the histories of the institutional embedding of human rights within nation states and large international organisations. This begs the question as to what might be the gains and the losses of exclusively centreing the human rights deliberations, initiatives and lobbying of nation states in global forums when it is, in fact, nation states which are the chief violators of human rights? Furthermore, what might be the correspondence between these histories of institutional discourses on human rights and the actually recognised rights either enjoyed in and/or violated by those nation states? Third, vernacular rights cultures signify an epistemic intervention into knowledge production from the standpoint of subaltern groups declaring and struggling for rights and human rights. The context of struggle is vital here, and, in this book, it is the contemporary subaltern political mobilisations for rights in India and Pakistan that provide the context of struggle. These rights struggles stand testimony to the fact that human rights are not only the stuff of institutional and legal rights talk but that they are productive and generative—producing particular rights bearing subjects and also political cultures of rights.

These subaltern struggles tie rights firmly to gendered struggles for economic, political, epistemic and ontological justice. An attention to these rights struggles and to the 'active social life' of rights (Abu Lughod 2010) clearly demonstrates that not only are human rights and rights politics conflictual but they are also gendered and intersectional. It also highlights that the subjects of rights that come into being through this rights politics are not homogenous and interchangeable, sovereign and unencumbered subjects of global human rights but vernacular subjects of rights who come into being under existing intersectional power hierarchies. Consequently, the politics of human rights in 'most of the world' is not one of simply enacting or reproducing the global subject of human rights or indeed of local translations of 'global human rights'. The term 'vernacular' signifies two strategic interventions. First, it crucially flags the fact that the exercise of ethical political agency that accompanies demands for entitlements is not individualist, discrete or indeed privately articulated, but one that is predominantly expressed in collective and also in religious, caste and gendered terms, even if this demand for expanded entitlements in the vernacular arises out of the failure of democratic representative politics and state developmentalism. The key point here is that the subject of rights is not the *a priori* subject, always already given, but comes into being through particular institutional, policy, political and discursive interventions and contexts. Second, a critical aspect of vernacular rights cultures as a framework of analysis is an attention to the languages—both literal and conceptual—of rights and human rights deployed by marginal groups to articulate entitlements and rights, paying special attention to the political imaginaries and subjectivities that these conceptual languages make available. A key intervention of this book is to track the deployment of rights in the vernacular across different subaltern citizen mobilisations in southern Asia.

But how is the study of vernacular rights cultures to be undertaken? And how is the conceptual work on human rights from the Global South to be done? This book introduces and assembles together a *feminist historical ontology* as a potentially enabling conceptual–empirical–methodological framework for documenting the stakes and struggles over rights and human rights in 'most of the world'. Through deploying a feminist historical ontology, I show how *haq* comes into being as the chief literal and conceptual term used to signify a right/human right, acquires meanings, produces rights subjectivities, while also putting in place possibilities for becoming a (gendered) subject of rights. A feminist historical ontology is invested in producing accounts of the coming into being of concepts in particular historical contexts but also how these concepts make up people (Hacking 2002: 99) and produce particular political imaginaries and political cultures of rights and human rights.

Readers will discern that through assembling together a feminist historical ontology as a methodological device, I am not only drawing on but also supplementing the work of the philosopher Ian Hacking. An important element of Hacking's historical ontology projects is the focus on words and concepts: of how concepts come into being and acquire traction at particular historical points. And, it is Hacking's focus on words and concepts and their role in 'making up people' together with my longstanding interest in the gendered processes of political subjectivation and in the self-fashioning exercises undertaken by subaltern subjects (Madhok 2013, 2018) that draws me to his work on historical ontology.

However historical ontology needs to be gendered and rendered more sociologically aware of the power relations that make up and sustain concepts in specific historical locations, including of the kinds of work concepts do. Quite simply, historical ontologies need to be read alongside a critical reflexive politics of location (Rich 1981; Mani 1990; Frankenberg and Mani 1993; Kaplan 1994; Hill Collins 2000; Probyn 2003; Mohanty 1996; see Chapter 3). A feminist historical ontology is this fusion of the two—of historical ontology with a critical reflexive politics of location. Accordingly, feminist historical ontologies produce an orientation towards generating conceptual accounts of encounters with the world that are responsive to a critical reflexive politics of location, to gendered power relations and struggles, and to the coming into being of gendered subjects.

Beyond Suffering Rights as Paradoxes: A Critical Productive Lens on Human Rights

Vernacular rights cultures focus on the productive[12] and generative nature of rights. To draw attention to the productivity of rights and human rights is neither to extol the virtues of rights nor to engage in a politics of despair. It is instead to focus on the double-edged nature of human rights—at once aligning with hegemonic power around the globe but also providing a language for mobilising against hegemonic power relations on the ground. Their double-sidedness produces the push and pull which characterises their operation: of enchantments and the disappointments; the enablements that rights put in place but also their regulatory effects; their mobilisational power and democratic potential but also their civilisationalism; the unremitting northern pressure behind their power but also their take up by the powerless and the precarious across the Global North and South; the politically conservative effects of rights and human rights but also the 'insurgent imaginaries' (Natera 2013) they produce, which not only engender challenges and 'interruptions' to the business of neoliberal politics as usual but also exceed the existing terms of recognition/inclusion/justice and rights. Consequently, a key strength of the study of vernacular rights cultures is to focus on this productive double-sidedness[13] of human rights politics and the intellectual resources they provide for forging political claims and subaltern struggles on the ground. Furthermore, it also enables analyses of the continuing, if contested, epistemic power of human rights in scholarly contexts and brings to attention the inordinate focus on specific privileged subjects who are always seen as paradigmatic subjects of rights and human rights, and on those 'others' who are almost always left outside of this academic scholarship on rights and human rights and, when incuded, are always required to make the case for being subjects of rights.

And, finally, studying vernacular rights cultures attends to the possibilities for but also equally the impossibilities of becoming subjects of rights within and through particular normative conceptual repertoires of rights.

Influential critiques of rights and human rights sometimes allude to the productivity of rights by drawing attention to the paradoxical outcomes that result from the deployment of rights. As Joseph Slaughter (2007) reminds, paradoxes are in effect the staple of critical scholarship on human rights. While none has been more productive in generating influential interventions on human rights than what is referred to as the foundational paradox of republicanism or the paradox between the rights of man and that of citizen, feminist scholars too have produced powerful critiques of the paradoxical politics and outcomes of rights and human rights. They have pointed to their contradictory, alienating, exclusionary and politically conservative effects, arguing that human rights are not only politically expedient but also politically retrogressive, that they are both inclusionary as well as exclusionary, and are at once regulatory and identity fixing. As Wendy Brown notes, 'to have a right *as* a woman is not to be free of being designated and subordinated by gender' (Brown 2000: 232). The double bind of human rights is that rights 'must be specific and concrete in order to reveal and redress women's subordination, yet potentially entrench our subordination through that specificity' (Brown 2000: 238). But, of course, critical scholarship on human rights does more than highlight their paradoxical outcomes. Queer theorists, for instance, note that the liberal imaginary of autonomy and sexual rights actively excludes those who do not 'fit' the normative lesbian, gay, bisexual, transgender, intersex, and queer (LGBTIQ) subject mould and, by doing so, upholds and maintains unequal geopolitical relations by assiduously policing and converting national borders into civilisational ones on the basis of recognition of sexual rights (Puar 2007; Sabsay 2016). Scholars also highlight the ways in which human rights constitute a 'central' element of United States (US)–led globalisation, capitalism and world trade (Mignolo 2000) and, are thereby, implicated and invested in upholding existing global power relations and racialised hierarchies of representation (Menon 2004; Kapur 2013). They have been characterised as a 'global secular religion'(Meister 2002: 91) and as being another word for neoliberal globalisation and free market economics (Badiou 2012); human rights are also critiqued as a form of 'transnational governmentality' (Grewal 2005: 125), as a form of biopolitical rights (Agamben 1998: 126; Cheah 2014: 215), as 'biocultural' (Chandra 2016: xxiiii) and as rights to 'humanitarian interference' (Rancière 2004: 298).

However, critique alone cannot account for the productive and generative struggles over rights and human rights in their historicity, specificity, dynamism and difference. As Ratna Kapur (2018) notes, the steady flow of critique upon critique of global human rights has successfully mobilised despair but done little to explore alternative epistemic routes through which to think of human rights politics; and where alternative registers have indeed been considered, these have invariably ended up in the altogether familiar staging of a chastised return to the fold of human rights. The work of critique, of course, is vital; it demystifies the workings of power to show why and how particular operations of power produce the particular effects they do. However, the work of critique can only ever be one part of the story, albeit an important and critical one. Critique must also lead to the formulation of alternative social designs and thinking that would not only enable the shift in perspective but also generate a more expansive repertoire of conceptual and methodological tools with which to think with. Therefore, the question is not only one of bringing new and different experiences of rights and human rights to the fore but also to devise different ways to think about these in ways that matter epistemically and take into account the epistemic difference these make.[14]

This book builds on and owes a great deal to the critical interventions on rights and human rights even if it uses their insights to construct a perspective that focuses not only on the critiques of human rights but also on the political cultures of rights. By shifting focus from the production of critique alone and towards thinking about the productivity of rights and human rights, this book draws, builds and critically engages with four different strands of recent, critical disciplinary-based scholarship on human rights. In particular, it brings together different geographically located ethnographic descriptions of the politics of *haq* with the philosophical work on rights and human rights on the one hand, and the anthropology and the political theory of a 'global' phenomena called human rights, on the other. It aligns itself with the recent historiographies of human rights that critique originary timelines that forge a long unbroken 'Western tradition' of international human rights (Hunt 2007; Moyn 2010; Jensen 2016). However, it also diverges from these progressive historiographies, which remain tied to investigating temporal questions and establishing different timelines for the origins, ascendance, and the breakthrough of human rights. It engages seriously with political philosophy and critical political theory that concerns itself mostly with the logics of equality, democracy and citizenship and in particular with the 'right to have rights' (Arendt 1958) and, also with the productive and the regulative work of human rights (Brown 2000, 2015; Slaughter 2007; Lefebvre 2018). In this case too, vernacular rights cultures instigate the need for further complexity and incite different questions. For instance, recent debates on the relation between rights and citizenship have focused on the 'logic of equality' (Rojas 2013: 581–95) or on acts of citizenship through which non-citizens seek the right to have rights that have already been declared (Rancière 1999; Balibar 2002). However, paying attention to the production of vernacular rights cultures reveals that mobilisations of subaltern and dispossessed groups do not just involve a logic of equality and inclusion through which these groups demand already existing rights. Rather, these mobilisations seek to alter the means through which rights are delivered but also transform the content and meaning of the rights that are already in place while also demanding that new rights are brought into being, as the right to food movement and also those to forest lands described in this book will make clear. As I will go on to illustrate through the rights ethnographies in this book, vernacular rights cultures inhabit particular political imaginaries and arise as movements that make demands for rights that are inflected with particular rights cultures, histories and contexts of political mobilisations. Although they can be transnational in nature—in terms of shared legal and political histories, resonances and even active linkages with similar forms of oppression and related historical cultural contexts, such as the newly developing links between the right to food movement in India and the Via Campensina[15]—they are rooted in an insistence that we do not lose sight of the historical, linguistic, conceptual and political specificity of rights claims and also of the political imaginaries that these inhabit. Finally, the study of vernacular rights cultures draws on the anthropological scholarship that engages thoughtfully with the limits of liberalism and legal constitutionalism in the post colony (Povinelli 2011; Comaroff and Comaroff 2012), on the 'active social life' of rights (Abu Lughod 2010: 1), of their 'vernacularization on the ground' (Levitt and Merry 2009: 441) and on the intersection of biopolitical technologies, law and the market (Biehl 2013: 419). But these too are by themselves insufficient for thinking about vernacular rights cultures and require further supplementation. For instance, the recent efforts to study 'vernacularization on the ground' (Merry 2006, 2009), where 'vernacularization' refers to the 'process of appropriation and local adoption of globally generated ideas and strategies of vernacularization' (Levitt and Merry 2009: 441), is an important intervention into studying the 'local uses' (Levitt and Merry 2009: 441) of global women's rights in different sites. Ultimately though, it suffers from a significant conceptual difficulty: it not only operates within and through the binaries of the epistemic and authorial Global North *versus* the non-epistemic and only ever translating local, that is, the Global South, but it also actively reproduces these. Vernacularisation as a verb reinforces the work of 'doing' rights on others and for those others to have the work of rights done on them. It does not allow for conversations on rights and human rights to flow in both directions and, thereby, forecloses agentival activity and authorship of rights from different and other epistemic sites, not least from the margins. A key component of vernacularisation of human rights according to Levitt and Merry is their 'translation' which is done by a 'chain' of 'vernacularizers' from the global to the national and all the way to the local. Levitt and Merry are careful to point out the differential power relations and vulnerabilities of vernacularisers that impact their effectiveness in different contexts to 'talk back' to the 'global values packages'. However, it is unclear from the examples they provide how this 'talking back' displaces either the epistemic centre of human rights, which they identify as the 'West' (and from where they travel to other places and are vernacularised), or indeed their content or forms and modes of expression. In other words, my point here is quite simply this: vernacularisation or indeed vernacularisers leave epistemic hierarchies put in place by global human rights intact. To think in terms of vernacular rights cultures, on the other hand, is to refuse an insistence on the unidirectional travel and simplistic translation of global right and human rights. Instead it is to demand a non-linear, intersectional and materially informed thinking arising from historically and politically specific struggles around world-making taking place in different locations, while also accounting for the transnational power dynamics in which these operate. Furthermore, while I think it is important and interesting to track how 'global rights' transfer, and 'translate' in different contexts, it is, however, only one strand/aspect of rights activism and must be accompanied by analyses of how not only certain rights became global/universal but also how these in turn are undergoing expansion and change under pressure from collective struggles. In other words, rights and human rights activism need to be viewed beyond prisms of discrete agent-based activism, even though individual agents play important roles in 'transferring and translating' rights.

Finally, the rights struggles described in this book are not only struggles against inequality and for justice, but significantly, these are struggles that are taking place in the high tide of neoliberalism. Neoliberalism is a 'loose and shifting signifier' (Brown 2015: 20) that takes up different forms in different parts of the globe (Rofel 2007). However, there are a few key characteristics integral and common to the different forms that neoliberalism takes around the globe: the downgrading of political arguments for economic and redistributive justice, the elevation of market rationality as the governing rationality for all social life, and consequently, the conversion of all social relations into market and financialised relations, and the elevation of an imperial, racialised and gendered *homo economicus*. An important feature of neoliberalism is its distrust of politics (Whyte 2018) and the steady erosion of political life including the steady demise of the political figure most associated with liberal democratic life, the *homo politicus* (Brown 2015). An important set of political arguments that have been considerably sidelined by the ascendance of neoliberalism are those of global economic justice and redistributive politics. We not only live in neoliberal times but also in the time of global human rights; the rise of global human rights shares a temporal affinity with the rise of global neoliberalism. Given that the overarching characteristic of the global present is one of unprecedented and exponential levels of global inequality, the shared temporality of the global ascendance of human rights and of neoliberalism as the accepted, albeit not uncontested, economic rationality have inevitably led to questions being asked about not only the nature of the relationship between neoliberalism and human rights but also that between global human rights and global inequality (Salomon 2013; Moyn 2014; Marks 2014; Brown 2015; Whyte 2018; Slobodian 2018). In other words, what has been the role played by global human rights in shoring up neoliberalism and also in politically sidelining global redistributive politics of economic justice?

As is well known, the dominant storylines of global human rights hierarchically organise global human rights into separate categories and 'generations' comprising civil, political and economic rights, and accords generational and normative priority to civil and political rights over other rights commitments endorsed in the Universal Declaration of Human Rights (UDHR, 1948). This categorical priority of civil and political rights can be seen in their ready operationalisation by international human rights and humanitarian organisations but is also evidenced in the fact that international human rights instruments have often been much stronger on 'status equality' and against discrimination on the basis of one's status, such as gender, race and sexuality, and somewhat less forthcoming on 'vertical' equality', which is that of income or wealth distribution (Balakrishnan and Heintz 2019: 396). Significantly, this generational story eclipses other stories of global human rights that contest the justice deficit of individuated civil and political centrism of the global human rights discourse and which have historically put questions of global inequality and global redistributive politics at the heart of international human rights law and politics. One such story spans the 1960s and the 1970s and is about the attempts of non-aligned and newly decolonised states to restructure the global economy via the establishment of a New International Economic Order (NIEO). The NIEO sought to restructure the critical vocabulary of international human rights by making economic justice and global redistributive politics as its key pillars. As Anthony Anghie (2019) explains, even though the NIEO used the language of rights, especially rights of states over their natural resources, these rights were not the individual human rights championed by human rights organisations. The advocates of the NIEO in the UN argued that poverty and economic justice were a key question for international human rights and that the prevailing global economic injustice was an active legacy of the colonialist extractivist policies and unfair control over natural resources, a legacy that was being actively carried forward by the work of post–World War II international institutions such as the World Bank and the International Monetary Fund (IMF) (Salomon 2013). Hence, what was urgently required was the setting up of the NIEO, which would provide an international legal framework for reorganising the colonial, unfair and unequal terms and rules of international trade agreements. The attempts by the supporters of NIEO to have 'economic justice reflected in international law' (Salomon 2013: 31) resulted in the UN General Assembly adopting resolutions on Permanent Sovereignty over Natural Resources, and the Charter of Economic Rights and Duties of States (Salomon 2013:37). In the end, however, the alternative vision advocated by the NIEO was short-lived and it could not ride out the combined storm of different oppositional forces that came its way in the form of the global debt crises of the 1980s, the exponential rise in commodity prices and, perhaps the most significant of them all, the oppositional strength of the conglomerate of the powerful industrialised countries (Salomon 2013: 46), intent on driving forward the mantra of the 'magic of the market'. If the ascendance of the neoliberal international order rudely interrupted the prospects for a deeper relationship between global distributive politics and global human rights, then what does this interruption and also the demise of the NIEO tell us about the relationship between neoliberalism and global human rights? There are different scholarly views on this. While Samuel Moyn (2015) writes that there is no intrinsic relationship between neoliberalism and human rights and that 'parallel trajectories' is the most effective way of describing the temporal alignment of global human rights and neoliberalism, scholars such as Susan Marks (2013) and Jessica Whyte (2018) disagree. According to Whyte, neoliberals

> saw in human rights the possibility of securing rights of investors and the wealthy in the face of challenges to their property and power. The human rights discourse they developed aimed to provide an institutional and moral foundation for a competitive market economy and to shape entrepreneurial subjects. In contrast to the anticolonialists who had fought to establish the right to self determination, the neoliberals saw the promise of human rights in constraining sovereign power, especially in the postcolony, and in restraining politicisation of the economy. (Whyte 2018: 24)

Now while these are very persuasive arguments, how do they enable us to give an accounting of the rights struggles of subaltern groups contesting the hegemonic power of neoliberalism and of global human rights through an insistence on a politics of economic justice, redistribution and intersectionally experienced citizenship? How to square the circle between the shared temporal fortunes of the rise of global human rights and those of neoliberalism without leaving out the struggles of subaltern groups against neoliberalism? In other words, how to provide an accounting of the global ascendance of neoliberalism without reproducing the power of the already powerful advocates and beneficiaries of neoliberalism? And, equally, how to tell stories about interrupting the juggernaut of neoliberalism without either advocating a philosophical return to the provincial and racialised ideals of the *homo politicus*[16] or indeed, by viewing the subaltern struggles against neoliberalism as the latter's radical other? This book argues that an accounting for the global ascendance of neoliberalism must also attend to ongoing political struggles against neoliberalism in 'most of the world'. These political struggles are historically and politically specific and reflect the push back against the different economic and political forms that neoliberalism assumes in different parts of the world. Paying attention to these political struggles is an important cautionary against the tendency towards overgeneralisations declaring the death of the politics of equality and justice everywhere. Importantly, however, it also brings into view the 'other' subaltern critical political vocabularies and imaginaries of rights and justice and alternative ways of world-making. Having said this, it is also important to guard against romanticising these political struggles against neoliberalism as either egalitarian, non-hierarchical or indeed as waged from outside of neoliberalism. If anything, these political struggles take place within specific historical conditions resulting from particular encounters with neoliberalism and are consequently, also shaped by it (see Chapter 4).

As a feminist scholar, I am acutely aware of the gendered and paradoxical outcomes of rights discourses, of their solely mitigating nature and innate inability to resolve harm on their own, of being identity fixing and also essentialising (Brown 2000). And I am only too aware of the dangers, injuries, asymmetrical power relations, violence and precarities surrounding the 'doing' of human rights around the globe. I am deeply attentive to feminist scholarship that has demystified the gendered/exclusionary/culture-reifying/ civilisational discourses that human rights lend themselves to. In particular, it has shown how a certain form of racial imperial politics plays out when human rights are deployed as championing women's rights—one where the discourse of 'saving' the natives from themselves, or indeed Spivak's formulation of 'white men saving brown women from brown men', comes in only too handy. And yet, an important paradox of the politics of rights is also that despite their paradoxical outcomes, the disappointments and the despair arising from their attachment to privileged raced and gendered bodies, they continue to be desired, claimed, contested and fought for by the marginalised, the precarious and the powerless. A dilemma for our present, therefore, is one of how to reconcile the often paradoxical conservatism of rights thinking, including their implication within imperial and racialised politics and in structures of coloniality, with the articulations and mobilisations around rights by subaltern groups in different parts of the world? In my view, feminist intellectual work on the politics of rights must be accompanied by an attention to the ways in which rights languages are put to use differently in different political contexts by subaltern groups. Rights are inherently political and must be seen as operating within fields of power, and, therefore, the task is not only one of examining the discursive formulations and the political use that rights are put to but also one of investigating the political cultures that rights create and the new forms of subjectivities and subjection these produce. Given the marginalised contexts within which vernacular rights cultures operate, the work of documenting rights talk and thinking in these contexts involves undertaking detailed ethnographic work that documents the conceptual languages in which the gendered subaltern groups stake their wager as 'active claimants of modernity' (Ram 2008: 145). In addition to the work of tracking and documenting subaltern rights languages, there also need to be analytical frameworks in place that allow for the conceptual capture of different political and normative strategies and imaginaries of rights. The conceptual work on rights from the margins is essential in order to not only stretch and dislodge the existing normative boundaries of the universal (Butler 1997), expand the existing languages of entitlements, impact and transform public policy but also to provide different visions for equality and justice.

Vernacular Rights Cultures in South Asia

In India and Pakistan, several strands of rights discourses circulate, of which three prominent ones are legal constitutionalism, developmentalism and religious or ethnic nationalism, the latter expressed more in the language of freedom and autonomy from the nation state than of citizen rights per se. Although 'divergent' (Oldenburg 2010) in their experience of democracy, representative government and citizenship, both countries guarantee fundamental rights to citizens,[17] albeit with qualifications[18] and with varying degrees of success and coverage. Both have superior judiciaries that have been less reticent in referencing and upholding international human rights law,[19] and while judicial activism is a recent phenomenon in the case of Pakistan (Newberg 2012), the Indian Supreme Court in the post-Emergency era has wrought a reputation for itself as a 'torchbearer of human rights' (Balakrishnan 2007: 157) even if 'its impact on the ground is not consistent'[20] and its recent judgments have substantially weakened fundamental rights protections in the country (Yamunan 2020). Moreover, both India and Pakistan have a visible and vibrant women's movement and an active institutional discourse on gender equality.[21] Finally, discourses of development and human rights have a discernible presence on both sides of the border, particularly in the NGO sector (Jaffrelot 2015).

The book tracks the deployment of *haq* across vernacular rights cultures in India and Pakistan. I draw attention to the four different political imaginaries and justificatory premises that underpin the deployment of *haq* rights within contemporary subaltern rights struggles in India and Pakistan. Many of the rights struggles I study, particularly in India, have had policy and legislative successes and several pioneering and innovative legislative acts are now in place guaranteeing citizen entitlements to information, food, employment and land rights. There also exists now a growing and sophisticated scholarship analysing the functioning, shortfalls as well as the impact of these newly introduced acts and policy measures (Drèze 2004; Shah 2007; Khera 2008, 2011; Bannerjee and Saha 2010; Drèze and Khera 2017; Nilsen 2018). Within this burgeoning scholarship and more generally, however, more attention could be paid to the conceptual and epistemic languages of rights that underpin the struggles by subaltern groups and of the nature of subjectivities and subjection these mobilisations engender, or indeed to the forms of rights politics these generate. In other words, we are yet to know of the justificatory premises of rights that inform and activate demands for expanded entitlements, and of the nature of rights languages that underpin 'self-making' exercises mobilised in becoming a subject of formal rights, and of the traversal of rights and human rights, and indeed of the ways by which statecraft, governmentalities and the market intersect and facilitate the dissemination of particular rights subjectivities. In short, we know very little of how rights languages are constituted and articulated by subaltern subjects. This book argues that it is not only the case that these questions spearhead the study of the emergence and operation of rights cultures in subaltern contexts in 'most of the world' but also that their study requires a different conceptual lens: one that is able to capture their dynamism but also their difference.

The different justificatory premises of rights or *haq* that I document in this book, and which span India and Pakistan, occur not in some conceptual bubble but are articulated and negotiated in contexts of sustained encounters and interactions with developmentalism, colonial and postcolonial law, militarism, statism and constitutionalism. By 'developmentalism', a term I prefer to 'development', I refer to not only a set of institutions, discourses and practices but also a 'condition' or a 'way of being'. Developmentalism is normative in its aims and includes both state and non-state actors. It speaks the language of self-empowerment and individual rights and has the transformation of subjectivities as its explicit aim. And, it mediates the experience and knowledge of constitutional settlement on postcolonial citizenship (Madhok 2013: 120).

In India, social movements are a variegated lot comprising 'identity' and 'interest' groups who more often than not practice a 'dual level political activism' that engages the government in order to influence public policy while also challenging societal norms and practices (Katzenstein et al. 2001: 267). Although some social movements see the state as the main oppressor, others participate in a much more 'situationally developed politics' (Katzenstein et al. 2001: 247) directing their campaigns at the judiciary for legal and policy reforms and for redressing injustices meted out by the state. I must hasten to add here that while this book focuses on the claim-making by subaltern mobilisations for rights, it is not a study of social movements in India or Pakistan.[22] In other words, it is neither a study examining the effectiveness of social movements in either of these countries to bring about social change or indeed reduce poverty[23] nor one that examines to what extent these social movements have 'served the constituencies of the least advantaged' (Ray and Katzenstein 2005: 2). The social mobilisations covered in this book are instead the key sites where rights talk takes place. They are dynamic, productive, generative and conflictual sites where the potential of rights as well as their limitations play out. To put it in another way: rights undergo transformation and expansion when claimed by subaltern groups but it is also when rights are claimed by subaltern groups that some of the particular limitations of rights become visible.

In India, my fieldwork has over the years spread to five districts of Rajasthan and has consisted mainly of recording narratives demanding *haq* by development workers, grassroots political workers and participants of various citizen mobilisations organising under the right to food movement as well as the independent rights activism of women development workers within a state-sponsored women's development programme in Rajasthan. The right to food movement is an umbrella organisation that includes a number of citizenship struggles, including those to the right to information, employment, forest rights and Dalit rights, among a host of others. Drawing on ethnographic tracking of these subaltern mobilisations in Rajasthan, I identify and document the political imaginaries but also three principal justificatory premises that underpin the deployment of rights and human rights, which are legal constitutionalism and citizenship; the cosmological, the historical and the prior; and finally, a gendered normative moral order based on 'Truth' (Chapters 4 and 5). I show how these justificatory premises resonate with several ideas of citizenship and rights or human rights within liberal democratic theories but also identify the marked differences between the liberal imaginaries of rights and citizenship and the political imaginaries of *haq*. Tracking *haq* further northwest and into Pakistan, the mobilisations of the Anjuman Mazarain or the AMP (Tenants Association Punjab) in rural Punjab, demanding the restoration of their ownership and sharecropping rights to the land taken over by the Pakistani military, provides yet another insight into the specific political imaginaries which produce particular vernacular rights cultures (Chapter 5). The justificatory premise of their deployment of *haq* is embedded in and derives its justification from Islamic jursiprudentialism and Qur'anic meanings and is consequently tied very strongly to the idea of 'right conduct'. It is interesting to note that although *haq* in this context derives its mainstay from a popular Islamic understanding, it is deployed outside of a strictly religious context and towards what might be seen as secular ends.

The political imaginaries I document in Chapters 4 and 5 are produced, articulated and negotiated within live political contexts of struggle and precarity and provide insights into how vernacular rights cultures are mobilised by filtering, mediating and interpreting rights through particular political imaginaries of struggle and claim-making. Importantly, these ideas, too, are not articulated in a discrete or an ahistorical way but emerge in particular political, institutional, historical and activist contexts.

Before I bring this introduction to the book to a close, I want to underline that there are at least six significant things to note about the contemporary applications of rights language or *haq* that I will document. First, the deployment of a right is not through a neologism but within the vernacular and as *haq*. Rights articulations do not occur as singular or even odd prototypes but draw on and are negotiated through existing moral vocabularies and the political grammar of norms, law, rules, entitlements, rights and identities. Second, vernacular rights cultures signal the overlapping and intersecting nature of the languages of rights and those of human rights, rather than insisting on either historical continuity or separation. In doing so, they resist theoretical foreclosure by sidestepping the paradox between the rights of man and the rights of the citizen that characterises much of the human rights debates in the Anglo-American and European world. If anything, vernacular rights cultures show that rights of man and rights of citizen are co-dependent, intersectional, struggled for and intricately interwoven rather than only paradoxical. Third, these rights cultures are co-produced through and invoked within multiple and diverse encounters with developmentalism, statism, legal constitutionalism, and activism; therefore, it is at the intersection of these and not as some freestanding abstraction, that *haq* as a contemporary idea operates. In fact, as the ethnographic descriptions demonstrate, these intersections are integral to the formation of vernacular rights cultures. Fourth, despite the extensive deployment of *haq* within citizen mobilisations, individual rights regulate neither interpersonal relations nor social life in either India or Pakistan. Fifth, the demand for gender equality or *haq* for women is a question that almost invariably needs to be addressed separately and seldom occurs organically within citizen mobilisations. Finally, the movements for *haq* I am tracking in this book are precariously positioned live struggles. The

Anjuman Mazarain continue to protest in the face of heavy securitisation of their lands; India's forest communities face the impending threat of a dilution of the hard won institutional guarantees and increased state violence, coercion and dispossession in order to make way for easier land acquisition for private investment and also further restrictions on forest land through their conversion into national parks; the right to food movement is seeing its legislative gains eroded with the ruling right-wing Bharatiya Janata Party (BJP)–led government threatening to cut back food security entitlements. In effect, the four different political imaginaries of *haq* that I document in this book—constitutional/ legal citizenship; justification of rights on the basis of morality and 'Truth'; justification based on the entitlements of the prior; and justification based on Islam—emerge within live political contexts of struggle and provide insights into how vernacular rights cultures are mobilised.

Conclusion

Through a focus on the generative and productive nature of rights, this book details how human rights are key sites of subjectification and conceptual innovation. In a significant sense, vernacular rights cultures are concerned with documenting political, epistemic and ethical agency. However, political mobilisations are not only sites for political agency, and a focus on vernacular rights cultures draws attention to the modes of subject formation set off by human rights/rights discourses. And, even as rights/human rights talk provides the site of subjectification (Rancière 2004), this subjectification does not result in the production of a homogenous subject of global human rights but a vernacular subject of rights.

The epistemic compass of vernacular rights cultures enables us to think carefully about the conceptual and literal languages for rights in 'most of the world'. It does this through a focus on the *other* conceptual and normative languages of rights. This focus on *other* languages of rights and of claim-making is crucial if we are to disrupt the politics of origins and the time–space provincialism it puts in place but also if we are serious about making epistemic difference matter. Making epistemic difference matter is also to say that *other* traditions and languages of rights must speak back to global human rights thinking and must not be reduced to a study of 'norm diffusion' (Dunford 2017)—where norms travel from the Global North to the South and are sought to be translated into local idioms. In other words, a focus on vernacular rights cultures is a call to think carefully about the normative, ontological and philosophical nature of the languages of rights that are deployed in 'most of the world'.

Notes

1. I am alluding in part to the subtitle of Partha Chatterjee's book (2004) *The Politics of the Governed: Reflections on Popular Politics in Most of the World*. I find Chatterjee's formulation of 'most of the world' a significant intervention into disrupting the binary of the West/Western and non-West/non-Western. This binary as I shall go on to argue in this book has crucial implications not only for human rights politics but also for politics of gender and sexuality in South Asia. Throughout the book, I shall be deploying this formulation 'most of the world' to refer to the epistemic and political worlds and thinking outside of Eurocentred and European, Anglo and North American contexts.
2. Priya Raghavan (2020) assembles a subaltern archive from some formal writing, mainly letters, petitions and rural newsletters that have been produced in the wake of some of the subaltern mobilisations.
3. For an account of the 'unselfconscious' making of vernacular literary cultures, see Pollock (1998).
4. For an important discussion on the subaltern and on subaltern groups, see in particular Nilsen and Roy (2015).
5. There is a now a substantial, well acknowledged and growing multidisciplinary scholarship on subaltern historiographies, geographies and politics. For a range of debates, see in particular Guha (1983), Spivak (1988), Guha and Spivak (1989), Prakash (1994), Rodriguez and López (2001), Chakrabarty (2002), Chatterjee (2004) and Nilsen and Roy (2015).
6. The term 'Adivasi' is the 'Indian language' term for the Indigenous. There is considerable nomenclatural controversy over the use of both 'Adivasi' and 'Indigenous' (Karlsson 2003; Sundar 2016). The term 'Adivasi' has associations with 'civilisational backwardness' and also with very problematic institutional terms and politics of recognition. In international circles, the recognition of the rights of the Indigenous, which grants specific rights of self- determination to Indigenous groups, has led the Indian government to oppose the term and to deny the presence of Indigenous groups in India (Xaxa 1999). It is also important to note that not all Indigenous groups identify as Adivasi; the latter is mainly used to identify Indigenous communities in India's mainland. The administrative category established by the postcolonial Indian state for governing all Indigenous groups is the Scheduled Tribe (ST). In this book, I will be using the terms 'Adivasi', 'Indigenous', and 'ST' as appropriate, the latter mostly to refer to administrative and governance matters.

7. The Dalits or Scheduled Castes were also previously called Untouchables.

8. I am grateful to Sherene Razack for encouraging me to engage with the politics of origins as a racialist discourse (personal communication, January 2019). See in particular James (1938, 1989), Fanon (1952), Trouillot (1995), Wynter (2003) and Suárez-Krabbe (2016). For an overview of the racism of human rights, especially of human rights law, see Bradley (2019) and on 'racially inflected' humanitarian politics and interventions, see in particular Razack (2004) and Wilson (2012).

9. See Barkawi (2018).

10. See in particular Fanon (1952), Bunch (1990), Charlesworth (1994), Kiss (1995), Trouillot (1995), Wynter (2003), Simpson (2014), Suárez-Krabbe (2016) and Bruce-Jones (2015).

11. For a detailed ethnographic account of subaltern encounters with the state, see Nilsen (2018a).

12. Although, not specifically on the productive nature of human rights politics as such, Saida Hodžić's book *The Twilight of Cutting* engages in 'illuminating the productivity and instability of repressive character of law' (2017: 248) on genital cutting in Ghana.

13. Rajshree Chandra (2016) refers to this double-sidedness of rights as the 'cunning of rights'.

14. There is now an emerging body of feminist scholarship which scrupulously locates theoretical and conceptual work in specific geographies, engages with intellectual registers of those geographies to produce theoretical and conceptual interventions on rights and human rights in productive and generative ways. Ratna Kapur's *Freedom in a Fish Bowl* (2018) positions itself in the aftermath of human rights critique to argue that while the work of human rights must carry on, this work must, however, be delinked from the epistemologies of freedom that it is embedded in. It intervenes to uncouple the link between predominant visions of liberal freedom and human rights, and to direct attention towards different intellectual registers and resources for thinking about freedom. She draws on non-liberal philosophical and agnostic spiritual traditions of Persian Sufism and also the subcontinental episteme of no-dualism—*advaita*. In each of these, Kapur argues that meaningful freedom becomes possible through self transformation and self reflection, and that ethical self care can provide us with a vision of what the futurity of rights might be. Located in very different intellectual, historical and political registers, Audra Simpson's book *Mohawk Interruptus* (2014) firmly situates the colonial logic of liberal freedom in the liberal multicultural governance of settler colonial states. Simpson argues that the presence and workings of settler colonial states exemplify both the operation of colonialism but also its failure. The insistence on and exercise of political sovereignty by the Indigenous and their refusal to disappear points

to not only that 'sovereignty may exist within sovereignty' but also that there is an ethical alternative to liberal multicultural recognition, which is that of 'refusal'. The ethical and political alternative of 'refusal' catapults questions of sovereignty, nationhood, citizenship, legitimacy and authority to the forefront of settler colonial politics to demand an 'accounting' that deals with Indigenous politics and how they challenge the perceived status of 'settled' state (2014: 11).

15. Interview with Kavita Srivastava, Secretary General, Right to Food Campaign (personal communication, Jaipur, July 2016). See also Dunford and Madhok (2015).

16. See Sylvia Wynter (2003) for a critique of the *homo politicus* as a raced subject.

17. India's constitution adopted in 1950 sets out fundamental rights in Part III of the document, and while Pakistan's constitutional history is more chequered having gone through three enacted constitutions but it too guarantees fundamental rights in Part II of the 1973 constitutional arrangement.

18. In the case of Pakistan, the establishment of Shariah federal courts qualifies the nature of remedies available to citizens. The operation of Muslim Personal Law in India similarly qualifies aspects of state civil law in relation to Muslims.

19. Pronouncing on gender equality, the Indian Supreme Court famously referenced CEDAW in *Vishakha vs State of Rajasthan* to lay down legal guidelines for the prevention of sexual harassment of women in the workplace (*All India Reporter of the Supreme Court* 1997: 3011). More recently, the Delhi High Court in *Laxmi Mandal vs the Deen Dayal Harinagar Hospital* (W.P.C.C. 8853/2008) drew on India's commitments to various international rights protocols in order to pronounce a legal basis for the protection of reproductive rights of women. In Pakistan's plural legal system, writes Shaheen Sardar Ali (2012: 22), 'human rights treaties appear to be invoked by the judiciary as effortlessly as customary and Islamic norms as well as constitutional provisions of equality and non-discrimination'.

20. Balakrishnan (2007) points out that this is due to the 'ideological character of the Court's particular approach to human rights and its biases ... in favor of the state and development, in favor of the rich and against workers, in favor of the urban middle-class and against rural farmers, and in favor of a globalitarian class and against the distributive ethos of the Indian Constitution' (2007: 158).

21. For discussions on the feminist and women's movement in India and Pakistan, see in particular Kumar (1999), Gandhi and Shah (1992), Ram (2000), John (1996), Menon (1999), Sunder Rajan (2003), Phadke (2003), Kalpagam (2000), Roy (2015), Khan (2018), Khan and Kirmani (2018), Madhok (2010), Basu (2005) and Shaheed (2010).

22. The study of social movements, at least in India, has emerged as an important and distinct area of study. See, for instance, Nielsen and Nilsen (2016).

23. Writing on social movements in India, Ray and Katzenstein (2005: 4) note that scholars writing on the state and poverty 'have not paid much attention to the social movements as actors who may buffer, accelerate, ameliorate, and challenge the shifting agendas of the state' (2005: 4). Rather, they have preferred to focus on the 'failure of poverty remediation', 'capture of state by elite interests', failure of state capacity, the relationship of political parties and the state and also intra party democracy, or indeed 'excessive democratization of Indian polity'.

2   Refusing the Politics of Origins

The Haitian Revolution is marked by an 'unthinkability', wrote Michel-Rolph Trouillot (1995). Its unthinkability was evident not only at the time of the event but continues to inform historiographies of rights and human rights ever since. But what makes this unthinkability, thinkable? The unthinkability of Black slaves revolting against Europe's colonial power has been systematically produced through an erasure of the event in retellings of the past but also in contemporary rememberings of the event. This unthinkability, a result of the 'entanglement of historicity with power' (Carby 2015: xii), is put in place by a particular racialised and imperial epistemic rationality—the rationality of Eurocentrism. This logic of Eurocentrism or what is also known in decolonial scholarship as 'coloniality of power' (Quijano 2000: 533) produces specific structures of polity, sociality, racialised humans, sexualities and epistemologies. An important consequence of this coloniality of power is that it institutionalises unequal circuits of intellectual labour production around the globe and generates a range of different forms of epistemic erasures and silences. An important form in which this silence and erasure manifests itself is through the relative lack of theoretical and conceptual attention that is paid to rights politics in 'most of the world', which are mostly viewed as illustrative of and also a derivative of the unfolding of global human rights. This logic of Eurocentrism robs rights and human rights struggles in the Global South of epistemic and political agency. The epistemological power and workings of Eurocentrism have been unpacked and discussed at length by a range of scholars (Said 1978; Amin 1989; Wallerstein 1997; Chakrabarty 2000; Mignolo 2012; Lowe 2015) and my intention in this chapter is not to rehearse the forms it takes or indeed its intellectual and political fallouts but rather to draw attention to only one aspect of this Eurocentred discourse on human rights which I call the politics of origins. Quite unlike the theorists of coloniality who critique the coloniality of human rights and call for delinking from Eurocentric frameworks of knowledge production, I am somewhat sceptical that we can 'delink', or produce a version of pure uncontaminated non-Eurocentric scholarship or even produce a 'third world perspective' (Barreto 2014) on human rights—in fact, I refuse claims of purity and authenticity for the principal reason that global human rights have permeated all sorts of discourses and have become by a large degree the condition for representation and voice, not least for subaltern groups, but have also been taken up by the latter to make claims and demand entitlements. Moreover, 'delinking' is a hard epistemic, ontological and political position to sustain in South Asia where colonial and postcolonial governmentalities led by the political logics of bureaucracy and development have unleashed dispossession, displacement, violence and coercion on subaltern groups on an unprecedented manner. However, this scepticism towards 'delinking' does not mean, as I shall go on to show later, that there is a singular, hegemonic human rights discourse that is travelling in an authentic or pure way from the Global North to meet other pure and authentic discourses in the Global South. In fact, quite the converse; the coercive entanglements of the histories of colonialism together with the penetrative capacities of state developmentalism and transnational capital have not only rendered talk of authenticity impossible but have also at the same time, laid bare the magnitude of epistemic and ontological violence unleashed on subaltern groups. Developmentalism and dispossession constitute important sites of subaltern rights talk in South Asia, and are also the grounds on which subaltern groups resist and challenge the irresistible power and the authority of the state.

The focus on vernacular rights cultures is a question of scale as it is of temporality, subjectivity, subalternity and political struggles. National and international institutions, their processes, rules, norms, discourses and functionings are central interests of vernacular rights cultures, not least because it is mainly at institutional structures—law, bureaucracy and the state—that human rights politics in 'most of the world' is directed at. The preoccupations of vernacular rights cultures, therefore, overlap with some of the concerns of institutional accounts of global human rights, even if their politics, tactics and actors are very different. It is worth stressing again that this is not to say that institutional accounts are not significant or helpful but only that they are only partial accounts, and therefore, to arrive at judgements, of either triumphalist or the unremitting failure of human rights on the basis of institutional accounts is to tell only one story, and it is often the story of those who occupy institutional positions of power and privilege. One such epistemically powerful story of human rights revolves around what I have called the politics of origins.

In this chapter, I have a twofold aim: to draw attention to a specific effect of this politics of origins, which is the pervasive time–space provincialism, historiographical, philosophical and moral, that characterises human rights scholarship. This time–space provincialism invests epistemic authority in the Global North, thereby leading to a lack of theoretical, philosophical and conceptual attention to rights struggles in the Global South.

If we are to decolonise human rights, I argue, then we will need to shift the epistemic center of human rights talk and disrupt its politics of origins and the time–space provincialism that it puts in place. This epistemic shift involves identifying the prevailing forms of Eurocentrism informing current human rights thinking but also generating scholarly work aimed at both tracking alternative genealogies of human rights and producing conceptual work that captures the stakes and struggles over rights/human rights in 'most of the world'. Consequently, the burden of the second half of this chapter, and also its second aim, is to outline the elements of this framework, which will enable this conceptual work aimed at decolonising global human rights.

The Politics of Origins

Broadly speaking, theoretical and empirical discussions of global human rights take place in a conceptually saturated and 'over-determined' discourse characterised by the politics of origins. Paradoxically, these can be entered into only through a clearing exercise or a refusal; a refusal that ironically only reproduces this originary discourse on human rights all over again. Keeping this risk in my mind, I shall outline what I mean by a framework of a 'politics of origins'. By it, I simply mean that the guiding assumptions framing rights debates and questions invariably begin with an orientalist and racialist assumption common to both the celebrators and detractors of human rights, mainly that the conceptual, philosophical and empirical experience of rights across the globe owe their formulation to the three revolutions of the modern West: the Glorious Revolution (1688), the American Revolution (1776) and the French Revolution (1789). Not only are rights politics viewed as Western derived, but they are also regarded as symbolic of this continuing Western tradition of human rights. The politics of origins is trapped in the binary and normative nomenclatural politics of assigning geopolitical and cultural labels: either of and from 'the West' or not of 'the West' and thereby, of the 'non-West'. The documentation of this global proliferation of human rights (or indeed its refusal) is hardly a descriptive project; it is, if anything, a normative one. On the one hand, human rights represent civilisational progress to which 'other' nations and peoples must aspire, even if it means justifying the spread or the protection of human rights through imperialist military invasions and 'humanitarian' interventions. On the other hand, there are powerful detractors of human rights who similarly place rights on a continuum of modernity, progress and linear historical time but prioritise economic development as a necessary precondition in the progress towards political and civil freedoms while refusing rights politics on the basis of cultural inauthenticity and non-origin. Both these positions involve significant historical and intellectual inattentiveness. Not only are global human rights a recent intellectual and political project within the Global North, and, one that has been mired in conflict and continues to be bitterly fought for, but discourses of rights and entitlements are powerfully invoked in the Global South too.

There is nothing partisan about the politics of origins. It is a shared discourse, partaken by the celebrators and detractors of human rights, by the progressive critics of human rights as well as by those who seek to 'vernacularise' rights. It also underpins the binary distinctions sketched between Asian values and Western human rights, universalism and cultural particularism, authoritarian economic development and Western political and civil centred human rights. These binary distinctions do the work of keeping epistemic hierarchies intact by actively reproducing the binaries of native/other and culturally authentic/foreign but also those of the epistemic-authorial global versus the non-epistemic always only ever receiving and translating local. Crucially, they effectively foreclose agentival activity and authorship of rights from different locations and repress democratic politics of claim making, dissent, freedom and justice.

Consider three relatively recent examples of this politics of origins from contemporary popular political discourse on gender and sexuality in India and Pakistan where the politics of origins enjoys significant hold in the subcontinent's historiographical, philosophical and cultural imaginations. My first example is from August 2016 when the Indian government announced that the surrogacy laws in the country needed overhauling. Intriguingly, for a country that has separate federal government ministries overseeing 'health', and also 'women and child development', neither cabinet ministers heading either of these departments were assigned to make the new surrogacy policy announcement but it was India's cabinet rank minister for foreign affairs who appeared before a press conference called for the purpose, to make this policy statement on the changes to the national surrogacy policy. The minister announced various changes to the surrogacy bill, many of which are explicitly exclusionary and homophobic and proceeded to justify these in the following way: '*We* do not recognise homosexual or live in relationships that is why *they* are not allowed to commission babies through surrogacy, it is against *our* ethos' (emphasis added).[1]

Or consider this example where Imran Khan, the then recently elected Prime Minister of Pakistan, in a widely circulated interview to a Pakistan news site, *Hum News*, had this indictment for feminism: 'A mother has [the] biggest influence on a person ... a real mother, that is. I completely disagree with this Western concept, this feminist movement ... it has degraded the role of a mother ... when I was growing up, my mother had the most impact on me.'[2]

India and Pakistan are no strangers to the politics of origins, of course. The two illustrations are paradigmatic of the manner in which the binary originary discourse of the West/non-West plays out routinely on questions of gender relations in the two countries. And, therefore, it is not that these representations of gender, sexuality and women's rights in India and Pakistan as 'Western' and 'alien' and culturally inappropriate constitute a matter of any surprise but rather they are the invariable lightning rods for mobilising the powerful epistemic and political hold of the politics of origins in the region and are routinely wheeled out to repress democratic claim-making.

Finally, consider this excerpted vignette from a speech on human rights made by the home minister of India's ruling BJP in 2019.

> India and the world have different concepts and situations regarding human rights. If we evaluate it with the world's standards, then perhaps that is not right ...[3] India has an inbuilt framework of human rights. Our family values have special protection of women and children, and villages look after the poor believing it to be part of their dharma ...[4] Ensuring a synergy between our cultural values and the modern approach to rights would make India the best in the world in terms of human rights.[5]

The politics of origins here is invoked to effectively discredit any critical scrutiny of human rights violations by the Indian state on the basis that international human rights standards are deficient and lacking and cannot be used to judge the workings of the Indian state. However, what is striking about the mode of reasoning on display here is that it does not deploy an outright rejection of human rights by invoking straightforward cultural relativism. Rather, it mobilises originary 'cultural values' arguments to reject international human rights standards by demanding to substitute these with culturally appropriate ones. And, therefore, the argument here is not that human rights are redundant or are not recognised in Indian culture, which it tediously and erroneously refutes by insisting on India's 'inbuilt human rights framework', but rather that international human rights standards themselves are in need of repair, retooling, and replacement by those which are culturally appropriate. This is a dangerous argument for at least three reasons: The politics of origins deployed here wilfully distracts from the deeply fragmented, fearful, exclusionary and hostile political and institutional cultures that the 'cultural values' discourse is embedded in but also reproduces and fortifies. In this case, the 'cultural values' mobilised here are resolutely identified as *hindutva*, racist, hetero-masculinist–patriarchal, anti-Dalit anti-Adivasi, and Islamophobic. Invoking 'cultural values' here is to essentially locate 'culture' firmly against the politics of democratic dissent and justice. In refusing the legitimacy of the critical scrutiny of human rights violations of the Indian state, what is in effect refused here is any political accountability or indeed responsibility for democratic functioning and for upholding the legal constitutional status of rights and entitlements. Finally, invoking 'cultural values' as the 'framework' for rebooting international human rights substantially undermines the political and legal legitimacy of the Indian constitution as the guarantor of fundamental rights and civil liberties of all citizens.

The politics of origins as played out in the three illustrations above remind yet again of the need for hyper-vigilance and caution in using categories of the 'West' and 'non-West' in discrete binary terms. They evocatively illustrate how the binary categories of the West/non-West produce disciplining and essentialising discourses that erase specificity and difference while clamping down on the democratic politics of dissent and justice. It is therefore, crucial to remain hyper-vigilant in respect of the ways in which these binary originary discourses reproduce not only particular gendered representations and power relations that must be refused, but also how their deployment both rearticulates and leaves unchallenged the hegemonic terms of global human rights talk that privileges some and excludes other struggles. My call for exercising a cautious–reflexive view in deploying the binary West/non-West while speaking of human rights owes in some part to the hostile criticism and reception directed at the women's and feminist movement in India and Pakistan, which is besieged by labels characterising it as foreign, alien and a Western import, and therefore, inauthentic, culturally inappropriate and illegitimate. However, as I have noted elsewhere (Madhok 2010), the argument that advocating women's rights and feminist politics constitutes inauthentic politics and an inauthentic social mobilisation because feminism happens to have its 'originary' moment in the 'West' is weak not least because women's rights were mooted and supported during the anticolonial nationalist movement itself (John 1996; Ram 2000). Moreover, the difficulties with women's rights in India and Pakistan are less to do with their being 'foreign' or 'out of place' with culture/tradition and more to do with their fragile and insecure inclusion into state legal constitutionalism, the actual experiential failure of rights on the ground (Rajan 2003) and the absence of accountability and non-individuation of citizen identities (Ram 2000).

Nevertheless, the irresistible power of the politics of origins has meant that even where women's rights have been explicitly under consideration, these are required to be in alignment with dominant definitions of authentic culture/ scriptural tradition and 'modern' Indian and Pakistani identity. It is hardly surprising therefore, that the debates on women's citizenship in postcolonial India and Pakistan have been circumscribed by an unyielding attention to balance out demands for women's equal citizenship rights with their religious and cultural roles (Kapur and Cossman 1996). Perhaps, nothing illustrates this constant accommodation of women's rights better than the insertion of the *Hudood* ordinances into Pakistan's legal system in 1979, introduced as part of the drive by the military dictator General Zia-ul-Haq to 'Islamise' Pakistan. These ordinances restructured the entire legal framework in Pakistan 'to institutionalize discrimination against women and non-muslim citizens' (Saigol 2004: 14). Among the new order of offences introduced by these ordinances were those of *zina*, which criminalised sexual intercourse outside marriage and conflated rape with 'illicit sex' and adultery. As scholars have noted, 'thousands of women were arrested under charges of *zina* over the next 30 years and it became the most common reason for their incarceration' (Saigol 2004; A. Khan 2018: 63). The feminist and women's movement was one of the few oppositional voices at the forefront of opposing the military rule of Zia-ul-Haq. During this period, it entered into a period of open confrontation with the military state over the dilution of existing women's rights and in its opposition to the 'exclusionary Islamic State' (A. Khan 2018: 111). However, this confrontation also brought into sharp relief the difficult and fraught negotiations over the binaries of secular and religious feminisms, between 'political' and 'non-political' feminists, and also between elite metropolitan and rural, provincial politics of women's rights. None of these binaries have met with any resolution, and if anything, have only intensified with the shift in global politics since 2001.

The challenge of resisting originary discourses on human rights is a pressing one. How, do we resist the binary politics of 'West' and 'non-West' and also think of the movements, rights claims and politics that take place in the non-Anglo-North American-European worlds without losing either their historical and political specificity or their geopolitical location and hierarchical relationship with majoritarian human rights discourses? In other words, how do we go about 'worlding' human rights without losing sight of their historical, linguistic and political specificities including the very specific ways in which these are mobilised? In my view, it is more productive to think of human rights as not wholly derivative from the three major revolutions in the West—the American, the French and the English—or entirely oppositional to Western notions and conventions of human rights. It is not helpful to regard them as entirely discrete in form, in that one would be hard pressed to find hermetically sealed or 'pure' rights traditions. Instead, human rights must be viewed as interlocked into relations that are historically, productively, intimately, racially, intersectionally, materially, and coercively produced and experienced. I must hasten to add here, that to say that we must be cautious and reflexive towards categories such as the 'West' when speaking of human rights is, of course, not to suggest that we ignore the geopolitical power relations upheld and signified by the 'West', nor that we lose historical specificity and the historically specific ways that global human rights discourses and politics have emerged, evolved, travelled, are translated and debated. It simply means that it is much more generative and productive to think of human rights in a transnational mode, recognising the unequal and uneven circuits of power in which they operate while also acknowledging the historically specific, intersectional, geopolitically situated and embedded political struggles for rights, with their particular conceptual categories, languages (both literal and conceptual) and modes of world-making.

Time–Space Provincialism

The politics of origins haunts both the celebratory accounts and the recent progressive critiques of human rights. If anything, it is reproduced and resurrected through critique. In particular, the epistemic power of the politics of origins is such that it sets up a particular paradox, a deadlock if you like, in scholarly accounts of human rights. On the one hand, the originary impulse enables different forms of time-space provincialism in human rights accounts. On the other hand, the critiques of this time-space provincialism resurrect the politics of origins all over again. By time-space provincialism, I simply mean that the epistemic centre of human rights intellectual thinking is temporally and geographically located in the West. So even if the timeline of the originary stories of human rights might shift, the location of the human rights story remained steadfastly in place with the result that the geopolitical context of epistemic enquiry remains stationary. To put it in another way, the politics of origins not only informs the discourse on human rights in originary terms but also frames its critiques. Through a critique of existing originary theses, it reproduces the politics of origins albeit in a different form—this time through refutation. The refutation itself can be either more straightforward—we know that there are other human rights stories (Sikkink 2017)—or more complex—presenting different timelines to show that human rights did not originate in the West from time immemorial (Hunt 2007; Moyn 2010; Burke 2010; Jensen 2015). The politics of origins is hardly confined to particular scholarly and disciplinary contexts and appears across different disciplinary sites where it has particular empirical and epistemic consequences.

Not surprisingly, a key theme of the politics of origins revolves around the question of temporality. In the last decade, this question of temporality has dominated the landscape of human rights scholarship. Of course, it was not that long ago that one would (and expect to) routinely come across teleological histories of human rights, which would mostly consist of how human rights made their appearance throughout the different epochs in the West from antiquity to modernity and how from their originary location in the West, spread to the rest of the world. In recent years, however, scholars have mounted insightful and sharp critiques of the seamless temporal links drawn between global human rights and Western civilisation. The key premise of these projects is that human rights belong to a more recent history and therefore, their work disputes the classical timeline of teleological histories. These recent historiographies of human rights chart a different temporality of human rights that fundamentally disrupts the originary impulse that aggregates a variety of 'Western' rights talk in different historical periods under the umbrella of global human rights (Hunt 2007; Moyn 2010). In her book *Inventing Human Rights*, Lynn Hunt (2007) plots the timeline for the emergence of human rights in the period from 1689 to 1776. It is during this time period in France, Great Britain and the United States, she argues, that the term human rights becomes operational as a 'common term', and a 'self-evident' one. The burden of Hunt's book lies in accounting for this emergence of 'self-evidence' (2007: 19) of human rights in these countries.[6] She explains that the growing self-evidence of human rights emerges from the increasing popularity and cultural circulation of the ideas of autonomy, bodily integrity and empathetic selfhood in public exhibitions, newspapers and popular novels. Together these forms of cultural production enable a 'leap of faith' and a particular ability to 'imagine' that 'someone else is like you' (Hunt 2007: 32). Now even though Hunt is very careful to point out that this 'self-evidence' of human rights applies to only a select few in society and does not include women,[7] children, colonial subjects and slaves, the inescapable question, however, is one of 'self-evidence' for whom and also 'self-evidence' towards what? These questions are essential because Hunt's timeline for the emergence of the 'self-evidence' of human rights is also the high age of empire and colonial order. As has been now powerfully documented, the enunciation of the declaration of the rights of man and citizen in 1789 was followed by a furious denouncement of the rights of all except propertied white men. And, the next decade and a half in the immediate declaration of the rights of man saw France, Spain and Great Britain send out their militaries in an all-out war to crush the greatest argument and demonstration of human rights and equality that arose in the wake of the *originary* and foundational moment of republicanism and human rights. As Michel-Rolph Trouillot powerfully reminds us:

> The Haitian Revolution was the ultimate test to the universalist pretensions of both the French and the American revolutions. And they both failed. *In 1791, there is no public debate on the record, in France, in England, or in the United States on the right of black slaves to achieve self-determination, and the right to do so by way of armed resistance.* (Trouillot 1995: 88)

The Haitian Revolution powerfully and unequivocally refutes any idea of the self-evidence of human rights (James 1934; Trouillot 1995). It also underscores the point that human rights have not been extended through a gradual recognition of the 'self-evidence' of human rights across the globe and for all but rather where human rights have held up, they have done so as a result of a long drawn and continuing political struggle for rights and human rights.

In an account of quite some contrast to that of Lynn Hunt's, Samuel Moyn (2010, 2014) writes that human rights do not emerge as a global imaginary until the mid-20th century. In fact, they only come into their own as recently as the 1970s. Moyn links this global ascendance with the rise of international human rights organisations such as Amnesty International during this period. The reason for their emergence, Moyn argues, is less to do with their 'self evidence' but rather because they are the 'last utopia' left standing amidst the ruins of all other political imaginaries in the post war period in the West. In a searing critique of the teleological accounts of human rights, Moyn argues that attempts to insert human rights into a long and unbroken European civilisational tradition—stretching from the Greeks to the European enlightenment—is a mistaken endeavor. He suggests that no such tradition exists in quite this form and points out that entitlements that were spoken about at different points whether in the natural law and rights traditions or indeed among the Greeks were hardly referring to a supranational framework of human rights that would transcend national sovereignty and belonging. Other scholars of human rights too have sought to locate the dynamism of human rights talk, not so much in the rise of international organisations and the rise of civil and political rights, or indeed in the efforts of Western lawmakers, peacemakers and lawyers but rather in the diplomatic exertions of newly independent states of the Global South. These scholars seek to shift the timeline of human rights from political imaginaries, cultural aesthetics and the rise of civil and political rights in the West in order to locate the rise of human rights in the human rights diplomacy of the newly independent postcolonial nations in the Global South. These accounts escape the time–space provincialism of their progressive peers as they work to shift the timeline and place of 'origin' of global human rights, even if they reproduce the framework of origins all over again. For instance, Roland Burke (2010) notes that there was a robust and visible support for human rights at the first ever significant meeting of the postcolonial nations that congregated as a 'third world entity', at the Bandung conference in 1955. Similarly, Steven Jensen (2016) writes that the 1960s laid the foundations for groundbreaking and radical interventions on human rights, especially those on race and religious equality which were led by the new postcolonial nations who insisted on such equality as core human rights. These historiographical accounts of human rights showing different timelines and actors are significant and do important work, not least in disrupting the civilisationalism that lies at the heart of the popular narratives of human rights. However, these critical accounts also show how difficult it is to escape the originary framework of human rights discourses. Even when they set out to refute the thesis, they end up reproducing the terms of the politics of origins all over again.

Philosophical Talks on Origin

Now, the origin question I have been tracking is central not only to historiographical accounts. Philosophical accounts of rights and human rights are no stranger to the politics of origin either. While historiographies of human rights are focused on establishing different timelines and actors, key accounts of human rights within political theory and philosophy are animated by the 'originary' or 'foundational' moments of Republicanism and the declarations of the rights of man and citizen articulated during the American and French revolutions. These scholarly engagements have generated important interventions focusing on the aporias, paradoxes and the violent exclusions inherent in the 'interval' between the rights of man and those of the citizen; between the normative 'we the people' and the declarative 'we the people'; between those who make the laws and those who obey them (Benhabib 1994: 6).[8] Hannah Arendt (1958) identified the most significant of these paradoxes, that between the rights of man and those of citizen—namely, if one did not have citizenship rights, then one did not have human rights. In recent years, the 'equivocal' (Balibar 2017: 29) nature of the declarations of rights of man and citizen have led philosophers to consider the democratic possibilities and limitations of these 'foundational' republican enunciations. Étienne Balibar (1994: 44) writes that there is a 'double identification' at the 'core of the revolutionary text'. The first identification is that of man and citizen— they are one and the same, no gaps between them. The second identification is between freedom and equality. It is this identification between freedom and equality—of one being the 'exact measure of the other', that Balibar calls 'equaliberty' (1994: 46–47).[9] Equaliberty signifies a 'universal right to politics' and a permanent tension between universal political signification of the rights of man and the 'struggle' and 'social conflict' required to construct the 'politics of rights of man'. Contrary to Balibar's equation of man and citizen, Jacques Rancière identifies a 'gap' and an 'interval' between the two, which is generative of what he calls 'dissensus'. The question of the 'political subject', writes Rancière,

> is not caught between the void term of man and the plenitude of the citizen with its actual rights. A political subject is a capacity for staging scenes of dissensus ... a dispute over what is given and about the frame within which we see something as given ... the putting of two worlds in one and the same world. (Rancière 2010: 69)

In conceiving 'dissensus', he takes Hannah Arendt (1951) and also Giorgio Agamben (1998) to task for their negative reading of the paradox of the founding moment of republicanism—that is, the interval between man and citizen in the declaration of the rights of man and citizen; for confining the subject of rights to already determined 'collections of individuals', who are either already citizens and already enjoy rights by virtue of having the 'right to have rights' (Arendt 1979) or those who are not and, therefore, only have the rights of man, which in effect amounts to having no rights at all. In contrast, Rancière (2004) argues that the 'subject of rights is the subject, or more accurately the process of subjectivization, that bridges the interval between the two forms of existence of those rights' and therefore, the interval between rights of man and citizen, neither signifies a 'theoretical lock', nor a 'void' or an 'abyss', but rather the possibility of political subjectivation and of democratic politics as 'dissensus' (2004: 302–04). Consequently, he proposes that the question of the rights of man be reset as 'the rights of man are the rights of those who have not the rights that they have and have the rights that they have not' (2004: 302). Central to this recasting is the recognition and the necessity of producing accounts of political subjectivation and collective action of those 'who have no part' (2004: 305), and who are represented as beyond accounts of democracy or anti-democracy, justice or injustice. Both Rancière and Balibar highlight the importance of political action in developing forms of community able to enact rights through demanding a right to have rights. For Rancière (1999: 30), political action is necessary in order to 'reconfigure the space where parties, parts or lack of parts have been defined'; it is through political action that the boundaries of exclusion—who is the subject of the rights of man or who is included within existing regimes of rights—are contested and redistributed. Similarly, for Balibar (2002: 6), the 'democratization of democracy' takes place through the 'struggle to enjoy rights which have already been declared.' Contentious politics are crucial, then, in providing access to or inclusion within already existing rights. Three things are of note here: first, it is striking that the pre-eminent philosophers thinking on human rights and political action turn to events from two hundred years ago in order to ground their arguments. Manfredi (2013) writes that there is often a tendency among left critics of human rights to contrast the contemporary human rights politics with an 'older revolutionary rights tradition' (Manfredi 2013: 6). However, what interests me here is the philosophical and epistemic erasure that this harking back to the originary sites of human rights politics located in Europe entails, which are held up as the normative and the desirable but also as the corrective to contemporary travails of human rights politics. The striking thing in these discussions is that 'Europe' as a standard background context remains stable and a constant normative referent, even in the midst of a growing acknowledgement that the meanings of rights far from being 'transhistorical' (Manfredi 2013: 8) are historically located, fluid and shifting. Second, even as Balibar and Rancière call upon the importance of political struggles in obtaining and continually reaffirming purportedly universal rights, there nonetheless remains an abstract, unchanging universal in the form of an axiom of equality (Rancière 1999) or of rights that have already been declared (Balibar 2002). Consequently, theirs is an analysis which accommodates political subjectivation only in the regime of already declared rights and focuses on those seeking inclusion into already declared rights. Third and following from the above, could it really be the case that the explanatory framework of human rights politics around the globe is the originary founding Anglo–American-European republican moment? Furthermore, how far can this overarching originary framework with its linguistic and philosophical aporias, paradoxes and democratic possibilities be used to explain the stuff of politics in 'most of the world'? I would be inclined to advance an answer in the negative. However, I am digressing from my main point, which is this—there are consequences to the erasure of empirical contexts of human rights mobilisations in 'most of the world'. Although tracking the present histories and experiences of rights and human rights in the Anglo, North American and European worlds is an important exercise, these are only ever 'provincial' accounts, and we have to work harder at resisting wilful ignorance and erasures of the mobilisations for rights and entitlements in 'most of the world' and also to produce conceptual and theoretical accounts of these mobilisations. The latter is a crucial imperative as it is only through conceptual descriptions of rights mobilisations in 'most of the world' that we will begin to counter the existing mismatch between the contemporary historical, theoretical and philosophical work on rights and human rights and the growing mobilisations on the ground in 'most of the world' (as the latter for most part fail to figure in this work). Finally, undertaking conceptual descriptions will also enable explorations of the stakes and struggles over rights in different parts of the globe.

Human Rights, Neoliberalism and the 'Depoliticisation Thesis'

There is, however, yet another epistemic impact of the politics of origins and its time-space provincialism that I want to draw attention to: I am referring here to the growing negativity, despair and epistemic erasure that characterises critical progressive scholarship on human rights. This negativity is, of course, not without good reason. A commonly occurring cause for this disquiet is the growing depoliticisation of our life-worlds as a result of neoliberalism and, human rights are often seen as deeply complicit in global ascendance of neoliberalism. The 'depoliticisation thesis' has become the standard lament and mode of critique within popular and academic imaginaries. It goes something like this: under neoliberalism, 'we' have become depoliticised subjects with little interest or stake in progressive politics of social justice or in anything other than consuming products and being consumerist subjects. Now this depoliticisation thesis comes in a number of forms, and the link with neoliberalism is not uniform in all cases. Influential philosophical critiques, for instance, link the growing depoliticisation to a philosophical turn to 'ethics'. And radical democratic theorists of the European left often bemoan the depoliticised nature of this theorising; critiquing it for being divorced from economic and political materialities, and for the evacuation of the 'political' from its work. In this context, the 'ethical turn' is usually used to refer to the writings of a number of theorists including, although, not only limited to, Michel Foucault, Emmanuel Levinas, and also to some influential strands of postcolonial scholarship, which are charged with inordinately focusing on identifying the ethical practices required for a democratic polity.

Predominantly, though, a key theme driving the 'depoliticisation' thesis is one of 'antipolitics' and especially the 'antipolitics' of humanitarianism. And, as I noted in Chapter 1, human rights have now become near synonymous with the practice of humanitarianism and with humanitarian actors who act on behalf of those 'victims' who cannot claim rights on their own (Rancière 2004). And, we know that in practice the human of human rights is in effect a citizen of a nation state who enjoys human rights as a feature of their citizenship (Arendt 1958). Moreover, it is also increasingly the case, that as human rights in the form of 'new humanitarianism' are assuming centre stage in global governance, they have led not only to an increasing displacement of international law but also to the depoliticising of rights and human rights by actively disassociating human rights from national citizenship (Mamdani 2010). In other words, human rights are increasingly no longer seen as political claims made by citizens but as a 'responsibility to protect' discharged by global powers towards 'populations', which it sees as its 'wards' (Mamdani 2010: 54).

Furthermore, the strong predisposition of global human rights towards civil and political rights and their championing of minimalist, individualistic rights counterposed to any collective politics of social justice has rendered them eminently suitable for neoliberal projects. Accordingly, in recent years, important questions are being asked of the neoliberal politics of human rights, (Whyte 2017, 2018; Moyn 2015, 2018; Marks 2013), and especially about their lack of strong and discernable distributive equality discourse. Scholars point out that not only has the astronomical rise of global inequality coincided with the global rise of both human rights and neoliberalism, and that human rights have, under their watch, seen and are seeing the most egregious forms of global inequality, but also that they have failed spectacularly to produce a discourse of social justice to counter this trend (Moyn 2018). And, consequently, there are now serious question marks hanging over the role of human rights in supporting and promoting neoliberalism's global designs and politics.

But perhaps, one of the most powerful critiques of neoliberalism and its 'antipolitics' is the one recently advanced by political theorist Wendy Brown. In her book *Undoing the Demos*, Brown (2015) writes that neoliberalism has recast the relationship between state and subject on the model of the contemporary firm, thereby, converting all political values into market values and reducing all social relations to commercial transactions, including those of political participation. Brown argues that this has serious consequences for political equality and for citizenship. Essentially, the juggernaut of neoliberalism marches on only to result in the death of the *homo politicus*.

I am not disputing that neoliberalism converts social relations into commercial ones, but I do not think that neoliberalism and the specific historical forms it takes in particular locations—Brown's examples are all located in the Euro-Atlantic world—is replicated in quite the same way in all locations and neither does it essentially replace all forms of the politics of equality and justice everywhere. To say this is not to deny the undeniable march of neoliberalism but rather to say two things: First, if influential theoretical and philosophical critiques of neoliberalism were to pay some attention to the ongoing struggles in the Global South, far from showing the impending death of the *homo politicus* they would reveal dynamic and bitterly fought struggles about how to redefine and expand the scope and meaning of citizenship. To draw attention to these struggles and mobilisations, however, is not to suggest that they simply mount a struggle against neoliberal policies, structures and institutions from an 'outside', as if they could. Instead it is to say that contestations of neoliberalism take place within specific historical conditions of neoliberalism in different locations and are consequently shaped by these specificities. Second, if we are to take seriously the calls to 'theorise from the global South' (Comaroff and Comaroff 2012) then we not only need to be attentive to how under particular historical conditions, certain subjectivities, subjects, precarities become routinely available and the different forms that neoliberal prescriptivism—for example, 'autonomisation' and 'responsibilisation' (Rose 1999: 174)—takes in different parts of the world but significantly, we must also pay attention to the forms of contestations, conflicts and counter-conducts that are generated under historically specific neoliberal contexts, and which work to disorient, destabilise and even interrupt deeply unjust concentrations of political, social and technological power (see Chapters 4 and 5).

Shifting the Perspective: Rights/Human Rights on a Different Scale

So, what does *haq* have to do with this tracking and the critique of a politics of origins? Quite simply, to focus on *haq*, as another language for rights and human rights, is to reorient historical, theoretical and philosophical thinking grounded in the politics of origins and to produce an epistemic shift towards enquiries that are attentive to the political cultures of rights in 'most of the world'. A focus on vernacular rights cultures and their disruption of 'originary rights talk', is to neither suggest that we divorce rights talk from how human rights operate as a form of hegemonic discourse globally for that would be to feign wilful ignorance or even worse, a 'colonial unknowing' and an ignorance of the circuits of power—histories, discourses and institutional politics within which all rights talk operates, and nor is it also to suggest that we deploy a 'global/local' framework for human rights or a global 'network' one for human rights.[10] Instead it is to suggest that we acknowledge the hierarchical epistemic and geopolitical power relations that exist between global human rights and vernacular rights cultures. Furthermore, this acknowledgment must be epistemological and needs to be directed at countering the epistemic erasures of human rights politics in 'most of the world'. Acknowledging vernacular rights cultures epistemically would mean avowing and responding to the forms of world-making including to the particular 'strategies' of utilisation of rights by subaltern groups which are linked not only to the historical and cultural identity of the groups making rights claims but also to the particular kinds of politics and institutional settings that they inhabit, critique and strive towards. Moreover, such an epistemic acknowledgement would also consist of drawing attention to the fact that these rights cultures exist in a relation of marginality and subalternity in respect to majoritarian rights discourses associated with the nation state, legal constitutionalism and developmentalism—even if these are also the pivots around which vernacular political cultures of rights operate.

Not unsurprisingly then, the question of citizenship is paramount in these rights struggles and the state is central in these accounts. However, does the focus on the state not end up replicating the state-centric nature of human rights scholarship, albeit in a different mode? If so, do vernacular rights cultures simply rehearse and demonstrate empirically the paradox of human rights discourse, which claims that human rights are in the final instance, citizenship rights? Numerous scholars, following Hannah Arendt, have elaborated on the philosophical implications of this paradox for human rights politics. Empirical studies of human rights too have followed through on the implications of Arendt's paradox by privileging nation states as their object of analysis. In contrast, I want to suggest that while it is certainly the case that vernacular rights cultures can be state focused, that is, they direct their rights demands at the state, it is also through paying attention to them that we can re-examine the ways through which the global architecture of human rights privileges nation states. By doing so, we can disrupt the particular form of nation state-centric rights talk privileged in global human rights discourse in three ways: first, the rights politics of vernacular rights cultures does not boil down to the Arendtian paradox—that citizenship is the primary route to rights—chiefly, because unlike the inclusionary impulse to demand already existing rights, mobilisations for *haq* alter the means through which rights are delivered and transform the content and meaning of the rights demanded (Dunford and Madhok 2015). Second, the demands for rights and their practice in the vernacular shows up the internally differentiated and intersectional subject of rights. It brings into view not the undifferentiated human of human rights but one who is gendered, raced and comes into being within existing caste relations. Finally, the evocation of *haq* draws attention to the manner in which nation states respond to the demands for human rights by subaltern groups. Therefore, rather than only focusing on the speech practices and acts of nation states in the international human rights policy making arenas, vernacular rights cultures also focus on the stakes and struggles driving domestic human rights policy making. This is not a matter of only identifying the match and/or the mismatch between international pronouncements of states committing to international human rights and the lack of corresponding domestic policy at home. Instead, it produces a differently oriented style of institutionally informed scholarship;

not just of dominant actors entering into majoritarian and dominant networks and conversations on human rights but one that includes the struggles, voices and claims making by subaltern groups. Consider, for instance, how recent historiographical accounts of global human rights have focused on the role of states in the Global South in the development of international human rights agendas, shining an important spotlight on the role of the Global South in pushing egalitarian agendas at various human rights conferences (Burke 2010; Jensen 2016). It would be interesting to see the extent to which these internationally expressed agendas voicing redistributive justice were reflected in domestic policy making during the same time period. In this context it is interesting to note that scholars working on rights and citizenship in India, for instance, have pointed out the absence of any grand domestic egalitarian agenda or redistributive rights talk during the period that India was making arguments for egalitarian redistribution in international human rights circuits, and that welfare and redistributive measures that were argued at 'home' were couched in terms of 'charity' to be bestowed by the Indian state rather than as rights that citizens were entitled to (Jayal 2013).[11]

Moreover, focusing exclusively on how nation states perform human rights in the international arena does not tell us much about the internal contestations over rights and human rights going on within those nation states or indeed about the ways in which subaltern groups within those states have deployed international human rights law and legislations either to claim rights from nation states or indeed to critique state power.[12] An important intervention which aims to fill some of this gap in human rights and policy scholarship is by Mala Htun and Laurel Weldon (2018). In their recently published book, the two political scientists ask the question—'when and why do governments promote women's rights?' In a cross-national study spanning 70 countries, they examine 'policies formally adopted by governments, including constitutions, supreme court decisions, and policy documents' (Htun and Weldon 2018: 255) in order to explain the 'variation and trends' in the institutionalisation of gender equality laws within and across countries.[13] One of the striking findings they uncover is that in 'cross national patterns of policy on violence against women and legislation promoting equality conformed', the single most important factor for instituting government policy on violence against women was the presence of vibrant 'autonomous feminist movements'. In other words, change came from feminist movements, which helped to 'consolidate international norms, which they leveraged to pressure for greater changed in domestic contexts' (Htun and Weldon 2018: 247).

This is an important intervention as it identifies the key factors responsible for the variation in institutionalisation of women's rights across the globe. However, the focus on public policy legislation w ithin states, while very important and revealing, essentially tackles legislation on already agreed 'global norms' around women's rights instituted in international instruments such as CEDAW, among others. And, even though identifying key actors responsible for the passage of legislations on gender violence is very significant, focusing on end points of struggles, that is, on policies enshrined in law, does not by itself tell us about the contestations around these policies, not least within feminist movements, and as to why feminist groups choose to pursue particular policies on violence against women, or as to which feminist voices have most power. Studying vernacular rights cultures on the other hand, opens up the possibility for policy making on rights and human rights to not only ever be about the 'vernacularisation' of global norms (Levitt and Merry 2009) while also acknowledging that subaltern groups are also not always able to influence policy changes. Subaltern mobilisations often escape full representation as rights-bearing subjects since their demands often exceed the possibilities and imaginaries set out in global human rights and state policy making. Therefore, a focus on vernacular rights cultures also entails the question of representation—and one concerning the actual representational capacity of nation states to effectively respond to the demands for rights and human rights of subaltern and marginalised groups within the nation state. The representational capacity of nation states is inordinately compromised by their willingness to facilitate dispossession and corporate extractivism such as land grabs but also through acquiring proprietorial rights over minerals and natural resources that collectively belong to subaltern groups. Indeed, the politics of vernacular rights cultures shines light on the low representational capacity of states to represent subaltern groups who have historically borne the brunt of its security and development apparatus. Therefore, the paradox of human rights in relation to subaltern groups is that although nation states are responsible for delivering human rights, they are less and less able to represent these groups, including their demands for rights and human rights. All of this does not make the nation state any less crucial to the study of the human rights. It only shifts the perspective on the appearance of the nation state within global human rights—as not an undifferentiated and fully representing entity but one that is internally differentiated and whose political legitimacy is under challenge by various groups including subaltern groups.

Political Struggles and Rights in the Vernacular

Thus far, I have argued that studying vernacular rights cultures requires a shift in our scale of analysis—in the direction of different forms of claim-making by subjects of rights who are neither only ever nation states, transnational organisations, nor 'humanitarian subjects/victims' of rights. These subjects of rights are not privileged transnational interlocutors, vernacularisers or translators of global human rights 'norms' or indeed global civil society actors but subaltern groups organising for rights. While the claim-making of these groups might invoke global norms and international human rights treaties, vernacular rights cultures are neither the direct products of nor principal sites of 'global norm diffusion'. Instead, they are dynamic, productive, generative, and conflictual sites where the democratic possibilities and the limitations of human rights creatively play out; where rights are claimed by subaltern groups and in the process get transformed and expanded, and where through the deployment of rights, the limitations of rights become visible. As such these grassroots mobilisations are key sites where subjectification takes place.

An intersectional gendered lens is crucial to study these forms of subjectification as it helps reveal the limitations and exclusions but also the intersectional failures of rights talk. A conceptual study of this rights talk involves producing a feminist historical ontology (see Chapter 3) of this conceptual language of claim-making while also showing how rights subjects come into being. Through claiming citizenship rights and participating in political mobilisations and struggles, it becomes evident that not all of those claiming rights can easily become the subjects of rights that they wish to be assigned as, even if they might be participating in a collective to demand these rights. In short, these collective demands can also bring into sharp relief the limits of collective struggles by highlighting their intersectional failures.

Political struggles are key sites for the articulation of rights in the vernacular. As I noted earlier, these rights mobilisations and rights struggles are directed at the nation state and even though these struggles invoke rights to demand entitlements from the state, the study of vernacular rights cultures does not accord authorship of rights and agency to the nation state alone. For it is the case that these struggles frequently invoke sources and justificatory premises of rights that are not informed by or limited to the state alone (I will examine these justificatory premises in Chapters 4 and 5). While this political activism is led by a concern for citizenship rights—and is primarily directed at the state—the framework deployed is not only one that corresponds to that of the 'right to have rights', that is, one of inclusion into the already existing framework of rights but rather one which is also invested in bringing new citizenship rights into existence. It justifies these new sets of rights not on the basis of citizenship alone, but also through a different moral and political vocabulary that is not derivative of the state or from citizenship rights. In directing their rights demands at the state, these marginalised, poor and intersectional subaltern subjects refuse the well accepted adage and conventional wisdom that regards the existence of minimum economic baselines as necessary predicates for political rights. More specifically, though, they encourage us to rethink the Marshallian categorisation and separation of citizenship rights into civil, political and economic rights as well as their hierarchisation. These subaltern struggles demand political accountability from state developmentalism and meticulously scrutinise the pervasive structural poverty and dispossession that it has unleashed, while also questioning the exclusionary gendered logics and differentially distributed vulnerabilities and effects it produces. For instance, in my ethnographies, subaltern groups routinely asked as to why it was that the money earmarked for poverty alleviation, drought relief and other welfare assistance failed to find its way into the pockets of its intended beneficiaries, that is, the poor? They interrogated why the state failed to uphold the minimum wage legislation or make regular payments for wages accrued under the rural employment guarantee programme. And they pointed to how the state condoned rampant caste and gender bias within drought relief programmes set up to provide employment to people in drought-affected districts and also to the flagrant procedural inefficiencies and corrosive corruption practices plaguing the Public Distribution System (PDS) and its network of fair price ration shops. More recently, with the introduction of compulsory biometric identification cards for accessing welfare, they have protested at the exclusion of millions of vulnerable citizens dependent on welfare for their very survival. All of these issues, they pointed out, were responsible for an institutionalisation of endemic poverty. According to them, this institutionalised endemic poverty was a result of an interlocking triad: a lack of transparency in procedural rules of government and routinised official corruption, the general failure of democratic accountability in political life, and everyday intersecting oppressions that impact and impede the quality of citizenship.

The fluent, powerful and complex articulation of citizenship rights by subaltern groups also questions the clear-cut divisions between 'subaltern worlds' and those of the elites. The vernacular rights cultures they produce disrupt the binary understandings of their politics by influential conceptual formulations such as 'political society'. Here, I am referring specifically to the distinction that Partha Chatterjee (2004) has drawn between political and civil society in order to study the politics in what he calls the 'rest of the world'. 'Civil society', Chatterjee writes, is constitutive of the elite, those who are well-versed in and consequently operate in the light zones of constitutionalism, freedom, equality, citizenship. In contrast, 'political society' is composed of those who exist in the dark zones—outside of and in violation of the law. In short, Chatterjee suggests a divide between citizens and populations. Drawing on the distinction between formal and actual rights, Chatterjee argues that, in terms of 'formal structure', everyone is a citizen and therefore member of civil society; however, he writes,

> Most of the inhabitants of India are only tenuously, and even ambiguously and contextually, rights bearing citizens … they are not, therefore, proper members of civil society and are not regarded as such by the institutions of the state … as populations within the jurisdiction of the state they have to be both looked after and controlled by various governmental agencies … these groups on their part accept that their activities are often illegal and contrary to good civic behavior, but they make a claim to a habitation and a livelihood as a matter of right. (Chatterjee 2004: 38, 40)

Therefore, the question for Chatterjee is, 'how can the particular claims of marginal population groups, often grounded in violations of the law, be made consistent with the pursuit of equal citizenship and civic virtue?' (Chatterjee 2004: 64). Chatterjee is describing a form of politics in which some urban poor are able to claim welfare entitlements through organising themselves into a critical mass either as 'associations' that demand their inclusion into existing citizen entitlements or nominate person(s) to 'mediate' on their behalf or speak for them. Theirs is a politics of inclusion that is 'contextual', 'temporary' and 'paralegal' that takes place on a 'political terrain, where rules may be bent or stretched and not on the terrain of established law or administrative procedure … here there is no uniform exercise of rights and citizenship' (Chatterjee 2004: 60).

Chatterjee's binary formulation of 'civil' and 'political' society has met with not insubstantial critique (Sinha 2015; Nilsen 2018a). In contrast to Chatterjee's theorisation of political society, the vernacular rights cultures and the rural political mobilisations described in this book display both a fluency in and an insistence on legal constitutionalism and the importance of rights, not only for purposes of inclusion into already existing entitlements but also for a politics of transformation and justice. Their acknowledgement of legal constitutionalism as an important instrument and resource for the recognition of entitlements exists alongside a clear recognition, particularly among Indigenous groups, that they are not subjects without rights and jurisprudential ethics of their own, and that they do not need to derive these from the legal constitutionalist doctrines of the state. Having said this, the politics of vernacular rights cultures is linked to the state in two ways. First, transformation is sought not on a 'paralegal' terrain but on the terra firma of citizenship rights. The mobilisation of a subaltern rights politics is directed at the state to both hold it to account for the lack of implementation of its welfare policies and to put in place a new and expanded set of rights (see Chapter 4). In recent years, these expanded set of rights have emerged in large part from rural mobilisations and have led to the successful passage of six new legislations guaranteeing citizen entitlements. These rural mobilisations have adopted a range of strategies in their push for an expanded set of citizenship rights, including accessing the law courts which have become 'consolidated as a critical site of politics' (Biehl 2013: 419). In short, there is nothing illegal or 'paralegal' about these mobilisations—in fact, if anything, they highlight the dynamic ethical engagements with rights and citizenship that subaltern groups deploy for an expansion of entitlements and for a politics of justice and equality that is not yet in place. In so doing, they disrupt the rather straightforward binary that Chatterjee draws between the civic politics of 'culturally equipped citizens' who deploy the language of rights and citizenship and those of the subaltern populations who operate on the 'terrain of political society', or on the margins of the legal constitutional state.

The second way in which the politics of vernacular rights cultures is linked to the state has to do with the self-making and forms of political subjectivation that developmentalism (both state and non-state led) as a form of governmentality and a technology of power engenders. Importantly, however, this rights politics is not only that of a politics of inclusion or one entirely focused on demanding relief in the face of state mandated exclusions (even though this is important and has material effects on those who are excluded). Crucially, it also enables the fashioning of particular forms of subjectivities and the coming into being of particular gendered subjects of rights.

The Justificatory Premises of *Haq*

As I noted in the introduction, I have been tracking the etymological roots, conceptual meanings and contemporary deployment of the Urdu/Arabic word *haq* in grassroots people's movements in India and Pakistan since 1999.

Ever since I first began documenting the use of the term by rural women in Rajasthan to demand their rights, I have been exploring the different kinds of intellectual resources and political imaginaries that *haq* offers, both for thinking about rights/human rights politics and also with respect to the sources of self-making and the processes of becoming a subject of rights. What, however, is the relationship between the contemporary meanings of the literal and conceptual term *haq* and global human rights discourse? And, how do we understand the conceptual meanings of *haq*? A useful way of documenting and analysing rights languages and also the conceptual meanings of *haq* is to locate these within the political imaginaries that they operate in and to examine the justificatory premises that underpin them. We need to ask what literal terms exist for entitlements and rights, what are their justificatory premises, what kinds of political and moral imaginaries they uphold and who are the subjects that are 'assigned' to rights and human rights? Not unlike other concepts, the conceptual meanings of *haq* are place dependent (Hacking 2002) and emerge out of a politics of location (Rich 1984).

A great deal of philosophical scholarship on human rights has engaged with what is sometimes known as 'foundations' for rights, and at other times, justificatory premises. Justifications for human rights concern themselves with the question of what the *basis* of rights should be or what human rights ought to rest upon. Consequently, several grounds for human rights have been offered. Among these, and not unsurprisingly, the justificatory premise of the 'human' has become a preoccupation of a lot of human rights thinking and consequently, has also come under serious theoretical scrutiny within critical human rights scholarship. Scholars have questioned the 'central reference point for human rights', which 'depend on some claim about what is distinctively human' (Phillips 2015: 3) and queried as to who is the human in human rights (Trouillot 1995; Wynter 2003)? The 'distinctively human' claims within philosophical discourse on human rights range from there being an essential 'human nature' with its capacities for rational thinking, autonomy and self-ownership to the crucial importance of human dignity. Grounding human rights in the intrinsic idea of the 'universal human' has neither been unqualified nor has it been universal in scope. If anything, the moral grounds for being 'human' have always been political and marked by hierarchical power relations and racialised, gendered and colonial worldviews. However, it is also the case that the 'human' invokes the powerful sentiment of sameness, and of being just like everyone else, and therefore, entitled to all that is accrued to everyone else. This sentiment and moral ground was first voiced in the eighteenth century declarations of rights of man and citizen and then two centuries later in the Universal Declaration of Human Rights (UDHR)—a reasonably long history of the sentiment by any account, and one characterised by its spectacular ineffectiveness in either making a universally applicable and a non-exclusionary philosophical case for human rights or for ensuring that human rights operate as an actually existing empirical reality for all peoples.

However, not all grounds or justifications for human rights are based on 'human nature', even when they are principally humanist. Contemporary scholarship on human rights and global justice have also introduced other justifications such as 'basic needs' (Miller 2012), 'capabilities' (Sen 2005; Nussbaum 2007), 'emerging world order' (Raz 2010) and 'cultural diversity' (Jones 2000: 33).[14] In contrast to seeking justificatory premises for human rights, Anne Phillips argues that the politics of the human is an 'enactment of equality' (Phillips 2015: 19), where equality is a 'political' and not a cognitive claim and crucially, one that is not dependent on a normative set of human qualities. Grounding the human in anything other than equality only opens up yet more grounds for exclusions and hierarchies, not least on the basis of 'gender coding'. Human rights are, Phillips argues, political and need to be claimed and not bestowed on those considered to be deserving them. According to her,

> It is not helpful to think of humanness as a reality that grounds our rights, a set of shared characteristics that we deem in some beings but not others, a list of characteristics we can use to work out who get the rights and who doesn't. Nor is it helpful to make our status as humans depend on not stressing some of our characteristics ... it is the language of equality, which is at the heart of the issue when we talk about the human—the right to be regarded as an equal should not depend on being able to prove one's membership of the category human ... the very act of claiming to be equal should be enough of a demonstration ... recognizing others as our human equals is not best understood as a process of recognition ... what links us (or could/should link us) is a politics of equality that refuses to attach hierarchical significance to difference. (Phillips 2015: 44–46)

I agree with Anne Phillips that human rights require a political rather than an abstract ontological commitment. However, it is also the case that the various justificatory premises offered for rights and human rights reveal interesting insights into their conceptual development and their exclusionary histories while also shining a light on those subjects who have been assigned to rights and are thereby regulated by them. Phillips (2015) is, however, right to insist that human rights have extended to others through political struggles for equality, rather than through the gradual unfolding of the idea of modernity. A focus on vernacular rights cultures accords a central place to the political struggles for rights by the marginalised. Crucially, it also focuses on the languages of rights and their justificatory premises deployed in these political struggles. The focus on the justificatory premises of *haq* is not to think of yet more justifications for human rights but rather to give an account of the conceptual and normative structure of *haq* and the rights and entitlements that it will allow itself to be assigned to. In short, I am less concerned with the philosophical debates about what might be the ideal justificatory premises (that is, what philosophical basis rights and human rights ought to rest on or whether there ought to be justificatory premises for rights or not) and more interested in documenting the actually existing justificatory premises of rights. Documenting the actually existing premises and the deployment of justificatory premises means to examine the nature of exclusions and the basis on which they are justified. It also involves examining the kind of subjects that get to be assigned to rights.

In my ethnographies, I have been able to identify and document four different justificatory premises of *haq* within contemporary political mobilisations. While some of these overlap with the liberal justificatory premises of rights and human rights, they are also different from these. The striking feature of these justifications is their dynamic nature both in terms of the subjects that they enable to come into being and the dynamic political cultures of rights they produce. The justificatory premises of *haq* signify that *haq* embodies particular imaginaries and discourses on ways of being. In Chapters 4 and 5, I identify and describe the four justificatory premises of *haq* and their 'applications' within contemporary struggles for rights in India and Pakistan. I show how they produce vernacular rights cultures through particular political imaginaries.

Thinking in terms of vernacular rights cultures enables us to consider the different political imaginaries, subjectivities and languages of rights and human rights that currently either fall outside the direct engagement of human rights scholarship or are culturalised by it as a 'local' variant of global human rights. The political imaginaries of *haq* produce particular rights politics and cultures of rights including new forms of subjectivities and also subjection. They produce forms of political subjectivation that do not map on easily with the forms of rights subjectivities, politics and demands, which are often seen to be the lifeblood of human rights politics. Significantly, they enable us to track the manner in which these struggles enable the deployment of rights and human rights in ways that expand not only the stories of human rights but also the work these do. It also enables a transnational optic on how to think about human rights and the political subjectivation these produce—as operating in multiple and intersectional circuits of power and not simply either discretely located at either only at the global and/or the local level.

Agency and Ethical Rights Talk: The 'Coming into Being' of the Subjects of Rights

In a meaningful sense, vernacular rights cultures are concerned with political and epistemic agency. The institutional histories of human rights, whether these are of nation states or of large international non-governmental organisations, either sidestep the question of political agency of those at the frontline of political mobilisations demanding rights and human rights or erase this political agency entirely. The agentival practices I draw attention to do not rehearse the 'action bias' of mainstream agency accounts, which visualise agency in terms of individual efficacy, 'choice' and the ability to produce unproblematic free actions.[15] Instead they focus on ethical conduct and ethical engagements with rights and human rights, including the making and remaking of the self that occurs through such moral and ethical encounters with rights. Here, I am aligning myself with scholars who foreground the productive and generative nature of discourse, including that of rights and human rights (Brown 1995; Slaughter 2007; Hodžić 2017; Lefebvre 2018; Butler 2015; Ranciere 2004; Mahmood 2005).

An attentiveness to the productive and generative nature of rights and human rights, and in particular, to the ethical dimensions of rights talk, is also sometimes known as the 'constitutive thesis'. This 'constitutive thesis' draws attention to the ways in which human rights generate opportunities for political subjectivation and incite particular kinds of ethical work on the self. There are several areas of overlap but also clear areas of differences between the scholarship on ethical subjectification and that of vernacular rights cultures. These differences yield different conclusions despite sharing similar starting points. The most striking difference concerns the identity of the subject of rights. First, studying vernacular rights cultures draws attention to the fact that while it is the case that rights/human rights talk provide the site of subjectification, this subjectification however, does not result in the production of a homogenous sovereign and free subject of global human rights or the *homo juridicus* but a vernacular subject of rights—one inflected by and produced under historically and politically specific configurations of power.

Second and linked to the above, the context and site of subjectification is hardly only ever international human rights law or policy talk. In fact, the context of rights talk is not so much one about the operation of rights in abstract global spaces but one of concrete, gendered and embodied rights and entitlements, mostly linked to the nation state and its failure to uphold justice and of the political struggles to expand and reorient rights.

Finally, the third arena of distinction from the 'constitutive thesis' on human rights is that vernacular rights cultures posit that the subject assigned to rights and human rights is a gendered subject and that the subject who 'comes into being' as a result of the processes of subjectification that human rights/rights discourses unleash is an intersectional one. The rights subject is an intersectional one, not only because gender is not a solitary category of analysis and exists alongside a host of other markers of hierarchy and differentiation but also because political struggles over rights and human rights are conflictual struggles, where the intersectional location and identities of subjects come to matter—and, becoming, in fact, primary sites of conflict. A case in point is that not only do women's rights need to be begged separately in political mobilisations (at least those under study in this book) but also that for Dalit and Adivasi women, these rights are actively refused (which is also the reason why rights politics is so conflictual for visibly intersectional subjects). In short, my point is that the ethical agency or the ethical rights talk and the work on the self that it entails is collective and also individual but, in both cases, it is also gendered. Making the gendered nature of social relations and rights talks visible enables us to ask not only as to who can be a subject of rights but also how these subjects are policed and regulated.

My interest in this book is not to uncover an *a priori* subject of human rights but rather to attend to the processes of subjectification that rights and human rights set off. Therefore, the question this book asks is not who is the subject of human rights but instead: how do subjects of human rights come into being? Underpinning this different question is quite simply the assumption that human rights are a normative and ontological discourse. Human rights produce particular subjects of human rights; they exhort 'self-transformation' (Lefebvre 2018: 9) and demand that rights bearing subjects in fact become the subjects they are designated to be (Slaughter 2007). The 'coming into being' of a subject of human rights presupposes particular kinds of ethical work done by the self on the self. The 'socialisation' and learning of the rules, conventions and traditions of human rights require particular kinds of discourses, practices and ethics through which individuals are turned into subjects of rights.[16] Alexander Lefebvre (2018), for instance, writes that human rights discourses set in motion an 'ethics of the care of the self' (Lefebvre 2018: 9), or operations on the self in order to become a subject of human rights. Ben Golder (2015) addresses the work that rights do within a context of governmental power and writes that they enable a 'critical counter-conduct' of rights. He writes that Michel Foucault's (2004) concept of 'counter-conduct'

> indexes a more nuanced concern with the ways in which practices of government simultaneously perform both these (objectifying and subjectifying, for want of better words) functions. We can readily perceive the relevance of such a formulation in the context of rights claims: the assertion of a right both functions to remake and contest relations with others but at the same time establishes a particular relation to, and conception, of the rights holder herself. (Golder 2015: 57)

According to Joseph Slaughter, UDHR law is marked by a teleological and tautological structure—of already presuming the 'legal person' it wants to bring into being. Or as Slaughter says, the UDHR law 'presupposes that the person *is a* person in order to effect the person as a person'; this person is 'both human rights' natural premise and their positive promise' (Slaughter 2007: 26). This 'human rights personality pre-exists society and law *and* comes into being through social interaction and the collective declaration of human rights' (Slaughter 2007: 79).

The question of socialisation is crucial, but not quite in the way that assumes that people will become the juridical legal persons that UDHR designates them to be. Rather, the socialisation into rights discourses results in the production of a rights subject who is neither the *homo juridicus* nor the *homo politius*—both are subjects allowed to appear as subjects of human rights, of course—but one who is intersectionally gendered, constrained and forged not only through the formal framework of the UDHR but rather in the vernacular. Consequently, these vernacular subjects of rights come into being not through only a process of global human rights socialisation but rather through conflictual and gendered processes of political subjectivation set off by a range of rights discourses and struggles, which can, at times, exceed and expand the terms set by global human rights.

As I noted earlier, in contemporary political philosophy, the question of political subjectivation has emerged as a key site for thinking about the democratic potential of human rights to enact claims/freedoms that are not yet in place— and, in particular, about the potential of human rights to produce forms of political subjectivation that could reconfigure and disrupt existing power relations (Rancière 2004; Butler 2015).

However, in order to think about political subjectivation of gendered subjects of rights and human rights in 'most of the world', theoretical accounts of political subjectivation will require three different kinds of supplementation. This supplementation becomes crucial because influential accounts of political subjectivation do not necessarily work with intersectional subjects or with a carefully calibrated account of the fields of power that makes political subjectivation possible. For instance, Rancière gives little account of specific contexts of power (also see McNay 2014) in which political subjectivation occurs and addresses next to none of the specific forms it might take for differently raced and gendered subjects. Moreover, while this political subjectification cannot be thought of outside specific contexts of power, it must not only focus on the modalities and sites of protest but also on the imaginaries, vocabularies and strategies of resistance, collective action and also its exclusions. The three kinds of supplementation I suggest are – First, to think more carefully about the 'other' human rights contexts within which political subjectification occurs. Second, in addition to producing a shift in the location, site and politics of theoretical thinking, this also means that the philosophical grounds for this political subjectivation cannot only be a politics demanding inclusion into already existing rights or only on the 'right to have rights'. In other words, in order to account for the political subjectivation that rights and human rights put into place, we will need to examine other political imaginaries in order to provide accounts of how rights not only materialise within different political contexts but also of the work they do in setting off new modes of political subjectivation. Finally, we will need to bring careful theoretical attention to the forms of differential distributions of rights that come to be attached to differently racialised and gendered subjects. This fact alone has significance for who can appear in public and in 'assembly' to participate in political mobilisations and also who can become the subject of rights.

Judith Butler (2015: 168–9) highlights situations where 'people engage in acts of self-making or self-constitution by appearing together in assembly.' By appearing and acting alongside others in public, they enact the right to appear. This right to appear may or may not be vocalised and for Butler, 'sometimes it is not a question of first taking power and then being able to act, sometimes it is question of acting and then laying claim to power' (Butler 2015: 58). Butler further writes,

> When bodies assemble on the street, in the square, or in other forms of public space they are exercising a performative right to appear ... showing up, standing, breathing, moving, standing still, speech and silence are all aspects of a sudden assembly ... that puts livable life at the forefront of politics ... where the legitimacy of the state is brought into question precisely by that way of appearing in public, the body itself exercises a right that is no right; in other words, it exercises a right that is being actively contested and destroyed by military force, and that, in its resistance to force, articulates its way of living, showing both its precarity and its right to persist ... it is, in fact, the right to have rights, not as natural law or metaphysical stipulation, but as the persistence of the body, against those forces that seek its debilitation or eradication. (Butler 2015: 83)

Here, political subjectivation may or may not require an articulation in the existing language of rights to inaugurate or to announce the 'right to appear' (Butler 2015: 25), but it is bodies acting in concert with others by assembling in public that produce possibilities for political subjectivation. Questions remain in Butler's account in relation to which bodies can occupy public spaces and of what the risks of appearing in public might be, as well as the nature of claims allowable in these public spaces. However, performing the 'right to appear' as a collective in public does effectively draw attention to the absence of actually existing freedom and justice, while also underscoring the possibilities of freedom yet to come. For both Rancière and Butler, it is the enactment of rights in concert with others in a public space that enacts what is not yet in place. Both theorists use the discourse of the rights of man and the rights of citizen as the standard background context for theorising moments of political subjectivation. Vernacular rights cultures, on the other hand, focus on the everyday moral, legal and political encounter of subaltern subjects with the nation state and consequently, it is the institutional and discursive power of the national state and especially its developmental apparatus that provides a potent site of political subjectification. I will examine these encounters and the processes of subjectification they set off in Chapters 4 and 5.

Political Subjectivation and the 'Right to Development'

Development constitutes an important site for which 'rights talk' in different parts of 'most of the world'. In international development policy making, the high point of human rights is marked by the passage of the right to development agreed in 1986, which coupled human rights and development to potentially activate modes of political subjectivation associated with human rights, not least through declaring 'the people' as rights-bearers of development along with nation states.[17] The human right to development has in the last three decades since its passage, become the framework of choice for global and national development bureaucracies and frames international action on poverty and inequality. But herein lies the paradox: while it is the case that development facilitates human rights talk, it is also through developmentalism (although not through it only) that human rights become govermentalised. As we know, however, governmentalised power is productive power. In this context, it is somewhat curious that even though ideas of rights and human rights now standardly accompany development, less scholarly interest is paid to the forms of political subjectivation these put in place and the democratic possibilities they set off in development contexts. For instance, whereas the adoption and implementation of the right to development and rights-based development is extensively studied, there is little written about the forms of political subjectivation these produce, including how subjects deploy rights/human rights to demand better and/or different forms of development. These demands for better or different development are not technical claims but political ones demonstrating, thereby, that human rights are not neutral and apolitical but contested and conflictual, and that they put in place, not only 'democratic possibilities' but also new forms of regulation and subjection (Brown 2000). In short, the right to development produces forms of political subjectivation and functions as a form of governmentality—transforming individuals into subjects and 'agents of development'. In keeping with all social phenomena, however, the forms of political subjectivation engendered by rights discourse are gendered, and when rights are 'seized' to make political claims by gendered subjects, these do not simply involve instrumental claim-making; what is claimed in effect, is also a particular subjectivity and relation to the self. It is for this reason that when gendered subjects engage in claim-making, it is almost always conflictual; their claim-making is more often than not read as oppositional to and/or disrupting of an established normative gender order.

For nearly two decades, I have been tracking the 'life trajectories' of developmentalism and of subjectivation in five rural districts of Rajasthan, northwestern India—of how individuals are transformed into 'agents of development'; and, how the 'technologies of power' associated with developmentalism, particularly rights function as a form of governmentality, with an explicit aim to shape, subaltern women's subjectivities. The paradoxical outcome of this rights-based developmentalism is that while it sets in motion new selfhoods, it also renders marginalised subjects even more vulnerable to conflict, intimidation, injury and to actual/threat of violence.

As I shall go on to show in Chapters 4 and 5, this form of rights-based governmentality releases new modes of political subjectivation and also political action. The mobilisations in South Asia, for instance, predominantly operate within imaginaries of developmentalism, whether as calls for a different form of development or as active resistance in the face of it.

Conclusion

The critiques of global human rights have by now been firmly registered. My aim in this chapter has thus not been to rehearse these critiques but to focus instead on the productive and generative nature of rights and human rights and to outline the elements of vernacular rights cultures that enables us to conceptually capture the productivity of rights in 'most of the world'. I have argued that the framework of vernacular rights cultures makes it possible for us to sidestep the politics of origins, which is the shared premise of both celebratory and critical positions on human rights—a politics of origins that erases and silences rights politics that falls outside of its remit. While one way to disrupt this politics of origins is to tell a different story of human rights, but there are important questions over how to go about telling this different story. I have suggested that this different story cannot be one of only drawing equivalences, translations and correspondences with majoritarian rights talk but must be one that is able to produce conceptual descriptions of deployments of rights talk in different contexts.

These conceptual descriptions are not meant to exaggerate differences or similarities but instead to shift the epistemic centre of human rights talk. While there are now growing calls for more empirical and theoretical work on human rights from different parts of the globe, and also for decolonising human rights, I have cautioned that this work cannot be seen as merely 'local' and always in translation. Global human rights scholarship needs to shift the direction of conceptual travel movement from the 'global to the local', which keeps the 'West' as the epistemic centre of rights/human rights thinking in place, to a more historically specific, intersectional and located, meanings and politics of rights and human rights.

Notes

1. See *Indian Express* (2016).
2. See Bansal (2018).
3. See *The Hindu* (2019c).
4. See *The Wire* (2019).
5. See NDTV (2019).
6. Lynn Hunt does not specify the location where this 'self evidence' of human rights emerges but I have deduced this from the places of publication of the texts she discusses in her book. Not having to name the location is the privilege only powerful stories of human rights can afford—other stories of rights and human rights are insistently asked to locate themselves as local derivatives of the hegemonic global human rights discourse.
7. The active exclusion of those who were central to the forging of autonomous and empathetic selves, that is, white middle class women, in the imperial metropolises who mostly read these novels is altogether incongruous.
8. In a critique published in the early 1990s, Seyla Benhabib faults Jacques Derrida and Jean-François Lyotard for privileging the 'originary or a 'foundational political act' (1994: 5) and for their 'formalistic' 'fascination with the aporias and the paradoxes of this foundational republican' (Benhabib 1994: 6) which they seek to stage through a 'linguistico-political' analysis (Benhabib 1994: 9) rather than through an analysis of the 'content of the acts of the declaration and independence' (Benhabib 1994: 11). According to Benhabib, the two philosophers focus on the violent exclusions inherent in the foundational moment—And 'this violence at the origin, this violent exclusion is concealed in every republican foundation' but returns in the form of disjunction between those who speak in the name of 'we' and those who are spoken about' (Benhabib 1994: 10).
9. According to Balibar, the declaration of the rights of man and of citizen '… integrally identifies the rights of man with political rights' (Balibar 1994: 45) or 'equaliberty' which is, in effect, the 'affirmation of a universal rights to politics' (Balibar 1994: 49).
10. I find both altogether unhelpful. See Goodale (2007) for a critique of 'global/ local' and 'network' frameworks.
11. Personal communication with Jayal (June 2018).
12. In South Asia, for instance, women's rights have been expanded through legal claim-making. As I noted in chapter 1 (see note 19), a notable example is *Vishakha vs State of Rajasthan* (*All India Reporter of the Supreme Court* 1997:

3011) More recently, the *Delhi High Court in Laxmi Mandal vs the Deen Dayal Harinagar Hospital* (W.P.C.C 8853/2008) drew on various international rights protocols to pronounce on reproductive rights of women. To my knowledge, this is also the first time that the term 'reproductive rights' enters the legal lexicon in India. More recently, the Indian state was taken to court on the matter of extrajudicial killings in the Indian state of Manipur (*Extra Judicial Execution Victims Families Association (EEVFAM) & Anr. v. Union of India (UOI) & Ors. (2016)* WP (CRL) 129/2012 PIL-W (Supreme Court of India, 8 July 2016), 86), which has been under military laws that authorise the right to kill to any non-commissioned officer of the military and police. It is important to note here that the Writ Petition explicitly deployed international human rights law, such as The Minnesota Protocol on the Investigation of Potentially Unlawful Death (2016) (OHCHR, 2017 [1991]), and also drew on the InterAmerican Court for Human Rights and the European Court for Human Rights for specific case law (Babloo Loitongbam, personal communication, 1 October 2017).

13. The authors put together a comparison across a typology consisting of four categories: status politics, doctrinal politics, class politics and non-doctrinal politics. Uncovering policy behaviour by states along these four categories, their research is able to identify the key actors and ideas responsible for adoption of gender equality policies.

14. According to Peter Jones 'both the foundation and the content of a theory of human rights has to be of a kind that makes sense against a background of diversity. But we can ask for more than that; we can also require that it should provide for that diversity' (2000: 33).

15. See Madhok (2013).

16. The assumption, of course, draws on the later works of Foucault. Consequently, this scholarship pays attention to the ethical work of rights and human rights covering a range of sites, from exploring the ethical work on individuals that rights discourses incite, to analysing the particular assumptions of the rights subject that underpins the UDHR, to examining the democratic potential of human rights and forms of political subjectivation these produce.

17. See the Declaration on the Right to Development, adopted on December 4 1986, G.A. Res. 41/128 U.N. GAOR, 41st Sess., at 3, Annex, U.N. Doc. A/Res/41/128 Annex (1987), https://www.ohchr.org/Documents/Issues/RtD/RTD_at_a_glance.pdf. The literature on the right to development is vast. My thinking on the right to development draws in particular from the writings of

Baxi (2007), Cornwall and Nyusembi (2004), Sengupta (2002), Marks (2004), Fukuda-Parr (2012) and Ilumoka (2006).

3 Assembling a Feminist Historical Ontology of *Haq*

How to study vernacular rights cultures? How to do conceptual work on human rights from the Global South? In this chapter, I assemble a *feminist historical ontology* as a potentially enabling methodological apparatus for documenting the stakes and struggles over rights and human rights in 'most of the world'. Driving my methodological investment in a feminist historical ontology of *haq* is a bid to take seriously a two-fold refrain that often accompanies progressive human rights talk: first, an empirical plea for a need to study human rights in different contexts, and second, a theoretical plea for a more sustained study of the normative meanings and practices of rights in different parts of the world. These are important goals, however, they shed little light on how to go about engaging in this work. In other words, how to actually do this work of documenting the normative meanings of human rights in different contexts? And how to conceptually capture the productivity, ideational energy of rights and human rights in different locations? Finally, how do normative meanings and practices of rights in different parts of the globe disrupt or facilitate epistemic encounters with human rights scholarship and politics in 'most of the world'? The questions I set out to answer in this chapter are: how to study conceptual, normative meanings as well as empirical practices and politics of human rights in 'most of the world', and further, how do these interact and speak back to the epistemic, political and normative drives and assumptions of global human rights discourses?

My contention here is that a feminist historical ontology might enable us to engage with these questions. Quite simply, a feminist historical ontology brings together the critical insights of historical ontology with those of feminist critical reflexive politics of location. In this chapter I will assemble key elements of a feminist historical ontology and lay out the theoretical and conceptual mechanics of the methodological investigations of *haq* that drive the work of this book. In what follows, I will first offer an outline of a feminist historical ontology of *haq*. My aim is to show how a feminist historical ontology informs a particular reading of *haq*. In assembling key elements of a feminist historical ontology in this chapter, my aim is not to enter into an exegesis of ontology or indeed of the 'ontological turn'. Instead, my intention is to show some of the intellectual connections and disconnections that a feminist historical ontology encounters as it sets out into the world to forge an intellectual path for itself.

A Feminist Historical Ontology of *Haq*

How does *haq* come into being as the principal word for a right in contemporary South Asia? What sorts of meanings does it acquire, how does it make up people, aid the production of subjectivities and produce new possibilities for relating to oneself? What kinds of political imaginaries does *haq* operate in and accords intelligibility to? What ethical commitments does it produce? What forms of subjectivities does it engender, and what are the kinds of people that *haq* 'makes up'? And, in what ways does *haq* enable but also constrain possibilities for being a (gendered) subject of rights? In Chapters 4 and 5, I will examine the subjectification processes where *haq* is implicated in 'making up people' (Hacking 2002: 99) but also how people actively make themselves up through deploying *haq*. The constitution of selves and of 'people' as moral and political agents is a historical, political, racialised and gendered exercise located in a specific time and place with its own particular sets of intellectual tools for 'making up' people. Furthermore, this 'making up' is not outside of authority or discipline or coercion but takes place in its shadow and light. In this book, the acts of subjectification and those of 'making up people' take place under the direction of the state and non-state directed developmentalism, statism and dispossession, legal constitutionalism, political struggles, 'military business' (Siddiqa 2007) and military siege, and it is at the intersection of these and not as some freestanding abstraction that *haq* as a contemporary idea operates. A feminist historical ontology of *haq* enables us to see the gendered lives of concepts and to produce shifts in theoretical descriptions of how concepts are described but also of the work they do. It enables us to examine the coming into being of a gendered subject of rights and the forms of self-fashioning that gendered subjects take up. Accounting for conflict and struggle is central to feminist historical ontologies. Not least because the recognition of intersectional gender relations demand an attention to the gendered nature of conflict and struggles. The struggles by poor subaltern women for *haq* in subaltern mobilisations, for instance, prise apart the edifice of collective struggles and formations that purport to speak for collective interests to show not only that these 'collective interests' are strongly gendered but also that when gender equality is raised as a basis of collective solidarity, more often than not, it is refused. Strikingly, these struggles show that the question of gender equality needs to always be begged separately and engaged with separately, as it almost never arises as an organic part of the overarching frame of collective struggles.

Since 1999, I have been tracking the etymological roots, conceptual travel and contemporary deployment of the Urdu and Arabic word *haq* in subaltern movements in India and Pakistan. *Haq* or *hukk* appears in Hindi and Urdu lexicon through the influence of Persian, which was the language of administration in most of precolonial India (Mir 2011). In the book, *India in the Persianate Age*, Richard Eaton writes that '... by the fourteenth century Persian had already become the most widely used language for governance across South Asia ... as a result, a wide range of Persian words infiltrated the vocabulary of many of South Asia's major regional languages' (Eaton 2019: 17). In contemporary times, *haq* cuts across geographical, religious and linguistic boundaries to become the principal word deployed to make rights claims in India and Pakistan. Remarkably cosmopolitan and with an extensive hinterland, *haq* is the predominant word used to signify a right in South Asia, Middle East and North Africa. A pre-Islamic term also available in the older Semitic languages, *haq*'s roots are said to lie in the classical Hebrew term *hkk*[1] and its earliest use in Arabic can be traced to pre-Islamic poetry where it means 'something right, true, just or "proper" and real'. In the Qur'an, its fundamental meaning is 'established fact', 'reality', 'justice and that which is true' and these meanings are also upheld in modern Arabic and Persian dictionaries.[2] It also means 'the divine' and as *al-Haqq*, it is one of the names for God (Smith 1971; Rosen 1980). In early dictionaries of the 'Hindustani' language, *haq* is translated as 'right' and as 'due' but later dictionaries record a much more expansive meaning of the term imputing qualities of 'equity and reason' (Fergusson 1773), and describing it as 'just, proper, right, true, correct, rectitude, right, title, privilege, claim, lot, portion, truth, true and God' (Platts 1884). The constellation of normative, ethical, moral, empirical, ontological and divine meanings that attach to it effectively signify that *haq*, in fact, embodies particular imaginaries and discourses on ways of being. In Chapters 4 and 5, I will be looking at political imaginaries of contemporary struggles for rights in India and Pakistan that produce vernacular rights cultures together with the justificatory premises that underpin these including their 'applications'.

However, here let me briefly explain what I mean by political imaginaries and what role they play in feminist historical ontologies.

By political imaginaries of *haq*, I refer to a set of dynamic gendered relations, ideas, practices, discourses, institutions and subjectivities, which attach to *haq* and in turn, those which it mediates, justifies, accords meaning to and upholds. By the plural imaginaries,[3] I am referring not to a single articulation but to a multiplicity of mediations of *haq*, each produced within particular political contexts of struggle; each stipulating a 'sense of how things usually go … interwoven with … how they ought to go' (Taylor 2002: 106). Thus, *haq* orients proper ordering of relations among persons, contains within it an image of a gendered moral order and mediates citizenship, political discourse and political struggles. Ian Hacking (2002: 17) defines a concept to be nothing other than a 'word in its sites'. Therefore, to focus on how concepts come into being in specific historical contexts is to focus our attention on a variety sites: 'the sentences in which the words are actually (not potentially) used, those who speak the sentences, with what authority, in what institutional settings, in order to influence whom, with what consequences for the speakers' (Hacking 2002: 17). However, we also know that concepts bring into view particular historical and moral worlds. Deploying a particular concept means deploying a particular worldview or political imaginary. In other words, if political imaginaries might be accessed through paying attention to words and concepts, then it is not hard to see that one might be studying historical ontologies of concepts and the processes of self-making and world-making these put in place.

Let me provide a few examples of the complex and capacious imaginaries of *haq* that are explored in anthropological writings on Islamic juristical languages and life-worlds in different locations especially on matters of legal adjudications and disputations. Clifford Geertz in *Local Knowledge* (1983) explores fact finding and rule applying in 'adjudicative processes' in different juridical traditions, namely the Islamic, the Indic and the Malayo–Indonesian and examines the ways in which different juristical life-worlds deal with a central juridical problem. This problem is the distinction between 'the is/ought, what-happened/was-it-lawful distinction' or that between fact and law. Contending that law is but one way of 'imagining the real' (Geertz 1983: 184), Geertz writes that *haq*, which he identifies as a key Arabic jurisprudential term, captures not only a 'distinctive way of imagining the real' but also a term whose capacious meaning bridges the fact-law divide characteristic of Western legal practices, invoking as it does a 'deeper connection' between the 'normative and the ontological'[4] or the 'right and the real' (Geertz 1983: 189). He uses illustrations from everyday Moroccan usage to illustrate the moral, normative, ontological, juridical and religious connotations of *haq* and identifies different ways in which *haq* is applied, where each 'level of application'—religious, metaphysical, normative/moral and a jural/enforceable claim—reveals a consistent 'identity between the right and the real' (Geertz 1983: 189) or that between the empirical and the normative.

Lawrence Rosen (1980) also notes the normative and the ontological connections of *haq* in his ethnographic investigations of *qadi* justice in a *qadi* court[5] in the Moroccan city of Sefrou where he observes the role and application of *haq* in legal adjudications. Through his ethnography, Rosen examines the influence of 'cultural assumptions' in shaping 'judge's modes of reasoning, factual assessments, and choice of remedies' (Rosen 1980: 217) to argue that not only is law (including in North America) 'suffused by culture and cultural is integral to law ... ' (Rosen 1980: 218) but also that law is a critical site for negotiating questions of equity and discretion. In the *qadi* courts at Sefrou, questions of equity and discretion invariably involve adjudicating over the operation and validation of *haq*. Rosen writes that Moroccan society is constructed around 'a series of interpersonal ties, freely negotiated and highly expedient which center on each individual ... it is however, clearly understood that every action one takes creates an obligation in the other, and the key to the formation of network of personal ties, as well as to a sense of how others are most likely to act toward oneself, is to organize and learn about such obligations in the most effective way possible. This sense of mutual ingratiation and indebtedness is broadly subsumed by Moroccans under the central Arabic concept of *haqq*' (Rosen 1980: 221). To speak of *haqq*, is to convey that sense of mutual obligations that bind men to men, and man to God. Each of these obligations is open to negotiation and the question of whose obligation or *haqq* is valid, 'true' or 'real' (Rosen 1980: 223) needs to be settled. It is in the *qadi* courts that the legal validation of *haqq is* established.

Cutting across southwest from Morocco to another Islamic legal context on the African continent, Susan F. Hirsch (1998) examines the discursive and dynamic constructions of gendered subjectivities and positionings in legal interactive speech over marital disputations in *kadhi* courts in coastal Kenya. Unlike Rosen, Hirsch's focus is less on *kadhi* negotiations of equity and discretion, than on the discourses available for 'marital disputing'. A predominant literal and conceptual language of marital disputing in Hirsch's ethnography is that of *haki*, the Swahili version *of haq* deployed by the disputants in Hirsch's ethnography. According to Hirsch, 'when disputants use *haki*, they produce distinct senses of the term that presuppose identifiably different discourses—one of specific, actionable laws and one of ethics or just behavior ...' and while, 'in the abstract, *haki* can embody *haqq* in all three senses' identified by Geertz: those of the real, reality and God, with ethics and just behaviour and with law and justice, 'but in Swahili marital disputes, most deployments of *haki* tend either towards rights or justice ... ' (Hirsch 1998: 86).

These ethnographic deployments of *haq* in the different Islamic contexts explore Islamic jurisprudential traditions where *haq* operates as an 'orienting' (Geertz 1983: 187) concept of Islamic law and theology. My ethnographic tracking of *haq* in the subcontinent, on the other hand, reveals that the use of *haq* is not limited to Muslim communities in the region nor indeed only to the application and adjudication of Muslim Personal Law, which incidentally governs Muslim communities in both India and Pakistan.[6] In fact, a striking aspect of its deployment in the region is its use across geographical, linguistic and religious groups. For instance, in Rajasthan, where I have been conducting fieldwork since 1999, recent census figures suggest that Muslims constitute just 9.07 per cent of the state's population and Urdu (popularly associated with Muslim communities in the subcontinent) is only spoken by 1.17 per cent of the people (Linguistic Survey of India 2011).[7]

The association of particular languages with religious communities in South Asia does not have long historical roots in the Indian subcontinent. The popular imaginary of Hindi and Urdu as being two separate languages and belonging to two separate literary traditions, and the association of Urdu with Muslims, and of Hindi with Hindus is of a very recent origin. The subcontinental politics, activism and historiographies of Urdu and Hindi literary cultures are also mired in a politics of origins. These originary 'myths' are in part a 'colonialist construction' and in part an 'emotional and political space of Indian (Hindu) identity of modern India' (Faruqi 2003: 805). Essentially, the originary myths of Hindi and Urdu revolve around 'two claimants of a single literary tradition' (Faruqi 2003: 806). The myth essentially goes like this: there was once a 'pristine' tradition of Hindi as a spoken and written language, which becomes Urdu as a result of Muslims who had come into India with the Muslim invasions developing a language of their own. The originary myth not only sets up two separate lineages, historical trajectories and literary cultures but also ascribes a religious identity to these. The question, however, is were Hindi and Urdu, in fact, two separate languages with their separate literary and religious traditions? It turns out that they were not. Hindi and Urdu were, and are, in fact, one and the same language. Shamsur Rehman Faruqi (2003) writes that the reference to 'Urdu' as a name for a language occurs for the first time around 1780 and that contrary to the prominent origin myths, no 'new language grew up in northern India as a result of the advent of the Mughals' (Faruqi 2003: 807). A discrete reference to Urdu only emerges during the reign of the Mughal emperor Shah Alam II, and although it does not supplant the official court language, which remains Persian, it registers a presence. In this period, Urdu is known as Urdu-e Mualla and refers to the language of those who lived in Urdu-e Mualla or Shahjahanabad, which was the emperor Shah Alam II's new capital. It was only a matter of time, however, that the colonial drive to provide the colonised with a 'history'—a history that reflected the 'political considerations' (Faruqi 2003: 812) of the colonial state would produce the colonial discourse of their being two languages, and in which it would be aided admirably by the subcontinent's socio-religious reformers and language 'activists'. As the historian Farina Mir (2011) writes, 'If the colonial state and socioreligious reformers emphasized differences, and a sense of religious competition, language activists also did their part to contribute to that discourse … What was new about the late nineteenth-century association of language and religion was that it linked vernacular languages and religious communities' (Mir 2011: 22). Overall, the production of an 'imaginary' (Faruqi 2003: 811) for Hindi and Urdu had deleterious effects on the latter and consequently, Urdu was systematically 'denigrated on moral and religious grounds' (Faruqi 2003: 814). The 'communal crusade' (Robinson, 1974)[8] against Urdu sedimented its 'Muslim' character, albeit on 'historically false and morally questionable premises' (Faruqi 2003: 811) with the result that Urdu has become overly associated and confined to a religious identity—that of a particular nation and a particular people: the *lingua franca* of Pakistan and the predominant language of the Muslims of the Indian subcontinent.

My ethnographies of subaltern struggles for *haq* in India and Pakistan demonstrate not only that the deployments of *haq* are not always in alignment with Islamic juristical settlements of *haq* but they also refuse the exclusively religious associations put in place by the originary myths surrounding Hindi and Urdu. If anything, the ethnographies of struggle over *haq* in the book *demonstrate* that the word *haq* in the region is not confined to Islamic jurisprudentialism or to its deployment by only Muslims in the region but has a wider presence that includes claim-making and seeking expanded citizenship entitlements from the state by subaltern groups across the subcontinent's religious and geographical landscape.

The context of struggle is crucial here because it is in the context of political mobilisations and struggles that the word *haq* acquires salience in contemporary South Asia. In India, my ethnographic tracking over the last decade has spread to five districts of Rajasthan[9] and has consisted mainly of recording narratives of development workers, grassroots political workers and participants of various citizen movements organising under the umbrella of 'the right to food' movement. In Pakistan, I have documented the deployment of *haq* by the AMP demanding land rights in the Punjab. The interesting thing I have noticed in all these years of tracking *haq* in citizenship mobilisations in both countries is that although the word *haq* is used in grassroots mobilisations, the word itself has somewhat limited mobility when it comes to invoking and supporting intersectional and complex inequalities. Here, I have in mind the ways in which *haq* does not by itself apply organically to articulations of gender equality. It does not help that the term *haq* itself is a masculine term and is rarely deployed as part of the everyday moral vocabulary of women in South Asia (see Chapter 4). This is not to say that articulations for gender equality or gender-based rights are not made; in fact, the book focuses predominantly on these articulations and their gendered nature but that the question of gender equality always invariably needs to be begged separately within political struggles. That demands for gender equality or *haq* for women emerge as a question that needs to be begged separately and seldom occurs organically within citizen mobilisations could also be seen as a limitation perhaps, of the ontological–normative structure of *haq*, which does not quite allow its easy translation into all demands for equality and rights. However, demands of *haq* for women are not only voiced, but its enunciation also brings into sharp relief the indivisibility and the intersectional nature of rights including the imbrication of individual with collective rights and their conflictual relationship.

The Curious Return of Ontology

But why a feminist historical ontology of *haq* though? What does ontology mean anyway? Is not ontology something that strikes fear and loathing in some sections of feminist theory? Is it not 'just another word for colonialism' (Todd 2016) and of yet 'another theoretical primitivism that presents itself as a methodological "avant garde"' (Rosenberg 2014). What does the coupling of 'feminist' with historical ontology bring to the methodological table? Is it yet another addition to the growing list of 'ontological turns' declared by an ever increasing number of disciplinary formations? Certainly, ontology means different things to different people depending on who you ask, and if the 'ontological turn' declared within several academic disciplines is any indicator, then it is clear that ontology means a range of different things.[10] The 'ontological turns' in various disciplines are heralded as re-signifying and bringing to prominence a range of entanglements with the 'contemporary', including the conditions of difference, exclusion, erasure and absence. It is a curious return because it was for the very same reasons that ontology fell out of favour. The charge brought against ontology then was that it enabled epistemic histories based on metaphysical and transcendental claims about reality and being, which refused difference and put in place logics of civilisational exclusion and absence. But this return of ontology has not come without a set of qualifications and reignifications. Consequently, there are a range of prefixes that now accompany the return of ontology and the ontological, a few among these are: 'political ontology' (Blaser 2013), 'politico-ontological' (Escobar 2018) and 'historical ontology' (Hacking 2002). The prefixes matter. They do particular kinds of work. In particular, they flag the particular deployments of ontology and the different intellectual investments in reclaiming ontology.

There are at least three things that are quite striking about the various disciplinary ontological turns. First, they seem to operate in disciplinary silos and show little awareness of the ontological crises going on next door. As a result, these accounts are marked by a fair amount of self-referentialism and there is little cross-referencing among them. For instance, depending on which 'ontological turn' you read, different people are credited with coining the phrase, and interestingly, none of them are feminist scholars. Similarly, depending on who you ask, the turn to ontology means very different things in different disciplinary quarters and sometimes, even within the disciplines. In the broad area of cultural studies, for instance, the 'ontological turn' has gone hand in hand with the 'affective turn' determined to bring the ontological reality of the body back into the centre of cultural analysis (Holzberg 2018). In the case of some anthropological interventions, the 'ontological turn' has been primarily about a turn to the 'native' or radical alterity. In economics, some are using the 'ontological turn' to draw attention to inadequate methods for capturing contemporary economic realities and within philosophy, 'historical ontology' is invoked to historicise philosophical concepts. Despite these separate objects of knowledge, there are also some overlapping themes across this 'turn', especially in regard to the 'origin' stories' that are told about this turn to ontology. Often, for instance, the turn to ontology is said to have arisen out of a 'crisis in representation', from the rise of science and technology studies and as a response to the ongoing ecological crises.

Among the different origin stories, however, perhaps none has gained more power and traction than the one that narrates the 'ontological turn' as a turn away from epistemology, in particular, deconstructionist epistemology. The charge laid against (deconstructionist) epistemology is three-fold: that it is theory for theory's sake, that it advances a Eurocentred view of the world and of the subject/human (Escobar 2018), and that it produces civilisational absence and erasures. Consequently, some proponents of the 'ontological turn' focus on the ontological erasures and absences that poststructuralist and deconstructionist epistemologies are said to produce. Some anthropologists also question the ontological orientation towards singularity and universal imaginaries, that is, of their being only one world, the modern one, and argue instead for the need to register different world-makings and pluriversal imaginaries (de la Cadena 2010; Blaser 2013; Escobar 2018). Despite the internal differentiations within this scholarship, a key concern driving the 'ontological turn' here is how to engage seriously with the question of radical difference.[11] In a series of interventions, the anthropologist Mario Blaser (2013), for instance, writes that the 'ontological turn' has emerged as a result of a 'crisis' in the hegemonic stories told by those who are 'modern' about themselves and the ontological present, that is, modernity.[12] Blaser argues that the story of modernity is a story of a 'hegemonic ontological' account of modernity that is propelled by a progressivist, teleological, evolutionary, linear narrative based on 'an ontologically stark distinction' (Blaser 2013: 554) between 'nature and culture' (Blaser 2013: 554) and 'modern and non-modern' (Blaser 2013: 554). The question of difference here is hierarchised and plotted along a linear direction of historical time and consequently, read as backward and primitive, a condition, which will eventually be resolved when everyone becomes modern. This particular ordering of the hegemonic ontological story of modernity therefore, refuses the question of 'radical difference' (Blaser 2013: 559) and different worldings by denying their existence through either refusing these any 'veracity' or by regarding difference as another subset or cultural variant of the modern story.[13] The question is therefore, one of how to bring these different worldings or ontologies into view? According to Blaser, this requires not only thinking about ontology but also on how to methodologically go about capturing these different ontologies. Consequently, Blaser argues that the way forward is to think in terms of ontology as a 'conceptual political project', or in terms of a political ontology, where political ontology means to be 'concerned with practices, performances and enactments and not with specific groups' (Blaser 2013: 552). Blaser writes that political ontology is concerned with 'reality making, including its own participation in reality making ... with telling stories that open up a space for, and enact, the pluriverse' (2013: 552–53).

The politics of the pluriversal and the ontological absence of the Indigenous is also a concern for Marisol de la Cadena (2010). In her case, the politics of the pluriversal requires the reformulation of two things: first, for politics to include the nonhuman and second, to interconnect such plurality without rendering these commensurable.[14] The ontological singularity that informs current understanding of politics renders different ontologies and worlds absent through marking them as inferior and as only ever 'others'. The problem of ontological absence is not one of finding resolutions through inclusion into existing 'politics as usual' but rather of changing the 'baseline of politics' and to reorient it towards a politics of the pluriversal. The new baseline would disavow singularity and make multiple worlds visible as legitimate actors and disputants within politics. The reconfiguration of politics would enable the Indigenous to take part as 'legitimate adversaries' and not be only at the receiving end of a biopolitical war that both liberalism and socialism have waged against their alleged 'others'.

Pluriverse also features in the title of Arturo Escobar's book *Designs for the Pluriverse* (2018) in which he argues that the contemporary crises of ecological devastation, dispossession and capitalist extractivism are the result of particular ways of 'doing, knowing and being', which in turn are a result of hegemonic forms of organising the world based on a particular design. This design is driven by a particular ontological orientation towards singularity of existence and of there being only one world—that of the modern. This ontological drive, which has a particular subject, a particular reality and a particular economy (capitalism) realises itself not only through producing and implementing this ontological design on a global scale (through development, humanitarianism and so forth) but also through putting in place a 'sociology of absences'. In other words, the other ways of world-making are not only ignored but in fact, wilfully rendered absent. Pluriversal thinking then, is an imaginary that replaces singularity thinking with a register of different ontologies engaged in different designs for world-making which are also in partial connection with one another. Escobar's designs for different ontologies are informed by Latin American Indigenous struggles. These movements, Escobar writes, are led by an ontology of radical relationality—a mode of existence that centres autonomy/autonomia and the community/communal.

Even though Escobar is careful to insist that 'community is understood in deeply historical open, and non-essentialist terms' he is also clear that this openness and non-essentialist understanding of the community rests upon a basic *system* (emphasis added) of relations, which has *to be* maintained for the community to preserve its autopoeisis, that is, its capacity for self creation. (Escobar 2018: 183).

I admire Escobar's wide-ranging, thoughtful and sophisticated book but the privileging of the non-representational political structure of social sovereignty organised around obedience to the 'basic system' of relations within community worries me. In my view, such a privileging evacuates power relations from the scene of politics. Therefore, the question is: do gender relations constitute basic relations within the 'community' that Escobar refers to? And, how does this basic *system* of relations register, negotiate and resolve gender relations, which are essentially conflictual and reflect different power hierarchies? To be fair, Escobar does cite the work of decolonial communitarian feminists describing their strategy as consisting of 'pursuing the twin goals of depatriarchalization (in relation to both autochthonous and modern patriarchies) and decolonization (in relation to liberal, modernising and capitalist hegemonies, including individualizing Western feminisms)' (2018: 182–83). However, it is not clear how the interventions of decolonial communitarian feminists inform pluriversal thinking and its social relations. And, I cannot help thinking how little space there is in these political ontological accounts for struggles over gender and sexuality (Tola 2018). An important aspect of the work of decolonial communitarian feminists is their critique of the biocentric, binary gender relations put in place by colonial formations, Indigenous patriarchies and universal feminisms and of the epistemic and ontological struggles against these. However, not enough of this important critique and interventions find much room in Escobar's account.

The Refusal to Disentangle Ontology from Epistemology

Contrary to the 'ontological turn' within anthropology, a feminist historical ontology refuses the disentanglement of epistemology from ontology. Epistemologies have particular ontological effects,[15] and therefore, not only is it difficult to unentangle epistemology and ontology—this is borne out by Black feminist and postcolonial scholarship—but also because there exists a mutually reinforcing relationship between ontology and epistemology, a relationship which is held together by a specific onto-epistemic glue. This onto-epistemic glue produces particular epistemic histories and subjects and puts in place a white onto-epistemic subject at its centre while negating others. As is evident, what is at stake here it is not so much the white onto-epistemic worldview of modernity, as critiqued by the 'ontological turn' in anthropology, but the white onto-epistemic subject of feminist theory that is the object of critique. Now widely documented within feminist scholarship, the white onto-epistemic subject does particular kinds of work—it shores up the white feminist subject, imbues it with capacities of autonomy and agency and invests it with epistemic authority. The strength of this onto-epistemic glue has meant that some of the poststructuralist inspired moves to displace the earlier ontological talk have done little to address the question of epistemic erasure of non-white subjects. What has been displaced, however, even if only partially, is the idea that there might be an essential experience of gender. Regardless of this shift, questions remain as to whose experiences count in producing poststructuralist accounts of gender and subjectivity.

If poststructuralist and deconstructionist inspired feminist critique have been unable to shift the white onto–epistemic glue that accords subject privilege to white women, has the recent 'ontological turn' within feminist cultural studies done any better in holding open the possibility of historical and ontological difference? Has the question of difference, absence and erasure been more productively engaged with through its 'ontological turn'? As it turns out, the answer is more or less no. In her important article 'Invoking Affect', Hemmings (2005) argues that within feminist cultural studies, the 'ontological turn' has aimed to (re)centre the body in feminist scholarship through a 'turn to affect'. Hemmings notes that the turn to ontology/affect in cultural studies is premised on two manoeuvres. First, it overstates the ills of deconstruction—its political flatness, the predictable nature of the analysis it proffers. Second, in its focus on white affects and white bodies it enacts an epistemic erasure of Black and postcolonial feminist scholarship. It is striking, notes Hemmings, that the proponents of the 'ontological turn' disavow deconstructionist concerns and direct attention towards ontology—to the body and its affects—but they do not acknowledge the Black and critical race scholars who have insisted on embodiment and racial affect.[16] The epistemological–ontological divide and the privileging of ontology over epistemology is worrying on several counts, not least because questions of epistemology have historically attached to the white subject and non-white worlds have been represented as those that are

devoid of theory but also of history (Said 1978). And therefore, histories of
epistemic violence on non-European/non-white worlds is not something that
can simply be reinstated through non-historical accounts of the body or an
ahistorical, undifferentiated account of ontology over epistemology.

Perhaps, among the most influential interventions by which feminist
scholars have laid bare the imbrication of epistemology and ontology is by
calling for a critical reflexive 'politics of location'. Now many feminist scholars
have written influentially about location as a place in space and in time but also
in history and epistemology. They have invoked location to draw attention to
unequal distribution of intellectual and institutional capital and production of
knowledge around the globe but also to the entanglements of theory building
with the heteropatriarchal, racist, capitalist geopolitics and power relations
that structure and inform knowledge production (Rich 1984; Mohanty 1995;
1991; Wynter 2003; Cusicanqui 2012). Questioning the location of knowledge
production is, of course, hardly confined to certain strands feminist thinking
alone. Within wider scholarship, location has been used to draw attention
to the interstitial and 'in between spaces' where differences are negotiated
(Bhabha 1994), to the 'provincialism' of the universalist pretensions of thought
(Chakrabarty 2000), to 'place based consciousness' (Dirlik 1999: 151–2), and to
the historicity of concepts (Hacking 2002). More recently, location has come
inform 'border thinking' espoused by the decolonial scholars (Mignolo 2000).
However, what is perhaps unique to feminist scholarship on location is its
insistence on location as a critical reflexive ethics. This critical reflexive ethics
comes into two forms: the first helps register and document the global power
relations that underpin the production of knowledge and privilege particular
sites of knowledge production and dissemination. It insists that the theorist
declare their location and position within the global circuits of intellectual
division of labour (Spivak 1987) and account for the epistemic tracks of their
location upon their theorising. In other words, a critical reflexive politics of
location demands an answer to the question: from where are you looking, and
whom/what are you seeing? And the second forges a dynamic, theorised and
historicised relationship between the self and the collective in specific locations
and contexts of struggle (Mohanty 1992), and also involves redrawing the
ethical relationship of the self or selves to the site(s) of knowledge production.
Adrienne Rich, the feminist poet and author titled her essay 'Notes on the
Politics of Location' and catapulted struggles over accountability, responsibility
and ethical politics to the centre stage of feminist knowledge production.
Exhorting white feminists to examine the 'thoughtlessly white' assumptions

underpinning their feminism, Rich directs her ire at the deadly 'sameness' of abstraction that 'allows no differences among places, times, cultures, conditions, movements' (Rich 1984: 221). As opposed to this ahistorical, 'lofty and privileged' abstract theorising which centres white women and engenders a 'confusion between [our] claims to the white Western eye and the woman-seeing eye' (Rich 1984: 219, 221), Rich demands that we recognise the location and 'name the ground we are coming from and the conditions we have taken for granted ... ' (Rich 1984: 219). A significant effect of this refusal to locate oneself in the geopolitics of theory production has been the prolific circulation of the universalising representational manoeuvres that produce visions of 'global sisterhood' without taking into account power differentials of race, class, caste, sexuality and geopolitical location (Mohanty 1995; Grewal and Kaplan 1994). As opposed to this feminist politics of 'global transcendence' with its refusal of global power relations, Chandra Mohanty calls for a feminist politics of engagement that is located in the 'temporality of struggles' and draws on 'historically interpreted and theorised' experiences of differently located and ongoing struggles over what it means to experience gender/gender oppressions in different locations (1992: 87–8). It is this centrality of and complicity within crisscrossing and dynamic entanglements of power structures and relations across different locations and their implications for knowledge production that distinguishes transnational feminist scholarship and practices from global and international feminisms (Grewal and Kaplan 1994; Mohanty 1995; Alexander and Mohanty 2010; Swarr and Nagar 2010). This focus on uneven and unequal entanglements of power relations dispels any attachment to location as signifying difference for difference's sake. If anything, invoking location as power saturated and as signifying specific relations of domination and subordination institutes a meaningful corrective to the easy slip slide into 'neo relativism', where difference and multiplicity are celebrated without any recognition of the fields of power in which difference and sameness operate and are invoked (Frankenberg and Mani 1993).

By insisting on knowing not only who is and can be the knower, but also what can be known, about what and from which locations, feminist epistemologists have engaged in unmasking, decentring and locating the Archimedean all seeing and all representing universal knower and also in identifying the contradictory and inconsistent assumptions that underpin epistemological thinking. For instance, a glaring contradiction in philosophical thinking is that it not only presupposes only particularly located persons as knowers (Code 2012) but also presupposes these particularly located knowers are also located nowhere. Parsing through these contradictions, feminist epistemologists have located knowers in particular social and historical milieus, shown the imbrication of the processes knowledge production within political and ontological entanglements (Alcoff 1993, 1991), but also consistently challenged the methodological individualism and the assumptions of 'human homogeneity' that underpin epistemological enquiry. But even as feminist scholars continue to successfully challenge epistemology's 'irrepressible connection with social power' (Fricker 2007: 2) and critique the epistemic exclusions that have denied (white) women a place at the epistemology table, questions of who, where and what possesses epistemic authority within feminist theory itself refuse to die down (Rich 1984; Spivak 1988; Crenshaw 1989; Mohanty 1991; Bhavnani 1993; Hill Collins 2000; hooks 2000; Lorde 2001; Chow 2003; Lugones 2010). And, here too, the prevailing forms of colonial unknowing together with the vice grip of positivist knowledge production has meant that there is both a great deal of reluctance to engage reflexively with the imperialist, heteropatriarchal, racialised and power laden theoretical entanglements at different locations, and even much less with the colonial burdens that inform theory building. The operation of epistemologies of 'white ignorance' (Mills 2007: 13) and those of 'colonial unknowing' have rendered not only these geopolitical, colonial, and institutional entanglements largely invisible but also unspeakable.

Crucially, however, influential strands of Black, postcolonial, decolonial and queer feminist scholarship have productively mined a critical, reflexive feminist politics of location in order to undertake critical conceptual work in 'non-standard' locations and contexts. Many of the key feminist conceptual categories that we have become accustomed to deploying in everyday theorising, empirical and in policy work, emerge out of critical engagements with the location of particular subjects. So, for instance, Kimberlé Crenshaw coins the term 'intersectionality' to mark the invisibility and erasure of Black women. Significantly, and this is crucial, intersectionality comes forth from a place that is a 'non-standard' background context for conceptual work but also for theory making. The complex inequalities, oppressions, social worlds, experiences and histories of struggle of Black women constitute the background condition here, and it is this unique location and context that intersectionality describes and visualises. After all, how often does one come across or deploy concepts that do not emerge and in turn reflect hegemonic and privileged raced and classed worldviews and histories? Another feminist conceptual intervention premised on the epistemic authority of marginal subjects whose 'shared histories based on shared location within hierarchical power relations'

(Hartsock 1983; Harding 1993; Hill Collins 1997:376) is, of course, feminist standpoint theorising. Standpoint thinking itself has been a hugely productive site for a range of important conceptual interventions. Sandra Harding has argued for the necessity of 'strong objectivity' for critically evaluating 'which social situations tend to generate the most objective claims', and for 'starting thought from the lives of marginalised peoples' (Harding 1993:56). Donna Haraway has written of 'situated knowledge', arguing powerfully that it is 'about limited location' and enabling 'us to become answerable for what we learn how to see' (Haraway 1988: 583). Also insisting on specific and different feminist standpoints, Patricia Hill Collins writes of a Black feminist standpoint as a 'subjugated knowledge' located in a context of racialised and gendered economic and political domination that emerges from an 'interdependence' of the everyday knowledges of Black African American women and 'the more specialised knowledge of Black women intellectuals' (Hill Collins 2000: 269). And Sharmila Rege (1998) writes of Dalit feminist standpoint that derives from and is located in Dalit women's struggles but crucially, does not originate from an authentic well of Dalit women's difference or experience. As opposed to the politics of authenticity, Rege argues that a Dalit feminist standpoint is not only a 'liberatory' feminist project but also one that is 'multiple, heterogenous, contradictory', which needs to be open to and in dialogue with all other liberatory projects.[17] In a slightly different vein, but carefully locating and starting from poor rural women's 'contradictory experiences of globalisation' within transnational circuits of production and consumption in Southern India, Priti Ramamurthy introduces us to the concept of 'subjects in perplexity', who 'experience both joys and aches of the global every day, often simultaneously (Ramamurthy 2003: 525). Perplexity, writes Ramamurthy, is the site of convergence of 'multiple ideologies that constitute subjects—cultural practice, temporalities and place ...' (2003: 525). Locating herself firmly within the political economy of knowledge production in Latin America, and critiquing statist ideologies of hybridity and multiculturalism deployed to manage difference, especially, Indigenous difference, Silvia Rivera Cusicanqui (2012) writes of the notion of *chi'xi*, which is the 'most appropriate translation of the motley mix that we, who are called mestizas and mestizos are' (Cusicanqui 2012: 105). A hugely capacious 'notion' of many 'connotations', *chi'xi* is irreducible to colonial governmentalising moves, capturing instead the 'parallel coexistence of multiple cultural differences that do not extinguish but instead antagonise and complement each other. Each one reproduces itself from the depths of the past and relates to others in a contentious way' (Cusicanqui 2012: 105). Crossing south central America and heading north to the borderlands of Mexico and southwest USA, is the location of Gloria Anzaldúa's conceptual offering: borderlands. Also, the title of Anzaldúa's pathbreaking book, *Borderlands* locates the history of a people living in a specific geography; a geography spanning and telling the history of Mexican-origin US Chicanas. Straddling specific border geographies, imperial histories, racialised political economies of dispossession and psycho-sexual socialities, it tells the history of the coming into being of a 'border culture' and of a 'hybrid subjectivity' informed and striated by histories of loss, psychic unrest, marginality, struggles to belong, displacement and perpetual transition. The borderland hybrid subjectivity is not one of a celebratory variety that confidently celebrates multiculturalism and diversity but is borne from an acute recognition of unequal power relations, alienation, 'cultural ambiguity', and 'perplexity'. But this 'psychic unrest', economic and historical alienation in the borderlands also produces an 'alien consciousness'—a borderland consciousness, borne out of a 'struggle of flesh, a struggle of borders, an inner war ... towards new possibilities' (Anzaldúa 1987: 100-01). By highlighting these conceptual interventions, my aim is not to provide an exhaustive list of location based concepts, which of course, by any means, these are not, but rather to argue that a careful attention to a critical reflexive politics of location makes it 'unthinkable' to delink the ontological and the epistemological.

Assembling a Feminist Historical Ontology: Concepts, Subjectification, Struggles

My aim in highlighting these feminist interventions on the imbrication of ontology and epistemology is to show why the work of ontology in a feminist historical ontology is not to signal a dismissal of epistemology but to instead underscore the impossibility of epistemology and ontology as discrete and radically disconnected. So, through articulating the idea of feminist historical ontology, how am I proposing to articulate vernacular rights cultures? Well, quite simply, my objective is to marry the critical insights offered by historical ontology with those of a feminist critical reflexive politics of location. As I have made clear, by invoking a feminist historical ontology, I am neither referring to the 'ontological turn' in the humanities and the social sciences nor am I referring to the dominant meanings of 'ontology' within sections of philosophical discourse. And while I think that the discussions of the pluriversal and of 'political ontology' are important interventions, especially because of their investments in producing concepts which are non-coincident with bourgeois modernity, ultimately though, they are unable to capture the question of the political category of gender and the gendered nature of conflict and struggle and are not entirely helpful in assembling a feminist historical ontology. As I will go on to show in Chapter 5, Adivasi mobilisations deploy *haq* in their struggles for survival, life and being, and against their dispossession and eviction from their ancestral lands by the overwhelming violence and coercion unleashed by the developmentalist state and the syndicates of transnational capital. However, it would be a mistake to think about their claims for rights as either representing a hermetically sealed off 'authentic' discourse or as entirely aligned with the state-led discourse of rights. By deploying the word *haq*, the Indigenous groups in my ethnographies claim rights in a language that is imbricated in a web of gendered relationality and cosmology, including a particular relationship to the state.

In assembling a feminist historical ontology, I am drawing on but also supplementing the insights on historical ontology offered by the philosopher Ian Hacking (2002) with those offered by a critical feminist politics of location. The supplementation becomes necessary since Hacking's historical ontology is neither informed by gendered power relations and nor is he particularly interested in the existing nature of Eurocentred epistemic discourses. And, in order for historical ontologies to reflect these two concerns they will require supplementing with a postcolonial, decolonial, critical race and intersectional feminist lens. In other words, historical ontology will require a reorienting towards a feminist historical ontology.

Ian Hacking interprets historical ontology to invoke among other things, the historical coming into being of concepts, of how they acquire meanings, make up people, produce new possibilities for relating to oneself, aid the production of subjectivities, and how people constitute themselves. Consequently, a historical ontology is concerned with the speaking of words in their places but also with tracking the 'coming into being' of objects that include not only 'material objects' but also classes, kinds of people, and indeed ideas' (Hacking 2002:2). For Hacking, the process of 'coming into being' is explicitly historical, and 'the beings that become' are: 'things, classifications, ideas, kinds of people, institutions ...' (Hacking 2001: 5).[18]

Incidentally, the term 'historical ontology' does not originate in Ian Hacking's work but is articulated for the first time in Foucault's essay, 'What is Enlightenment?', where Foucault refers twice to 'historical ontology'. According to Hacking (2002: 2), by historical ontology, Foucault means a study involving truth through which we constitute ourselves as objects of 'knowledge', with 'power' (how subjects constitute themselves as 'subjects acting on others') and with 'ethics' (how subjects turn themselves into moral agents). In effect, historical ontology refers to the material, intellectual and conceptual resources and practices through which subjects constitute themselves. However, Hacking's own conceptual enquiries do not just mirror Foucault's own work, even if he does deploy the term 'historical ontology'. What is interesting about Hacking's interlocution of Foucault's work is that he deploys Foucault's insights to objects, sites and problematisations that exist outside of Foucault's 'corpus' (Koopman 2015: 571). To put it differently, Hacking uses Foucault's methodological tools—that is, historical ontology—to produce enquiries, which were never part of Foucault's repertoire. Instead he applies historical ontology to a different field and towards a different end, that is, towards historicising philosophy and towards producing new objects of knowledge. This deployment of Foucault's methodological apparatus, or his analytic, rather than his conceptual repertoire is somewhat uncommon. In academia, we have become accustomed to scholarly investigations that take up Foucauldian concepts (biopolitics, governmentality, discipline, subjectivation, and so on). However, we are less so, when it comes to work deploying Foucault's analytics (archaeology, genealogy) towards non-Foucauldian enquiries (Koopman 2015). In this regard, Koopman and Matza suggest that in contrast to the popular take up of Foucault's concepts—it is, in fact, Foucault's methods or his analytic that are more mobile and can travel a 'range across contexts' (Koopman and Matza 2013: 838). The reason for the greater mobility of Foucault's methods in contrast to his concepts is attributed by some to Foucault's 'relentlessly empirical approach' (Patton 2011:41), evidenced in his attentiveness 'to peculiarities, to small differences, to the moments when shifts in truth, authority, spatiality or ethics make a difference for today as compared to yesterday' (Rabinow and Rose 2006:205). As Koopman and Matza insightfully note, 'analytics, which range across contexts, are light, whereas concepts, which are always tied to their sites, are heavy'(Koopman and Matza 2013: 838).

My reason for discussing this taxonomy of Foucault's concepts, categories and analytical categories is to make clear that to study vernacular rights cultures is not to engage in another or a new 'model building' around human rights or indeed in producing a new theory of human rights. But why study concepts and not produce a theory of human rights? As I noted earlier, the problem is not one of not having enough theories but of not having enough concepts. Concepts are the 'building blocks' of theory, they make our world 'visualisable and discussable' (Rabinow 2011: 122) and they need to be in place in order to produce theoretical accounts. The problem in producing 'theories' for 'most of the world' is that the concepts that are put to use in these theoretical descriptions are 'provincial' (Chakrabarty 2000) and produced in specific temporal, spatial and historical contexts. And, therefore, in order to produce theorised accounts of different forms of world-making, many existing concepts would either need to be retooled or new ones would need to be generated.

A feminist historical ontology is a critical analytic and an ethical tool for producing concepts and theories from the Global South or in non-standard background conditions, that is, away from contexts which are taken as standard, assumed or unquestioned. Through an insistence on historical and contextual specificity, responsibility, intersectionality, interdisciplinarity and attention to epistemic, ontological and political marginality, a feminist historical ontology refuses a technical application of theory and holds open 'historical difference as constitutive of the possibility of thought' (Wiegman and Elam 1993: 3). In its insistence on a critical reflexive politics of location, a feminist historical ontology demands that the theorist answer the question: from where are they looking, and whom/what are they seeing?

Drawing on while also supplementing Ian Hacking's thinking on 'historical ontology' enables me to put together some key elements of a feminist historical ontology. As I noted earlier, a feminist historical ontology does not see a disjuncture between the ontological and epistemological. It does not turn away from the epistemological towards the ontological but instead shows their imbrication matters and produces consequences. The work of a feminist historical ontology is to make explicit the ways in which particular concepts come into being, the political cultures they put into place, the kinds of people they make up but also the accounts we produce of these. It helps draw attention to the different, historically specific and located languages of rights and human rights—both literal and conceptual in different parts of the globe. It attends to the political imaginaries these languages make available, and the subjectivities, conceptions of personhood and the claims for subject status that underpin them. An important way of documenting and analysing rights languages and the political imaginaries within which they operate is to examine the justificatory premises that underpin the political struggles around claim-making. As I shall go on to show in Chapters 4 and 5, the deployment of *haq* and the struggles that ensue are gendered struggles but also located within specific political struggles for rights. A key objective of a feminist historical ontology of *haq* is to challenge reigning epistemic preoccupations that characterise the theoretical and philosophical scholarship of global human rights, which mostly fails to pay near adequate theoretical, philosophical and conceptual attention to the struggles for rights and human rights in the Global South. As a result, rights struggles in the Global South seldom inform theoretical and philosophical debates on global human rights on the one hand, and on the other, when they do appear in the scholarship, they are more often than not subjected to a technical application of normative theory.

Consequently, in assembling a feminist historical ontology of *haq*, I turn my attention not only to the forms that these subaltern political struggles take and the sites they occupy but also to the intellectual resources for claim-making these deploy and use. Furthermore, a feminist historical ontology of rights and in this case, of *haq*, is explicitly oriented towards tracking and documenting how rights and human rights are mobilised in the vernacular; to exploring how concepts come into being and are deployed to claim rights; to attending to the political cultures of rights these concepts mobilise and put in place; to analysing and cataloguing the forms of subjectification these concepts engender and the political imaginaries they enable; to theorising the forms of rights politics and the erasures and silences that these put in place; and finally, to accounting for the ways in which the gendered articulation of concepts and in this case, of rights and human rights, can exceed both the purpose and nature of their mobilisation. In other words, a feminist historical ontology is explicitly concerned with critical epistemologies and ontologies of rights politics in different geographical and historical contexts.

As I noted earlier, it is Ian Hacking's focus on words and concepts and their role in 'making up people' that draws me to his work on historical ontology. In part, this is to do with my longstanding interest in speech practices and processes of political subjectivation Madhok (2013)—for instance, reorienting agency in terms of speech practices rather than free action, in order to counter the 'action bias' in our theoretical formulations of agency—but also in trying to think closely about the stakes involved in the 'politics of presence' (Phillips 1995), and in the 'performative politics of assembly' (Butler 2015) for differently gendered, raced, low caste and Indigenous subjects sitting in public assembly and staking a claim to the language of rights, and the ways in which their assembling in public disrupts the normative constitution of the public space while also making rights politics so conflictual for them.

However, even while I write this, I am acutely aware that Hacking is not interested in the coming into being of gendered concepts, nor in the gendered nature of power relations, imaginaries and subjectivities they put in place or even in the gendered processes which make up people. Even though Hacking is deeply invested in the particular historical sites at which words develop into concepts, he does not acknowledge the feminist politics of location. A feminist historical ontology on the other hand, explicitly argues that concepts are not only historically and contextually specific and tied to particular historical sites but also that they are intersectional and gendered. Gendering Hacking's historical ontology, allows one to see not only that *haq* is a masculine concept, which very often than not means, that gender equality needs invariably to be begged separately; and the latter has been without exception, the case in all the citizen mobilisations I am tracking in this book. Quite simply, this means that *haq* puts in place particular gendered political imaginaries of rights, which in turn, engenders a whole new arena of a politics of struggle over *haq*.

Accounting for conflict and struggle is central to feminist historical ontologies. Bringing a gender lens to historical ontology is to exercise awareness of the inherent power relations in the meanings that concepts take up but also in the work they do. Gender is an intrinsically political concept and struggles over gender relations are political struggles and involve multiple levels of conflict. A gender lens is manifestly important and crucial because bringing a gendered perspective means one is constantly aware of the intersectional and conflictual nature of rights but also of the limits of the normative ontological possibilities offered by *haq*.

Finally, I want to draw attention to the ethical commitment of working to and for justice that drives a feminist historical ontology. In particular, I want to highlight two issues in this regard: The first is to do with the thorny question of representation and the other is concerned with the relationship of marginal epistemologies to the politics of the marginalised. Driving both is the ethical question, which is this: how to acknowledge the intellectual contributions of the counter-hegemonic ideological work that feminist scholars and activists do in the Global South? And, furthermore, how to demonstrate ethical responsibility by not appropriating the epistemologies of subaltern movements of the Global South on the one hand, and/or by not displaying historical amnesia about their temporality, location, and counter-hegemonic contributions, on the other? In other words, how to practice vigilance against an easy forgetting of the counter-hegemonic work that is done by subaltern grassroots struggles for rights in the Global South? Consider for instance, how some influential feminist critiques of neoliberalism not only display 'startling [historical] amnesia' (Briggs 2008:85) when characterising feminist politics in binary terms as either struggles for recognition and/or redistribution, an analysis that does not take into account either the temporality or the nature of the struggles against neoliberalism by women in the Global South, which have insisted on both recognition and redistribution, and not just one or the other (Briggs 2008). Further, in the event when these social movements in the Global South are acknowledged, the terms of acknowledgment focuses predominantly on their influence on producing a shift in 'Europe's mind' (Briggs 2008) and consequently, re-centres 'Europe' as the subject of history all over again.

The question of feminist scholarship and its internal colonialisms, wilful erasures, and lack of intellectual acknowledgement of its others is hardly confined to the unequal production and acknowledgment of feminist intellectual labour between the Global North and the Global South. It also characterises feminist production in the Global South, where upholding gender binarism, biocentrism and heteronormativity, and the erasure of Dalit and Indigenous feminisms is rife. This is not to say that the context of theory production in the Global South, both feminist and mainstream, is not a context of marginality, or that theory produced by women of colour in academia is not maginalised. It is only to say that there are multiple intersectional hierarchies and circuits of power and privilege that come into visibility when we undertake multidirectional critique and start paying attention to a critical reflexive politics of location, one that is both historically located but also carefully acknowledges the multiply intersecting and entangled circuits of power.

In studying vernacular rights cultures, I am of course, studying the rights politics of subaltern groups with a view to shine a light on the conceptual deployments of rights within their political struggles, and how to make these speak back to received understandings of global human rights discourse and politics. In particular, two concerns inform my intervention in the debate on decolonising human rights in this book. First, I am very aware that the subaltern groups I am studying are mobilising to make demands from the state, which is also the all-powerful actor in this struggle. And second, given the existing coloniality of knowledge production, it is also the case that these subaltern struggles are unlikely to inform the theoretical concerns of global human rights scholarship. Both insights lead me to argue that the decolonising imperative of human rights is a twofold one: to produce human rights scholarship aimed at shifting the epistemic centre of human rights, and to generate conceptual work supportive of those challenging complex inequalities and the intersectional nature of oppression at the frontline. And, even though I share many of the critiques of global human rights, I also believe strongly that these critiques are by no means enough. We cannot afford to rest at producing sophisticated critiques alone and need to find epistemic practices, forms of activism and political practices that will challenge, or at the very least be theoretically and politically non-complicit with structures of power opposed to rights, justice, and freedom. This conclusion might seem at one level to be quite easy, instinctual, default and even commonsensical. Yet I have reached this position after many years of observing and documenting subaltern struggles for rights and human rights, and also navigating and negotiating powerful, persuasive and astute critiques of rights, many of which I agree with. Three things have been vital for me to reach this position: the vibrancy of the subaltern movements on the ground, the dynamic deployment of a vocabulary of rights in the vernacular and, finally, the epistemic urgency of conceptually capturing these movements and normative meanings of rights politics in the vernacular while also insisting that these have something to say to the human rights discourses. This 'speaking back' is key here as it is this that orchestrates the epistemic shift in the thinking on global human rights.

Conclusion

This chapter takes up seriously the challenge of understanding the normative meanings of rights in different part of the globe. In Chapter 1, I noted that in recent years, decolonising academia has acquired theoretical and political urgency. This urgency has mostly taken the form of methodological, pedagogical and epistemic critiques: of finding different methods, of producing different histories and intellectual trajectories, and of teaching different curriculums. While these decolonising moves are crucial, I have argued that the work on alternative trajectories and different genealogies must be *supplemented* by scholarship aimed at conceptual production that is able to capture the stakes and struggles of subaltern subjects in 'most of the world'. This is significant and crucial, if we are to disrupt and shift the epistemic centre of intellectual work and thinking.

However, how does one undertake the task of conceptual production in 'most of the world'? In this chapter, I assemble a feminist historical ontology and argue that it facilitates the production of conceptual accounts of our encounters with the world, which are responsive to a critical reflexive politics of location. Feminist historical ontologies are finely tuned to accounting for gendered power relations, conflicts and political struggles.

They insist on firmly situating concepts in specific histories, gendered politics and practices. Through a focus on how concepts come into being in particular historical locations, make up people and political imaginaries, feminist historical ontologies make visible the new forms of subjectivities and forms of subjection that they produce. In this book, through deploying a feminist historical ontology, I am of course, studying the conceptual life trajectories of *haq*, the work it does, the ethical commitments it produces and the forms of subjectivities it engenders. In short, I am looking at some of the gendered possibilities for becoming a subject of rights that *haq* puts in place.

Notes

1. Its root in classical Hebrew is '(a) "to cut in, engrave," in wood, stone or metal, (b) "to inscribe, write, portray" . . . (c) "to prescribe, by decree," (d) "due to God or man, right privilege' (Glasse 2001: 82).
2. See Mashkur (1978).
3. I draw on Taylor for whom social imaginaries are 'ways people imagine … how they fit together with others, the expectations that are normally met, and the deeper normative notions and images that underlie these expectations' (Taylor 2002: 23).
4. Geertz does not explicate how he deploys 'ontological' and I read him here as alluding to *haq* as consisting of a discourse on the nature of being. See David Graeber (2015) on some of the ambiguities surrounding the use of the term in anthropology.
5. The jurisdiction of the *qadi* courts in Morocco is limited to matters pertaining to personal law governed by its 1958 Code of Personal Status and thereby, only to those of marriage, divorce, filiation, inheritance and child custody.
6. The Pakistani legal context is more complex with the setting up in 1980 of the Federal Shariah Court, which has the authority to determine 'as to whether or not a certain provision of law is repugnant to the injunctions of Islam' (Hussain 2011: 15).
7. For census data on Muslim population in Rajasthan, see http://www. censusindia.gov.in/2011census/C-01.html (accessed 21 October 2020).
8. See Robinson (1974) and Faruqi (2003).
9. A British Academy Grant (SG-39747) made fieldwork in Rajasthan (2005–07) and research assistance in Okara and Khanewal in Pakistan between 2007 and 2008 possible.

10. While I use 'disciplines' here, I do not mean to suggest that there is a wholesale turn to ontology in these but only that there are sections within disciplines that have declared an 'ontological turn'.

11. For anthropology's 'ontological turn', see Holbraad and Pederson (2017).

12. Drawing on Ranajit Guha, founder of the Subaltern School, Blaser (2013) argues that this crisis can be read into the challenges to neoliberalism by Indigenous groups but also in the growing realisation in some quarters that the current ways of understanding and making the world are no longer adequate. Furthermore, solutions to these growing crises can no longer be sourced from within 'modern' paradigms.

13. However, Blaser notes, quite paradoxically, a single ontological story is reproduced in well-meaning and important anthropological critiques of culture in the 1970s, which in critiquing the 'static, backward, timeless' view of 'culture' end up reproducing the hegemonic ontological status of modernity through assertions that there are 'no really existing traditional societies' (Blaser 2013: 549).

14. Drawing on the rise of Indigenous movements in Peru and Ecuador, de la Cadena notes that the politics of these movements have been categorised as 'ethnic' and their demands as 'cultural'. However, their demands and politics are premised on an ontological refusal of the nature–culture binary that not only exceeds this categorisation as 'culture' but also the current formulation of politics.

15. The philosopher Sylvia Wynter has written powerfully about the entanglements of epistemology and ontology (2003, 2015). Walter Mignolo (2015: 108) notes that for Wynter 'the human is the product of a particular epistemology, yet it appears to be (and is accepted) as a naturally independent entity existing in the world (Mignolo 2015: 108).

16. Different bodies invoke different affects. Moreover, Hemmings argues, Black and postcolonial scholarship has shown that affects are not only the 'good' ones but also are sites of violence and racialisation. Citing the work of Audre Lorde and of Frantz Fanon, Hemmings demonstrates not only the white ontology of this 'ontological turn' but also the active erasure of the 'fact of blackness' in their work. In effect, what Hemmings is pointing to is the lack of historicity in this work and the ease with which it proceeds in its historical forgetfulness—the ease with which we forget bodies and scholarship of colour.

17. For critical interventions on Dalit feminist standpoint, see Guru (1995), Datar (1999), Lata (2015) and Arya and Rathore (2019).

18. For Hacking an important question is 'how do new ways to classify open up, or close down, possibilities for human action'? (2002: 99). Describing himself as a dynamic nominalist, he writes that

The claim of dynamic nominalism is not that there was a kind of person who came increasingly to be recognized by bureaucrats or by students of human nature, but rather that a kind of person came into being at the same time as the kind itself was being invented. In some cases, that is, our classifications and our classes conspire to emerge hand in hand, each egging the other on ... i.e. the category and the people in it emerged hand in hand. (2002: 106–07)

4   The Political Imaginaries of *Haq*
'Citizenship' and 'Truth'

In April 2001, India's leading current affairs magazine, *Frontline*, reported that 47 Adivasi people had died from hunger in Kotra Block of Rajasthan's Udaipur district (Mishra 2001). The report struck a raw nerve and made for difficult reading then, and it still continues to be a difficult read. It made for a difficult read not because the fact of hunger was unknown in postcolonial India[1] or that newspaper reports had skipped stories of hunger but more because the fact of hunger has been invisibilised and rendered banal through what Sudipta Kaviraj (2010: 225) has termed 'the logic of bureaucracy'. Policy makers prefer to use the bureaucratic term 'drought' and not the affective term 'hunger' in their reports. The erasure of 'hunger' and 'starvation' from national policy discourses represents nothing less than a national scandal for not only is hunger a constant feature of India's postcolonial timeline but also because the failure to recognise and address it unequivocally has resulted in an exponential growth in the experiential everyday reality of hunger and starvation. It is no surprise, therefore, that recent figures show that India ranked 102 out of 117 countries on the global hunger index (Global Hunger Index 2019). In contrast to the institutional reticence to acknowledge hunger, drought is a term that lends itself much more amenably to bureaucratic discourse, where it works to successfully elide the empirical fact of hunger and starvation through folding these into neat columns describing the 'social and economic consequences' of drought. The annals of India's drought policy weigh heavy with references to the administration, definitions and the management of drought but shed little light on the actual nature of harm and the experience of hunger and starvation brought on by drought.

However, in 2001, this bureaucratic logic governing the administrative representation of drought and its downplay of hunger received a major legal and political challenge. This legal challenge to the bureaucratic logic of drought came in the form of a public interest litigation (PIL) filed in the Supreme Court of India by the Rajasthan branch of the People's Union for

Civil Liberties in April 2001. Rajasthan is India's most 'chronically drought prone' (Bokil 2000: 4171) region. Since 1901, the state has experienced a minimum of 48 drought years (Rathore 2004), and at the time of filing the PIL in 2001, the state was already in its third consecutive year of rainfall failure (Bokil 2000: 4171). The PIL (a form of judge-led or 'juridical democracy' that became operational in India in the post-emergency period for 'activating' fundamental rights and providing protection from 'excesses of state power')[2] questioned whether the right to life guaranteed under Article 32 of the Indian Constitution also included the right to food (Banik 2010). In its response, the Supreme Court passed interim orders for the country-wide implementation of the 'mid-day meals' scheme under which a cooked meal would be provided to all children attending government aided schools. For all practical purposes, the legal challenge, through the submission of the PIL, converted the bureaucratic logic of drought management into a political and legal question, and into a substantial question of human rights.

The legal challenge in 2001, however, was by no means the beginning of this line of questioning. For a decade by then, Rajasthan had been at the forefront of grassroots mobilisations demanding official accountability, transparency and for the citizen's 'right to information'. These mobilisations catapulted the rights of citizens to official information and to transparency in matters of governance into mainstream political discourse, arguing that these were essential for drawing attention to the horrendous bureaucratic apathy, corruption and mismanagement of state resources and for enforcing administrative accountability, not least in the face of growing dispossession, destitution and hunger. Approaching the Supreme Court through the mechanism of the PIL, though, was but one among a combination of strategies of activism and engagements pursued by activists that included public protests, drought awareness and village level drought action committees and significantly, it led to the formation of a grassroots mobilisation forged from ongoing existing movements in the state to demand the 'right to food'. As a result of these efforts, The Right to Food network, a decentralised network built on local initiative and voluntary cooperation, was formed in 2001 as an umbrella group of several NGOs predominantly based in Rajasthan in order to frame a people's response to governmental apathy and inaction in the wake of successive droughts. The cruel irony of this institutional abandonment and bureaucratic fostering of precarity, hunger and dispossession was that it coincided with a surfeit of official stocks of food grains in the country.

As a consequence of these mobilisations on the 'right to food', the administrative term 'drought' has come to be associated, and in not insignificant measure, not with official apathy alone but also with political mobilisation, legal interventions and legislative actions directed at the developmental state. The decade-long mobilisation demanding the right to food reached its climax with the federal government deciding to legislate on the legal right to food. Accordingly, in March 2013, the Indian cabinet approved the National Food Security Act, a scheme looking to provide subsidised nutrition to two-thirds of the Indian population at an annual cost of INR 1.3 trillion. Although the legislation suffers from several shortfalls, nevertheless, in light of increased destatisation and prevailing neoliberal inspired economic orthodoxies prescribing one size fits all models of self-sufficiency, autonomy and entrepreneurial citizenship, it is indeed remarkable that this citizen activism has resulted in expanding the rights dispensation of the postcolonial state to secure for its most vulnerable citizens, what is by all accounts, an 'old fashioned' social welfare legislation.

The legal right to food is but one among six recent legislations guaranteeing social and economic rights and entitlements.[3] Since the early years of the new millennium, India has witnessed substantial expansions in the architecture and the coverage of 'social security' in the country (Drèze and Khera 2017).[4] The temporality of these social welfare legislations and legal rights, which bear not an unlikely resemblance to old fashioned social welfarism, passed in an era marked by the high point of global neoliberalism and also at a specific neoliberal economic juncture in India's political economy constitues something of an achievement but also a 'paradox' (A. Sharma 2013; Jayal 2013; Madhok 2017). As a range of scholars (Chatterjee 1996; Jayal 1999; Kaviraj 2004) have pointed out, the central objective of the postcolonial Indian state has historically been economic development and not economic and social welfare. Even though welfare appears regularly in the first sets of five-year plans (Palriwala and Neetha 2009), and is a clearly constitutionally marked objective stated in the non-justiciable parts of the Indian constitution known as the directive principles of state policy, its presence in terms of policy formulation and outcomes from 1947–2001 is at best marginal and sketchy. As Jayal (1999, 2013) argues, welfare discourse during the first four decades of Indian state developmentalism was essentially conceived in terms of 'charity', 'beneficence', 'relief' and 'poverty alleviation' rather than a citizenship right. And, therefore, it is quite striking that this language of welfare as charity undergoes a significant shift in the first decade following the neoliberalisation of the Indian economy in the 1990s. Thus the paradox that is often pointed to here is essentially this: that the point of 'opening' of the Indian economy to global and neoliberal market-led forces is also one that coincides with a re-articulation of welfare in terms of citizenship rights and entitlements in Indian political discourse. But how does one explain this paradox and this shift in political discourse of state welfare from charity to one that is a legal right of citizens? A number of different explanations can be mobilised here. For instance, this shift in discourse can partially be traced to transnational circuits of policy making that began emphasising human development and human rights (UN 1986; UNDP 1990, 2016),[5] and in particular to the global agenda in the post-Washington consensus era where civil and political rights have come to be regarded as 'essential parts of institutional structures' and mechanisms necessary for the functioning of the 'liberal market order' (Whyte 2018: 15). And, therefore, it is sometimes argued that contrary to the 'roll back of the state' under neoliberalism, the state is positioned ever more centrally in mobilising private investment and enforcing the rules of neoliberal market regulation. The shared temporality of the rise in fortunes of both neoliberalism and global human rights has led some scholars to ask if human rights are indeed the 'handmaiden to neoliberal power'? (Özsu 2018: 144; see also Moyn 2015). In this context, where civil and political human rights are seen as key to advancing neoliberal economic agenda, it is worthwhile asking as to what might be the record of human rights-based initiatives in countering global inequality? Furthermore, since institutional discourses and practices of development are a key conduit through which the global politics of inequality operates, it is also useful to ask what might be the relationship between the rise of discourses and strategies advocating rights-based and rights-led development, neoliberalism and growing global inequalities? To reprise briefly from Chapter 1, recent critical scholarship has shown that global human rights have, in fact, done little to counter the rising inequality around the globe. The general disinterestedness of global human rights in questions of inequality has been attributed to the 'minimalist' and 'moralising' nature of human rights discourse steeped in a 'politics of fatalism' (Brown 2004) and one that is disinclined towards either maximalist ends of championing equality or a structural reorganisation of social and political life demanded by a commitment to equality and justice. In India, what is striking, however, is that rights-based development is not only an official, top down, global institutionalist discourse but is also one led by grassroots citizen movements demanding the people's right to development; and, the vitality and dynamism of these rights mobilisations is evidenced in their substantial influence over national policy making resulting in the successful passage of legal entitlements to welfare (Khera 2013). Quite strikingly, though, the neoliberal landscape in India is characterised by a curious coexistence of state directed market-led neoliberal reforms to the economy resulting in rampant and exponential levels of inequality, precarity and dispossession, alongside a simultaneous expansion of the state charter on legal welfare rights. If anything, neoliberal economic policy making and the politics of expanded rights struggles and entitlements operate on parallel tracks within India's neoliberal trajectory, resulting in neither the displacement of India's neoliberal economic reforms and its resultant inequalities, nor in the withdrawal of demands for expanded citizen rights settlements. The sociologist Alf Gunvald Nilsen (2021) writes that the explanation for the paradox of expanded welfare rights under neoliberalism lies with neoliberalism's reinvention of itself as 'inclusive'. Consequently, 'inclusive neoliberalism' refers to the coupling of market-oriented accumulation strategies with social policy interventions that aim to protect poor and vulnerable groups from marginalisation and dispossession. It is this 'inclusive neoliberalism', writes Nilsen, that has allowed the Indian neoliberal project to include rights-based legislation alongside its robust commitment to neoliberal market reforms. However, while this 'inclusive neoliberalism' did little to obstruct the expansion of the legal charter of welfare rights, it actively facilitated the rise of endemic and pervasive inequalities and a 'high incidence of poverty', particularly among Dalit and Adivasi groups, who are also the most structurally oppressed and disadvantaged groups in India (Kannan 2018). So, it is the case that roughly three decades of relatively high growth rates under economic neoliberalisation have not 'trickled down' to those bearing the brunt of 'multidimensional inequality',[6] and despite a 'vastly accelerated' growth, actual poverty levels in the country have seen only a very 'sluggish' decline (Drèze and Sen 2013: 217). As the economist K. P. Kannan points out, the six year period between 2004 and 2010, which were also years that saw accelerated economic growth, 69 per cent of the population earned PPP \$2 per capita per day and were classed poor and vulnerable, with the 'highest incidence of poverty' distributed among Dalit and Adivasi groups followed by Muslims (Kannan 2018: 35). More current statistics continue to show that this stranglehold grip of inequality is firmly in place with just over 60 per cent of the population continuing to live on \$3.10 a day (Oxford Poverty and Human Development Initiative [OPHI] 2018). As is now well documented, while inequality is pervasive around the globe, what sets apart inequality in the Indian context is its 'unique cocktail of lethal divisions and disparities' (Drèze and Sen 2013), where extreme economic inequality is experienced at the intersection of structural oppressions of caste, class, Indigeneity and gender inequalities, which mutually reinforce and reproduce each other (Drèze and Sen 2013; Kannan 2018). Perhaps the impact of recently struggled for expansions in legal welfare rights could be read not so much as representing a 'comprehensive vision' in either the social policies on universal welfare and social security or indeed directly impacting on poverty reduction, not least as their implementation on the ground has been uneven and marked by political unwillingness, but rather as directly targeting the deep structural intersectional inequalities of caste and gender (Drèze and Khera 2017: 563). And, therefore, even while cold statistics show the firm grip of inequality, which has grown unfettered and in tandem with the rise of rural movements demanding expansive citizen entitlements, there are also other stories coming out of the experience of the rights-based legislations which draw attention to discernable shifts within gendered relations of oppression and dispossession; changes and disruptions not always captured by cold statistics alone[7] or anticipated by the rights legislations.

However, the ushering of this new welfarism and new legal rights has neither meant that the argument on the need, design and implementation of India's social security apparatus has in any way been won; and, nor has it led to a firm political consensus or policy commitment towards these. Over the years, these legal rights have been rendered precarious and fragile through official apathy, 'indifference', refusals to allocate funding and by the repeated recalibrations of these entitlements in the name of removing 'corruption' and improving 'efficiency'. The passage of these new rights—while showing not insignificant results in terms of access to social security, social equity benefits and 'significant gender related benefits'—have ramped up popular cynicism and criticism of these 'social protections'. This criticism has been particularly pronounced within sections of urban media circles and city dwelling middle classes who complain of their unaffordability, but also among a section of economists and social policy analysts for their inefficiencies, 'leakages', non-accountability and corruption on the one hand, and over the economic ideas and design underpinning these on the other. Consequently, technical and theoretical questions with respect to exclusion errors versus inclusion costs; universal versus targeted distribution; and social benefits versus market costs,[8] have come to preoccupy detractors as well as supporters of these citizen rights.

Significantly, though, the grassroots rural mobilisations spearheading these new rights legislations and legal rights have produced new political cultures of rights. These political cultures of rights are explicitly non-party political, articulate political claims in a language of rights, and mobilise and demand public policy legislation in respect of these rights claims but do not, at least in the final instance, regard the state as the dominant mainstay of citizen rights. These rural mobilisations have revitalised and animated the meaning and work of legal constitutionalism through invoking citizenship rights but in doing so, have also expanded the meaning and spectrum of rights on offer. Interestingly, the language through which these rights have been demanded has not been the formal, abstract and distant language of legal constitutionalism alone, but a language of rights in the vernacular; a moral language imbricated in the relational structures, which it both upholds but also seeks to disrupt.

My focus in this chapter, is not so much to rehearse or shed any new light on the legislations themselves but rather to examine the critical vocabularies of rights that have spearheaded this demand for rights-based legislations. In particular, I examine the political cultures that this deployment of rights has produced, the political imaginaries these have generated and the political subjects of rights that have come into being as a result. As I pointed out earlier, these subjects of rights are complex and conflictual subjects primarily because although *haq* has emerged as the principal language to make unhesitant claims for very specific entitlements from the state, it does not translate easily into one that also makes claims to or defines inter-personal relations. The boundary-keeping around these subjects of rights and the policing and regulation of these rights subjects begs the following question: to what sorts of claim-making does *haq* lend itself? And, who are these subjects of rights that *haq* makes up? The rural mobilisations predominantly deploy *haq* to claim citizenship entitlements, and not surprisingly then, citizenship is an important justificatory premise of rights. However, upon querying who this citizen is, the homogenous category of the citizen starts to unravel along intersectional gender, caste, religious and class lines.

Going forth in this chapter, I draw on my ethnographies of the right to food movement in Rajasthan and identify the political imaginaries and the two dominant justificatory premises that underpin the deployment of *haq*. Through ethnographic descriptions, I show how *haq* produces particular subjects of rights. The first subject of rights I focus on draws heavily on the justificatory premise of citizenship but this idea of citizenship and the relationship with the state that it summons is a qualified one. The second justificatory premise of *haq* I explore in this chapter is articulated by primary women development workers in a state sponsored development programme for women in Rajasthan known as the *sathin*s and is grounded in the moral idea of 'Truth'. The Hindi word *sathin* literally translates as female companion or friend, and the *sathin*s were recruited by the state as 'agents of change' to bring development to the women in Rajasthan's villages. As I will go on to illustrate in the second half of the chapter, in the narratives of the *sathin*s, *haq* is said to embody the moral idea of Truth and therefore, demanding *haq* is to stake a claim to Truth and to be considered morally credible and believable subjects.

Significantly, this chapter also shifts the empirical context within which conceptual and theoretical work on rights and human rights takes place. As this chapter demonstrates, the background context for rights claims in 'most of the world' is not so much the global human rights discourse championed by transnational organisations and policy makers, but a rights discourse mediated through the nation state and its deployment of rights and human rights and explicitly oriented towards furthering its policy interests of development. In short, the developmental state is a key agent and facilitator in the production of rights subjectivities and in providing the context for rights struggles. However, as I show in the chapter, the political mobilisations on the ground around citizenship rights have not only resulted in the fashioning of new and innovative rights thinking, rights politics and citizenship claims, but also produced innovative forms of 'counter-development'.

Mobilising for the Right to Food

As I noted earlier, the right to food campaign came into being in Rajasthan. The reasons for Rajasthan's pre-eminent position in matters of citizenship struggles are not altogether clear. In terms of development outcomes and indicators, Rajasthan is among the persistently poorly performing states in India. Going by cold statistical print alone, the social and economic indicators in the state, especially in respect of gender, make for grim reading. Recent statistics indicate that maternal mortality rate in Rajasthan is on a downward trend but still considerably lags behind that of other Indian states. The child sex ratio already among the worst in the country is worsening (there were 888 girls for 1,000 boys in the 0–6 age group in 2011) and there are only 926 females for every 1,000 males.[9] The literacy rate for women in Rajasthan, in 2012, was 57 per cent, with 37 per cent of 15–17 years old girls not enrolled in any school (World Bank 2016). The latest available statistics point to a 31 per cent gap in the literacy levels between rural and urban women (World Bank 2016) and a further disparity in the literacy rates of Scheduled Caste women (44.6 per cent) and those belonging to Scheduled Tribes (37.3 per cent).[10] However, these depressing social indicators only tell some of the story, for somewhat paradoxically, and in spite of these dismal statistics, it is also the case, that Rajasthan has a vibrant women's movement and boasts of a high visibility of women in the public sphere. Moreover, it elects the highest percentage of women to *panchayat* bodies in India, and currently 56 per cent of the total elected representatives in its local government bodies are women. While the numbers elected to its state legislature are not impressive, however, in electing 12 per cent women to the legislature,[11] Rajasthan leads far ahead of the better socioeconomically performing states in India. Finally, it is also worth noting that in the latest elections to the state legislature, 74.66 per cent women exercised their vote, outstripping the state's total voting percentage of 74.21 per cent.[12]

Overall, despite the mismatch between social and political indicators of gender wellbeing and keeping in view the plurality of social contexts inside rural Rajasthan, the statistical evidence reflects the fairly common social practices, experiences and conditions one witnesses first hand in its hamlets and villages: that girls are very seldom in secondary education let alone in primary schools, that iniquitous caste practices determine interpersonal social relations, that access to public amenities is strictly regulated according to one's position in the caste hierarchy, that child marriages abound and are celebrated in annual religious festivals, and that female infanticide occurs in several communities, helping to account for the state's skewed sex ratio. All these iniquitous and discriminatory practices take place in the persistent background of widespread and acute structural poverty and hunger.

Although my fieldwork focused on the articulations of *haq* amongst rural participants of rights mobilisations, it is important to keep in mind that these were not spontaneous but a result of intricately organised and coordinated rights initiatives by NGOs and social activists with a longstanding presence in the area. From the mid-1980s onwards, the streets of Jaipur began witnessing large popular mobilisations voicing protest over a diverse array of issues. These included public demonstrations against institutional inaction over the *sati* (widow immolation) of a young woman, Roop Kanwar, at Deorala in 1987; women's groups calling for more stringent laws on sexual harassment and violence in the workplace in the wake of the gang rape of a village development worker in 1992; and civil society organisations demanding state legislation in favour of minimum employment guarantees and citizens' 'right to know', with the latter seen both as a tool against corrupt bureaucratic practices and as a means of enforcing accountability and transparency within governmental mechanisms[13] (Madhok 2009; see also Jenkins and Goetz 1999).

Approaching the courts was but one of the strategies pursued by the right to food network. In effect, the right to food movement has engaged in a diverse set of advocacy and mobilisational practices, organising public hearings, rallies, *dharna*s, *padyatra*s, national conventions on the right to food, action-oriented research, media advocacy and political lobbying of elected members of parliament. They have been particularly effective in lobbying the state administration for increasing drought relief and assistance in villages and mobilising popular support in favour of a social rights legislation guaranteeing the 'right to work'. A forerunner of the right to food movement was the Akal Sangharsh Samiti (ASS) or 'drought action committee', a platform of 50 organisations across Rajasthan, that scrutinised the implementation of state-led drought relief schemes. The ASS held public hearings and surveyed the living conditions in drought affected areas, which challenged the statist narratives of drought relief. Many of my Dalit women field respondents, for instance, spoke of the struggles to be included in drought relief programmes, and especially by drought-hit women-headed low caste households. Despite the many difficulties outlined by these Dalit women, however, what remained remarkably clear was their resolute demand for a more expansive social rights legislation. Let me provide an excerpt from one of my interviewees in this regard:

> On 5 June 2003, we attended a public rally at Jaipur where we demanded our *haq*. We said we wanted *kam ka adhikaar* (right to employment/work or employment guarantee). This right to work or employment guarantee is very important to us for in the face of severe drought, successive crop failures, disappearance of water, food and livestock feed, how are we meant to live?
>
> When the drought came, I went to the village *sarpanch* [a *sarpanch* is the elected chairperson of the *panchayat*, which is a democratically elected village level local body] to enquire if there had been a muster roll for a local road works programme sanctioned for our village under the drought relief programme organised by the *sarkar* [*sarkar* refers to the state and/or government]? I came to know that there had in fact, been one that had been sanctioned but we never got any employment or relief under it ... there is so much *rajniti* (politics of caste) in these things ... the upper castes—the Jats, Thakurs, Meenas, Kumhars were getting the employment but people of lowest castes—the Bairwas and Rehgars—could not even register themselves on the employment rolls.
>
> In all of this politics, we must not forget that it is the people who are the wealth creators ... and the government in guaranteeing a right to employment would only be giving us what is rightfully our due.[14]

What is evident in this narrative is an intersecting and a non-hierarchical view of rights, which refuses a strict categorisation and discrete understanding of rights in terms of social, economic and political rights. In fact, a common theme that emerged in my fieldwork interviews was how the employment guarantee or the 'right to work' and the 'right to food' was fundamental to render substantial the constitutionally enshrined right to life. In addition, what was also evident was that it was no longer enough for the state to be charitable and welfare oriented but for welfare to be a matter of legal right. This intersecting nature of legal rights moves away from the *ad hoc* and uncertain provision of 'lifelines' for survival provided by the state in times of 'drought' and other 'crises' and towards claiming formal and substantive legal provisions to welfare rights that would ensure wellbeing and welfare at all times and not only mere survival in the face of starvation and acute hunger.

The intersecting nature of rights is also emphasised by the right to food campaign. Their website has a vast amount of information on the various social welfare rights they are involved in. Although the campaign started in 2001 with a petition demanding that government food stocks should be used to prevent hunger and starvation, it also demands equitable land rights and forest rights. However, despite its insistence on an integrated set of rights that include the right to ownership of land, unlike other more transnationally focused campaigns and networks such as the Via Campensina, which focus on food sovereignty and the rights of the producers over both land and the means of producing the food (Dunford 2016), the right to food campaign focuses mainly on the institutional mechanisms and duties of the state, believing that the primary responsibility for guaranteeing basic entitlements to food rests with the state. The campaign emphasises popular mobilisations as a way to pressurise states and aims to use 'all democratic means' to make people's basic rights political priorities for the state. It regards the right to food as interrelated with broader entitlements. As its foundation statement says: 'we consider that everyone has a fundamental right to be free from hunger and under-nutrition. Realising this right requires not only equitable and sustainable food systems but also entitlements relating to livelihood security such as the right to work, land reform and social security'. It has, therefore, focused on legislation and government schemes, including NREGA, the integrated child development services, mid-day meals scheme, and the public distribution system.[15] The mid-day meals proposal and campaign, for example, is indicative of the way the right to food intersects with other rights in a way that elides any clear hierarchy of rights. The demand for the provision of mid-day meals for all children enrolled in state schools argues that educational attainment in deeply segmented societies and poor households is clearly dependent on some kind of provision of food, and powerfully demonstrates the intersection of a right to education and a right to food with various equality outcomes, including promoting school participation, preventing classroom hunger, fostering social equality and enhancing gender equity (Roy and Dey 2012).

A Tale of Two *Jan Sunwais*

Perhaps, the most recognisable, significant and innovative form of public mobilisation organised by the right to food movement is the *jan sunwai*. As the Hindi word suggests, a *jan sunwai* is literally a public hearing where people gather together to scrutinise particular public policies and to demand a public audit of these, especially of the public expenditure on public projects. The 'public hearing' institutes a public monitoring mechanism and consists of airing people's testimonies, experiences and observations on the existence and actual workings of policies and development projects in their villages.

The *jan sunwai* is predominantly the brainchild of the Mazdoor Kisan Shakti Sanghathan (MKSS), or the Association for Workers and Farmers (Mishra 2003), also a part of the right to food network, which has been involved in a long-drawn struggle for the right of ordinary citizens to gain access to state financial records and to state audits of development projects. It spearheaded a social movement espousing the right to public information and of people's right to know about the government's economic functioning, which led to the passage of a federal law known as the the Right to Information Act in June 2005. The right to information (RTI) movement formally began in the early 1990s to highlight the gross failures of the state to uphold minimum wage legislation particularly within drought relief programmes set up to provide stipulated employment to people in drought affected districts and to focus on the flagrant inefficiencies and corrupt practices within the state PDS. The people's right to public information was seen as a key political tool with which to scrutinise reasons for endemic rural poverty and as a means for enforcing democratic accountability and transparency. However, the activities of the MKSS have not been limited to exposing the everyday forms of official corruption but have also come to reveal the 'multifaceted nature of corruption' within the legal and political system through championing innovative social techniques of mobilisation and public appraisal.

On 2 December 1994, the MKSS organised its first ever *jan sunwai* at Kot Kirana *panchayat* in Rajasthan's Pali district. The *jan sunwai* declared itself as a public forum for the people to speak openly about the corruption in development works carried out in the villages. The people came to the Kot Kirana *jan sunwai* where they assembled to hear the nature and scale of the discrepancies between the official records of the development works carried out in their name and those that actually existed on ground. They heard in astonishment, anger and dismay at the names of all the people in the official records who were supposedly the beneficiaries of development schemes and, who in reality were anything but that. More often than not, a *jan sunwai* follows a set order of events. They usually begin with the reading out of the agenda and introducing the representatives of state bureaucracy and also of the various civil society organisations participating in the *jan sunwai*. Soon after there is usually a performance of a few high energy and catchy motivational and movement songs highlighting the importance of exercising citizenship and the work that a *jan sunwai* does in holding the state to public account, not least in respect of citizen entitlements. This is soon followed by a reading out aloud of the individual testimonies about the ongoing development works. These testimonials of corruption on the ground more often than not draw attention to the current state of development projects and their corrupt practices; to the existence of ghost schemes and ghost development works, to fake muster rolls of public works programmes, to bogus receipts and expenditure logs and to the various corrupt practices of state officials, ration shop owners, and elected local government representatives. After these testimonials are read out, the invited officials are asked to provide explanations and to give an account of the current state of affairs in respect of these, and/or to provide clarifications.

The *jan sunwai*s are public monitoring mechanisms which focus on the public shaming of the powerful. And not surprisingly, the questioning of both power and also the powerful at the *jan sunwai*s led to a 'backlash' orchestrated by powerful groups, who found themselves now increasingly coming under public scrutiny. In the early years of their institution, the *jan sunwai*s were actively boycotted by the local administration and elected representatives who also organised collective threats against the villagers offering testimonies at these[16]. However, as the public demands for a 'right to information' gained momentum, the *jan sunwai*s too increasingly came to be viewed favourably both by the state administration and also by the people. Importantly, though, and as Neelabh Mishra (2003: 41) notes:

Each such success made a breach in the wall of feudal fear that characterises a typical Rajasthan village, helped put the finger on the convergence between feudal inequities and the pathologies of contemporary practices of development and politics and thus helped make the *Jan Sunwai* a continuously growing mass movement.

Over the years, the *jan sunwai* has become not only one of the most recognised forms of public monitoring of public policy, but it has also come to be adopted by many international institutions, national and local governments, who along with several Indian states, including Rajasthan, have adopted social audits (Roberts 2006).[17] Their institutional incorporation notwithstanding, the *jan sunwai*s are contentious and conflictual exercises with the ever present threat of violence. In 2004, I attended two *jan sunwai*s held on consecutive days at the end of January. Both *jan sunwai*s were organised by the MKSS but both were different in the atmosphere, attendance and the kinds of issues they brought to light. The first, held on 29 January in Jawaja in Ajmer district focused on the state of local public health facilities, and in particular, on the misappropriation of funds and the general mismanagement of the government hospital at Jawaja. The *jan sunwai* took place under a large marquee where rugs were laid out for the gathered public to sit on. For the attending invited officials and other civil society representatives, a long set of tables were arranged in a rectangular fashion with accompanying chairs lined up next to each other on one side. The entire scene was staged in such a manner that the assembled officials and invitees sat facing the assembled public. There was a visible presence of women who had come out in large numbers to the *jan sunwai*.

In line with the established order of events, the *jan sunwai* at Jawaja began with a round of introductions of those who were sat at the table and the reading out of the agenda of the *jan sunwai*. Next, the testimonials from the affected villagers of the *panchayat* were invited from those in assembly, and these came in thick and fast with many people coming over to the microphone to speak about their particular hardships at the hospital. A substantial number of the testimonials had also already been collected beforehand and subsequently were read out by the MKSS representatives. The testimonials highlighted that the 'ladies bathroom' in the hospital was always shut and out of operation so that women suffering from malaria or those who were pregnant or who had come to the hospital for the 'delivery' of their babies had no option but to relieve themselves outside in the open without any privacy. It was noted that the funds sanctioned under the state tuberculosis prevention scheme for procuring an ambulance for the hospital and also for buying computers for the hospital had in fact been used by the District Collector[18] for buying an air-conditioned 'Ambassador car' for his office and a personal home computer. It was pointed out that statutory 'free' treatments to people who were below the poverty line (BPL) at the hospital were never free, that women had to pay for deliveries and for abortions; and that doctors demanded money to treat snake bites and dog bites, even when these are meant to be provided free of cost. The general atmosphere at the *jan sunwai* was one of chaotic bonhomie and enthusiasm, and after receiving replies and assurances from invited state officials that these issues would be looked into, the *jan sunwai* gradually dispersed.

In contrast, the *jan sunwai* held the next day on 30 January at Kelwara village in Rajsamand district could not have been more different. The MKSS had organised a *jan sunwai* at Kelwara to institute a public meeting on the right to food and to scrutinise the progress of the development works in the *panchayat*. The *jan sunwai* took place near a check dam, and in the outdoor precincts of a one storied building. Unlike the *jan sunwai* at Jawaja, there was no marquee this time but rugs were laid out on the ground for the public, with the tables and chairs arranged similarly in long rectangular lines in a fashion similar to those at Jawaja the day before. A larger gathering was in assembly at Kelwara and there was also very high level official presence. The state administrative hierarchy present included the Assistant District Magistrate (ADM) and the Block Development Officer (BDO) of Kumbalgarh who were present throughout the entire proceedings of the *jan sunwai* along with other officials of the development bureaucracy. There was also a large number of civil society representatives, a delegation from the Ford Foundation and a smattering of journalists including one from the *Washington Post*. In my estimation, there were about 350–400 people assembled at the *jan sunwai* and there were not as many women present as there had been at Jawaja.

After the initial introductions, the *jan sunwai* began with a two-minute silence in homage to Mahatma Gandhi (he was assassinated on 30 January 1948) followed by a reminder to the gathered public that the objective of the *jan sunwai* was not to oppose the administration but to demand accountability.[19] And that at the same time, the state administration was also required to apprise the *jan sunwai* about the progress of official investigations into the corrupt practices of various development programmes across different *panchayats* that had been unearthed and laid bare at the previous *jan sunwais*. Highly aware of the potentially conflictual nature of the discussion agenda at hand, the organisers repeatedly reminded the assembled public that the main aim of the *jan sunwai* was not to instigate conflict between the public

and the state officials or *sarkar* (government) but to demand answers from
the administration. Early in the proceedings of the *jan sunwai*, the state
officials in attendance at the *jan sunwai* at Kelwara were asked for an update
on the outcome of the *jan sunwai* held three years ago at Janawad in 2001.
The Janawad *jan sunwai* of 2001 and the contents of the investigation that
followed it have been widely covered in the regional and national press but
the details are worth repeating. In broad strokes, the state's own official
investigation into the endemic corruption in development projects in Janawad
found that during the period of 1994–2001, out of the INR 1.25 crore (1 crore
is equivalent to 10 million) that had been sanctioned to Janawad *panchayat* for
development projects, 70 lakhs (700,000) had been misappropriated.[20] The
scale of corruption aside, what was truly spectacular about the Janawad *jan
sunwai* was that it brought to light the astounding levels of official resistance
to make public any documentary evidence of the development projects in
progress or their incurrent expenditure. For nine months prior to the *jan
sunwai* at Janawad, the people of Janawad assisted by the MKSS knocked
on the doors of every state official and elected representative linked with
development in their *panchayat* to demand information on the expenditure
on development projects sanctioned in Janawad between 1995 and 2000. In
their bid for official information, the people submitted applications to relevant
state officials, wrote to prominent functionaries of the *gram panchayat* and
the Rajasthan state bureaucracy including to the ministers in the government
with repeated reminders of their obligation to provide information under the
revised rules of the Panchayati Raj Act (1996). When all their efforts came
to nothing, the MKSS organised a *dharna* (protest demonstration) outside
the District Collector's office in Rajsamand. In the end, and after a year
long struggle, the people of Janawad did receive the official documents they
had been demanding but, even then, these were only made available in an
incomplete form with some crucial paperwork missing.

The official update on the Janawad corruption scandal was, however, not
the only major issue on the agenda at the Kelwara *jan sunwai*. Previously in
2003, a *jan sunwai* also held at Kelwara had looked into the irregularities in
the dealings of ration shops in the *panchayat*. By 2003, the public welfare
system had already undergone a series of neoliberal reforms to meet the fiscal
constraints of a market friendly economy introduced in India in the early
1990s. A heavy brunt of these reforms to public welfare was shouldered by
the public distribution system (PDS) which underwent a major overhaul in
orientation in the 1990s when it became a targeted system focused on two

categories of beneficiaries: those 'Below the Poverty Line' (BPL) and those 'Above Poverty line' (APL). In December 2000, a third category, 'Poorest of the Poor' (Antyodaya) was added. Over the years, the PDS has been transformed into a highly complex, segmented and scaled down entitlement. A prominent feature of the PDS is the dense network of ration shops which distribute subsidised grains[21] to those officially classed poor (BPL). Ration shops are the lifelines of the village poor and in Rajasthan, there are 26,000 such ration shops. In 2003, the Kelwara *jan sunwai* had drawn attention to the gross irregularities in the record keeping practices of ration shops in Kelwara, which showed that the subsidised grains had been sold to the intended beneficiaries when in fact, they had not received any of their food grain entitlements.

On 30 January 2004, the *jan sunwai* at Kelwara demanded to know if there had been any improvements in the functioning of the ration shops in the *panchayat* since the previous *jan sunwai* held in the *panchayat* a year ago. Over the year, there had been public reports, which had raised doubts over these improvements, and as some of these public testimonials on the corrupt practices of the ration shops in Kelwara were being read out, there arose a noticeable disruption in the gathered crowd. The ration dealers and shopkeepers who had come to the *jan sunwai* began shouting objections to some of the testimonies and started raising their hands and voices demanding a chance to speak. On being asked by the *jan sunwai* organisers to let the proceedings continue without interruption, the ration dealers started raising slogans and began to move forward through the mostly seated crowd in a bid to approach the invited guests sat on the other side of the assembled tables. Soon, a discernable wave of panic arose among the assembled crowd who scrambled to get up in order to get out the way of the advancing ration dealers. I heard some urgent and impassioned voices asking people to leave the site and the *jan sunwai* quickly. However, since there was no easy and swift exit away from the thronging crowds which had now spilled out onto the main street, I followed a few people I knew and climbed up to the rooftop of the building in whose precincts the *jan sunwai* had assembled. Looking down from the rooftop, I could see that a few policemen were trying to calm the gathering while also trying to control the ration dealers. There seemed to be nothing more to do but to wait for the upheaval to die down. And, after just under half an hour, the ration shop dealers stood aside. The *jan sunwai* resumed its work with the MKSS organisers reading out falsified sale entries in the ration registers and also checking entries in the ration books of the villagers.

For many days after the Kelwara incident, I kept thinking about the everyday nature of 'feudal fear' reigning in Rajasthan's rural villages. As powerful interventions by Dalit feminist scholarship makes clear (Irudayam et al. 2011; Kowtal and Soundarajan 2014; Rowena 2013), this 'feudal fear' is borne from specific and systemic gendered relations of violence, dispossession, injury[22] and upper caste entitlement. Demanding rights is a conflictual business and the organisers of the *jan sunwai* were highly aware of the fear and intimidation involved in these settings. As noted earlier, the organisers expressed this awareness by repeated exhortations to the gathered public to not be fearful and to speak of their experiences without fear. But these assurances did little to allay the heavy cloak of anxiety and fear circulating in the crowd. The fear and trepidation was palpable at the Kelwara *jan sunwai* despite the fact that there was a full attendance by high officials of the state, by journalists and other subjects with fair amounts of social capital, none of whom deterred the ration dealers from flexing their muscles, of course. However, rights are not only exercised in either full public view or indeed under full security of one's life and bodily autonomy. For subaltern groups, demanding and exercising rights are conflictual, risk saturated exercises precisely because the act of articulating rights is also to draw attention to the structural oppressions of social life that effectively deny, oppose and delegitimise rights for these groups and where to exercise rights is to simultaneously also stage an act of defiance against these structural oppressions. Consider, for example, the case of Manohari Bai, a Dalit woman and a member of Marudhar Ganga Society, a local NGO working for Dalit rights based in Jodhpur district. At a *gram sabha* in her village, and in full public view, Manohari Bai exercised her citizen's right to information and asked after the proposal to build a girl's school in her 'ward'. but she did so in a setting without the high-profile presence of administration officials and civil society actors.

In her interviews with me, Manohari Bai recounted the horror that broke loose when she stood up and asked the question about the girl's school. Barely had she finished asking her question that she was mercilessly beaten by the *sarpanch* (a Choudhury by caste and his supporters) and her clothes were violently torn off. She describes the incident in the following interview:

> In 2002, sometime in August–September, I went to the *gram sabha* meeting where I stood up and asked about what had happened to the proposal for the girls school which had been approved in our 'ward' no 14 [a village *panchayat* is divided into smaller units called 'wards']. The *sarpanch* said, '*chup ho ja, tu*

kaun hain bolni wali' (you must shut up, who do you think you are to pose these questions?). Then all violence broke loose. There were 500 men who shouted obscenities at me and I was beaten up, my *dupatta* and other clothes were torn off me whilst all the time the people kept shouting *'randi baith ja'* (sit down you whore). My attackers were mainly Rajputs and Jats but there was also one Mali and even a *sarkari karamchari,* I mean he was a *Patwari* … I went to Osian, and then after a month and a half the police registered a case against them. The police only registered my case after I pleaded my case with the Chief Minister and he ordered a case to be registered. The police did register a case after pressure from the Chief Minister's office, but they put a FR (False Report) against it. In the courts, the magistrate was pressured by the police and the *sarpanch* and he dismissed the case. I didn't give up though and I took the case up to the High Court in Jodhpur. I am now waiting for a date for a hearing to be announced.[23]

Apart from Manohari Bai's graphic account of the violence and conflict that demanding rights entails, her narrative also points to the indivisible and intersecting nature of rights. For instance, demanding the 'right to information' from elected representatives or indeed public officials about public work programmes on health, education or work programmes can in many cases involve a simultaneous claim for gender and caste equality whilst in the same breath drawing attention to corruption within the local and state bureaucracies, the judicial system and to the flouting of procedural norms within the administrative, executive and legislative system itself. Perhaps, it is the indivisible nature of rights (and the futility of analytically trying to isolate them into categories)—of political and civic entitlements intersecting and interwoven with individual rights—that makes rights politics so conflictual.

The Justificatory Premises of *Haq* as Citizenship

Given the institutional focus of the right to food movement, it is not entirely unsurprising that in the narratives of the grassroots participants of the right to food movement, by far the most ubiquitous justificatory premise underpinning *haq* was that rights accrued to one through citizenship. In effect, one can detect two different but related ideas of citizenship in the narratives of *haq*: the first is a discernably 'active' view of citizenship that regards rights as crucial for political participation and for exercising citizenship, while the second is a more or less straightforward legalist notion of citizenship that predicates rights upon legal constitutionalism. An unmistakably 'active' view of citizenship replete with notions of self-governance, accountability and responsibility is clearly enunciated by the political and field workers of the MKSS.

The interview below is excerpted from a long conversation with two prominent members of the MKSS. According to them:

> As citizens, we have *haq* over this road, the road is built with our money. It is 'our' money because we pay income tax and we pay also tax on whatever we buy such as rice, *dal* and cooking oil. That is how the *sarkar* (the state/government) builds hospitals and schools. It builds these with 'our' money. The money that people think is *sarkari* or the building that is deemed to be *sarkari*, we say to them: it is not *sarkari*, it is 'our' building and it is 'our' money. 'Our' democracy must be safeguarded for that will make our rights safe. 'Our' effort should be that the constitution continues to guarantee the rights of citizens.[24]

In a different vein, I encountered what might appear at least initially as predominantly a statist notion of citizenship. Consider the following excerpt from an interview with Prem Bairwa, a Dalit woman and member of the village council in Kotkhawada in Jaipur district. In addition to her role as a member of the local village council, Prem Bairwa is affiliated with a large and well-funded NGO[25] that explicitly describes itself as a 'facilitator in the development process' (Cecoedecon 2017); she is also closely associated with the National Campaign for Dalit Human Rights (NCDHR), a national level advocacy organisation in India.

According to her:

> As a council member, I have a *haq* in the *panchayat* (village council) to get development done in the village. Do only men have the right to speak and conduct political business; are not women to enjoy these rights equally? It is a fight for my *haq* and a fight I have to fight myself. The government has given these rights to women; Indira Gandhi started the *mahila raj* [government ruled by women]. Before her, there were no women's rights. In case the government changes 'our' rights then we have to fight the government. After all, it is 'us' who make the government.

At the outset, these two views of citizenship appear to resonate with liberal citizenship (subjects with rights) and also with those of civic republicanism and its ideas of self-governance, rights and public service. They also seem to uphold the 'umbilical' relationship (Moyn 2010: 38) between rights and the state. Yet, all these conclusions would be too quick for at least two reasons: first, liberal citizenship is based on a contractual arrangement between individuals and the state on the basis of negative liberty, and civic republicanism with its valorisation of political participation takes homogenous political communities as self-evident. Neither liberal selfhood nor the assumption of single axial political identities inform the justificatory premise of *haq* as citizenship, not least, since the rights subjectivities engaged by *haq* are not always individuated and also because citizenship's common unitary identity fractures only too easily in the actual practice of rights and citizenship especially by marginalised subjects. Second, it would seem that these deployments of *haq* conflate legal rights with entitlements—a widespread academic tendency that cuts across disciplinary divides (for example, Morris 1993; Hirschl 2000),[26] where rights and entitlements are mainly (and interchangeably) understood as positive legal rights attached to corresponding obligations, liabilities, addressees and duties. However, paying close attention to the narratives above shows that claims of *haq* exceed this predominant and legalist understanding of rights and entitlements. If anything, the deployments of *haq* in my ethnographies embrace legal rights but also draw attention to entitlements and to extrajudicial claims. Within analytical philosophy, the distinction between rights and entitlements is not only one between legal and moral rights but concerns the more general question of the structure of rights, the relationship between rights and obligations and the justifications of rights itself. Consequently, the relationship between rights, claims and entitlements has engaged philosophical discussions and many philosophers make some careful and intricate distinctions between these (for example, Wasserstrom 1964; McCloskey 1965; Feinberg 1970; Hohfeld 1978; Raz 1986; Sen 1986; Nickel 1987). Some view rights not as claims or powers (McCloskey 1976: 99) but rather as 'entitlements to do, have, enjoy or have done' and consequently, independent of a corresponding duty holder in place from whom rights can be claimed *against*. Others envisage rights as 'valid claims' backed by mandatory positive legal sanctions with a corresponding duty holder and/or addressee in place and/or, where there might be (as in the case of moral rights) a claim for recognition based on existing moral principles. Joel Feinberg (1970: 255), who is most closely associated with the above view, regards rights as 'valid claims' which are always 'correlated with another's duty' but he also makes allowances for a 'manifesto' sense of rights in some contexts, which are entitlements without corresponding duty holders in place. As is evident, the chief distinction between valid and manifesto claims is over where to place the burden of obligation but also that the relationship between rights and obligations or duties is more often than not overdetermined by the question of law: rights are judged 'valid' or 'weak' depending on their relation to law. In other words, when there is no strong link between the two, there is unlikely to be a right, at least in the strictest sense (Hohfeld 1978).

The activist narratives in my ethnographies deploy *haq* to denote 'valid claims' in so far as they claim *haq* over clearly identified sets of legal obligations and a stipulated addressee, that is, the state. Yet, often, demanding *haq* is also to claim recognition for an altogether new or a different set of rights or for an expanded set of rights. For instance, the political demands of the right to food movement and of the MKSS for the right to public information were raised as qualified versions of 'manifesto' demands which were subsequently successfully converted into 'valid claims' with the passage of federal laws on the same; these were qualified manifesto rights in the first instance, because unlike Feinberg's (1970) definition of manifesto rights, these were directed towards a specified addressee, that is, the state and were therefore not unspecified. While it follows that deployments of *haq* certainly coincide with legal rights, albeit with certain qualifications, what does this legal coincidence lead us to infer about the nature of the justification underpinning *haq* here? In other words, does *haq* only ever hold in the presence of legal rights? Or to put it another way, does *haq* depend on declared legal rights to sustain its meaning and authority? At first reading, the above narratives appear to uphold a correlative link between rights and legal constitutionalism, in the sense that *haq* or rights are premised upon, depend on and are justified by legal constitutional citizenship. However, if we were to examine how *haq* mediates citizenship in these narratives more carefully, we would find that *haq* does not quite posit a symmetric and correlative relation between itself and the positivist legal order of the state. In fact, upon close inspection, one will note a peculiar conceptual insight: whether these narratives rest their justificatory premise of rights on law, the state or on the constitutional rights and obligations of citizens, they, in the final instance, retain with the people the right to change both the law and government and the constitution if these fail to uphold the rights of citizens. For instance, in advocating constant vigilance over the state on citizen rights, both Prem Bairwa and the MKSS activists align *haq* with legal constitutionalism but also withhold its subsuming into the latter. In other words, although the justificatory premise of rights in the two narratives draws on law and the constitution and on legal citizenship, in both cases, there is a clear enunciation that even though law and the constitution are required for these rights, *haq* has an independent justificatory premise separate from the formal legal regime of rights and lies in what Brett (2003: 98) has termed a 'zone of non-coincidence between individuals and the positive legal order of the state.' *Haq*, therefore, refers to and is based on an ethical, normative, moral and empirical idea, which exists independent of the law and has a moral authority of its own.[27]

Counter-Development, Counter-Conduct and Human Rights

It is worth noting that the *haq* narratives that I have been documenting thus far are articulated in the context of development. As I pointed out in Chapter 2, development is an important site for rights talk in 'most of the world'. Development, however, is not only simply a 'top down' state owned and led discourse but is one that has come to be an all embracing, shared discourse that all sections of society are expected to share. In effect, development operates as a form of governmentalised power, producing subjects for development, setting off forms of political subjectivation and also authoring its own critiques. As a form of governmentality, development institutes a specific mode of critique and even resistance to development, which it channels through a form of 'perpetual questioning' of development. This 'perpetual questioning' of development, in line with Foucault's idea of counter-conduct, sets off what I shall call 'counter-development', which in producing and engaging with critiques of development, reproduces the object of its critique, that is, development. Counter-development, marks not a sharp break with development but rather configures development as a site of continual contestations over how to improve, expand and seek, among other values, those of rights and justice in and through development. This counter-development emerges through modes of political subjectivation that development and its accompanying ideas, in particular, human rights, put in place. These in turn engender new fields of possibilities—making it possible both to imagine different forms of sociality and challenge existing ways of doing development, while also making it impossible to imagine a time and a politics outside of development.

Counter-development enables us to focus on the productive power of development and the forms of political subjectivation it engenders. However, and this is very important, counter-development, like other modes of counter-conduct, is gendered and not explicitly oriented towards emancipatory efforts (Roy 2017) but may, in fact, stall on the question of gender equality. While I will examine the unfolding of counter-development or counter-conduct in development along gendered lines in Chapter 5, for now I want to focus on explaining the idea of counter development in some more detail.

The term counter-development is a non-technical application of Foucault's concept of 'counter-conduct' to development contexts. In his Collège de

France lectures on 'Sovereignty, Territory and Population', Michel Foucault introduces a new 'resistant concept' (Golder 2015: 54), which he calls 'counter-conduct'. Describing it as a 'specific web of resistance to forms of power that do not exercise sovereignty and do not exploit, but "conduct"' (Foucault, 2004: 200), Foucault offers possibilities of 'wanting to be "conducted differently" and "towards other objectives"' (Foucault 2004: 194) not exhausted by either 'dissidence' or 'misconduct'. Arnold Davidson (2011) writes that 'counter-conduct' is the 'conceptual hinge' that brings 'together the ethical and the political axes' in Foucault's work (Davidson 2011: 26), where the ethical or the 'exercise of the self on the self' (Foucault 2004: 205) aligns with the biopolitical or the conduct of power through the social body, that is, biopower. Through conceptualising 'counter-conduct', Foucault draws attention to the ways in which forms of 'revolt of conduct' or resistance deploy existing modalities and 'certain themes' of power against 'structures of power' (Foucault 2004: 207).

In recent years, governmentality[28] scholars have turned their analytical scrutiny to the concept of counter-conduct in Foucault's late work. Partly led by an increasing dissatisfaction with the politics deficit in governmentality accounts they aim to theorise the relationship between power and resistance and forms of resistance under governmentalised power. Accordingly, these scholars turn to counter-conduct in order to ask: how to conceptualise agency and resistance to power where resistance does not lie outside of power but is both constitutive and constituting of it? This philosophical question is, of course, hardly new; feminist theorists have long asked how subjects produced within relations of power rise to challenge those very relations through which they are constituted? (Weeks 2011; Butler 1997). For some human rights scholars the relationship between governmentalised forms of power and human rights is of increasing importance. But, is it really the case, and as some governmentality accounts suggest, that human rights are but another governmentalised technique of freedom? And if it is indeed so, then, how do we account for the politics of resistance or indeed for the production of 'insurgent imaginaries' under governmentalised power? Or as Selzmecki puts it, 'if freedom is indeed the vehicle of power, then how could demands for freedom enshrined in rights declarations manifest a challenge to power?' (2014: 1077). One can identify at least two different strands of thinking that offer a response to this philosophical puzzle, and interestingly, both turn to Foucault for their explanation: the first set of responses deploy Foucault's idea of counter-conduct in order to produce complex accounts of politics and resistance under governmentalised power (Odysseos 2016); and, the second considers the democratic potential of human rights by engaging Foucault's idea of subjectivation (Rancière 2004; Butler 2015). Ben Golder (2015) develops an account of Foucault's late politics of rights, which he calls a 'critical counter-conduct of rights'. The prefix 'critical' in 'counter-conduct', flags two things: Foucault's distance from a liberal politics of rights, and his philosophical understanding of critique, where 'meaning and operation of forms of governing are not set in stone but rather available for contestation, appropriation, and reversal...' (2015: 154). Consequently, to think in terms of a 'critical counter-conduct of rights', then, is to think of the ways in which rights can be put to 'different, and contrary, uses' (Golder 2015: 159) but also, to view rights as establishing a particular relation to oneself and with others, and as being 'simultaneously forms of regulation and resistance' (Golder 2015: 57).

Somewhat relatedly, a second set of responses draw attention to the democratic potential of human rights for enacting claims/freedoms that are not yet in place—in particular, to the potential of human rights to produce forms of political subjectivation that could reconfigure and disrupt existing power relations. As I argued in Chapter 2, it is this possibility of political subjectivation that underpins Jacques Rancière's (2004) critique of Giorgio Agamben and Hannah Arendt. Rancière's reformulation of the foundational paradox of the rights of man and citizen helps draw attention to moments in which the powerless and the oppressed rise up to demand and claim rights. And, as I also noted earlier in the book, Judith Butler (2015: 168–9) highlights situations, where 'people engage in acts of self-making or self-constitution' by assembling together and appearing and acting alongside in public concert with others, that produce possibilities for political subjectivation. For both Rancière and Butler, it is the enactment of rights in concert with others in a public space that posits what is not yet in place. However, while philosophers such as both Rancière and Butler use global human rights as their standard background condition for theorising moments of political subjectivation, I argue that it is, in fact, developmentalism that provides the context and articulation for human rights in 'most of the world', and thereby, for political subjectivation.

Counter-Development and the 'Perpetual Questioning' of Development

Broadly, the *jan sunwai*s that I described earlier can be described as a form of counter-development. Let me, however, give another example of what I mean by counter-development from my more recent rounds of fieldwork. Between early December 2015 and March 2016, the right to food movement organised a public audit of the existing development and social security provisions in Rajasthan. The movement demanded the adoption of a public accountability law,[29] aimed at instituting efficiency and official accountability and at curtailing the endemic corruption in the delivery of welfare and development. The public audit itself was conducted through a 100 day long *jawabdehi yatra* (answerability–accountability caravan) across all 33 districts in the state and was spearheaded by the MKSS.

The immediate political context for the *jawabdehi yatra* though, was the assault on the new legal welfare rights including the NREGA and the NFSA by the combined efforts of the new BJP (Bharatiya Janata Party) governments at the federal level (Ghosh 2015), and at the state level, in Rajasthan. Under the *mantra* of 'good governance', the new BJP state administration which came to power in 2013 in Rajasthan had immediately set about recalibrating existing lists of all those entitled to welfare provisioning, including under the NFSA, 2013, on the basis that it operated on inflated statistical figures and was marred by corruption. It tore up the lists of all those identified as beneficiaries eligible for entitlements under the NFSA, 2013, drawn up by the previous Congress administration[30] and put in place a new enumerating exercise, which would be 'transparent' and free from the corrupt and false practices of the previous government, and one that would weed out the non-entitled populations. This new identification survey took about eight months to complete and severely disrupted existing welfare programmes and resulted in the removal of 10.2 million people from existing welfare lists (A. Khan 2018). In light of the severe ongoing drought affecting 19 out of the 33 districts of Rajasthan,[31] this recalibrating exercise resulted in very serious consequences, not least for those already extremely vulnerable and highly dependent on state welfare for survival. Controversially, however, not only were great numbers of poor and vulnerable people excluded from welfare entitlements but also now in order to access the PDS and welfare schemes, a biometric based identity card known as Aadhaar was made mandatory.[32] Proclaiming the end of paper ration cards, the Rajasthan government's website announced that all transactions through the Targeted Public Distribution System (TPDS) were now electronically handled via the computerised machines (PoS or point-of-sale machines) installed in all 26,000 PDS shops in the state. Moreover, people in the state were now required to present their biometric ID cards at the ration shops and only upon their biometric data, mostly a thumb impression, registering a match, would their PDS allowance be released.

The *jawabdehi yatra* spent three days in each of the 100 blocks of the state documenting complaints about the corruption and inefficiencies plaguing the various development policies and welfare schemes operational in mostly rural areas. Its overwhelming focus was to set development right; and it focused on the importance of doing development differently and in accordance with the stipulations laid down in law. The majority of the complaints documented by the *yatra* concerned difficulties in accessing the PDS through these newly mandatory biometric cards. The PoS machines require uninterrupted links to the internet; not all villages in Rajasthan are wired, and even when there is an internet connection, its reception is very poor, especially in remote villages, where shop owners transported the machine to higher grounds or a hilltop in the hope of connecting to the internet! And even when there was a working internet connection, often the thumb impressions of people were faint and did not register a match—as was often the case with the elderly and daily wage labourers who are also among the most poor and precariously positioned. Additionally, complaints were also registered concerning the poor condition of state schools and the lack of government teachers, the disruption to pensions and access to other social welfare schemes. Overall the *yatra* recorded 7914 grievances, of which it registered 2551 on the state government's public grievance portal known as the Rajasthan Sampark Portal.[33]

The scrutiny and questioning of the developmental activities instituted by the *jawabdehi yatra* was not geared towards dispensing with developmental welfare but rather to ensure that they were carried out in the right manner and in keeping with laws guaranteeing citizen rights and entitlements. Nowhere was development as an idea or an instrument of state policy under question. Instead, it was the actions of BJP governments, at the federal and state level, to weaken existing legal guarantees of citizens' entitlements that was the object of scrutiny and critique. Therefore, what was at stake here was not the object of development[34] but the proper and right manner of doing development which was seen to be in jeopardy.[35]

As such, the *jawabdehi yatra* is not an exceptional response to neoliberal policy making and its rollback of hard-won citizen guarantees won through grassroots struggles and mobilisations. It is rather a part of the broader context and history of the 'push and pull' of rights in the long running discourse on developmentalism in postcolonial India, which took a decisive 'rights-based' turn coinciding just at the point of the liberalisation of the Indian economy in the early 1990s. Now rights-based development in India imbricates both state and non-state institutions. It interpellates citizen rights and entitlements as sites of 'judicialized activism' (Bornstein and Sharma 2016), mobilisation, juridical biopolitics,[36] welfare policy making and counter-conduct. The 'perpetual questioning' of development has resulted in blurring the distinction between activist concerns and activities on development and those of state actors.[37] In India, various state governments now routinely adopt activist mobilisational modes in order to generate popular support for development, and both state and non-state actors share discursive codes of rights-based development, transparency, corruption and empowerment.

On 12 February 2019, news wires began reporting that the recently elected Congress government in Rajasthan had published a draft copy of the Rajasthan Social Accountability Bill, 2018, and made it available for public consultation (*The Hindu* 2019a, 2019b). The draft bill, 2018, is undoubtedly an institutional and a political response to the long-standing demand by citizens groups in Rajasthan even if a commitment to citizen's social accountability legislation was also a part of the 2018 assembly election manifesto of the Congress Party. The chief demand of the *jawabdehi yatra* in 2016 was for a public accountability law that would hold state officials to account for the provision of welfare entitlements, and the bill certainly fulfills this. Among the notable features of the draft bill are 'time bound' delivery of welfare, penalties for state officials who fail to deliver goods and services within the prescribed time period and for a *jan sunwai* or public hearing of these grievances within 14 days of their complaint (Government of Rajasthan 2019).[38] Although, it remains to be seen as to what the final accountability provisions of the bill would be and what the bill will actually do once passed, but if the social accountability legislation is ratified by Rajasthan's legislative assembly, then it would be the first such law in India guaranteeing a time bound provision of citizen entitlements.

Before ending this section on counter-development, I want to provide a note of caution against viewing counter-development in terms of a 'reversal' of power or indeed as only directed 'against' and as such countering hierarchy and power. Counter-development is double-edged: it can not only be invested in making development more expansive and responsive and rights cognisant, but it can also be directed explicitly away from realising rights to gender equality. I shall come back to this point in Chapter 5 in some more detail but for now, I want to turn to the gendered forms of political subjectivation that human rights and developmentalism give rise to.

Developmentalism, Political Subjectivation and the Remaking of the Gendered Self

The counter-development I have been describing is but one form through which we can see the governmentalised power of rights and also of development. Another site to study their productive power is to focus on the forms and processes of subjectivation released by human rights and development, and in particular, on how subjects refashion their selves under developmentalism.

In recent years, scholars have turned their attention to processes of subjectification under development as a form of governmentality[39] to argue that development is not merely a technical project engaged in provisioning services and infrastructure but is also invested in the improvement and welfare of populations (Li 2007) through producing particular subjects and subjectivities for development (Madhok 2013). As a form of governmental power, developmentalism operates through conducting 'conduct' and educating desires of persons. These techniques comprising both discipline and ethical self-fashioning include overt directives, laws, incentives and policies but also work through 'responsibilisation' and ethical practices of the self, which in turn are also heavily surveilled. Developmentalism, as I pointed out earlier in Chapter 1, comprises not only institutions, practices and discourses but also a particular ethical mode of relating to the self. Ethical and experiential encounters with developmentalism constitute critical sites for tracking the normative and political life trajectories of developmentalism and of the ethical and political project it unleashes. Such a tracking can lead to an attentiveness to the forms of subjectivities released by development as it authorises itself in these sites, to the new modes of subjection it generates, and to the forms of political cultures it gives rise to. Moreover, we can examine how developmentalism attaches itself to differently gendered and racialised subjects, produces particular subjectivities but also makes the performance of these particular subjectivities a condition of representation within development (Madhok 2013).

The narratives and the justificatory premises of *haq* articulated by the primary development workers known as the *sathins* within a state sponsored development project for women set up in the mid 1980s by the state government of Rajasthan provide us with insights into the processes through which rights subjects come into being and the forms of political subjectivation unleashed by development, but also into new forms of coercion, policing and regulation that accompany these processes. The *sathins'* moral engagements with individual rights and developmentalism evocatively highlight *haq*'s legal 'non-coincidence' as well as its moral authority. Significantly, their invocations of *haq* also reveal the gendered nature of social and caste hierarchy and intersecting power relations that *haq* is embedded in and upholds, but also its intellectual capaciousness and elasticity when put to very different critical political work by very poor and dispossessed Dalit and Adivasi women.

The *sathin*s are predominantly Dalit, low caste, and vastly politically literate even though most have no formal literacy skills. They enjoy considerable visibility within gender and development bureaucracy and feminist circles in India. They rose into unexpected prominence in the early 1990s and began attracting unusually high levels of attention from the media and other civil society groups. I use 'unexpected' here to underscore how rare it is for rural women in India to gain any visibility, and, given the very low interest in theorising rural women in the Global South in both feminist scholarship and activism in South Asia, and around the globe where rural women's everyday lives mostly only get a glance in as 'case studies' or target groups' of various development interventions. The *sathin*s come into being in the first instance within a state sponsored development programme launched by the state Government of Rajasthan in 1984. The Women's Development Programme, Rajasthan (WDP) set up entirely new administrative structures and assembled different civil society and feminist groups to assist with the responsibility of training and developing rural women. It put together a training programme with metropolitan feminist positioned as 'trainers' and the rural women selected as *sathin*s, as the 'trainees'. The involvement of the civil society and feminist groups resulted in suturing different ideational scripts for the programme, which invariably pulled the *sathin*s and the programme in different directions and which in the end, all too easily unravelled at the seams at various times of crises. Within the WDP, despite efforts to the contrary, the inclusion of feminist actors as 'trainers' reproduced power hierarchies between the trainers and their trainees and left little room for critical practices of reflexivity on the role and position of feminist interlocutors of state developmentalism and especially, on the ways in which technologies of state developmentalism can render precarious subjects even more vulnerable and exposed to risk and injury (Madhok 2010; Madhok and Rai 2012).

The training design of the *sathin*s was technical but also normative. The *sathin* was to be a development worker with a difference; she had to embody the ideals of development that she was meant to carry out. Accordingly, the developmentalism beamed at the *sathin*s directed its energies at changing subjectivities and creating new values and patterns of behaviour, emphasising individual rights, self-empowerment, self-improvement and the performance of individual agency (Madhok 2013). Becoming a *sathin* required aligning with and embodying this normative impulse of developmentalism. In effect, this required a certain reorienting and re-crafting of the self in line with the expectations of personal transformation, in matters not only ethical and moral but also of comportment, speech and sartorial. These exercises in the refashioning of subjectivities and the constituting of oneself as a development 'subject'—the self-conscious operations or 'technologies of the self' (Foucault 1994) that the *sathins* perform upon themselves in order to wrought a desirable subjectivity—helps focus attention on the 'technologies of power' associated with developmentalism as a form of governmentality (Li 2007), aimed at 'shaping', 'guiding', and 'modifying' subjectivities (Burchill 1996: 19).

I first met the *sathins* in 1999, nearly 15 years into the inception of the programme, and ever since then have been intermittently following their entanglements with developmentalism. The majority of them have now retired or no longer work for the state. I was a graduate student out on my first ever fieldwork trip when I was introduced to them, while they were already very well known in Indian feminist circles and in state development bureaucracy; several *sathins* had even attended the 1995 UN women's conference at Beijing. At that time, many feminist activists regarded them as iconic feminist subjects and uniquely subversive and transgressive agents of transformation; while the state, who was also their employer, considered them as spectacularly unsuccessful and disobedient employees.[40] As I began documenting and organising the narratives of the *sathins* accounting for their 16 years of work in the WDP, the most unmistakable, exciting, intriguing and dynamic stories they entrusted me with were invariably those that recounted their struggles over rights. These stories described their first encounters with individual rights, of their strange alienness but also the difficulties and conflicts they encountered in putting rights to work. They belaboured over why a public commitment to rights became an important part of their identity as *sathins* and why this identification required them to wrest *haq* away from statist interpretations of rights; and why it mattered that they justified *haq* on a premise that they could morally and politically defend. Their stories of rights struggles are difficult stories to narrate but also to hear; these are stories of disappointment, despair and frustration, of heart-breaking betrayals, disenchantment and catastrophic violence. But at the same time, these are also inspirational stories of collective struggles and solidarities.

Two events catapulted the *sathin*s to the forefront of feminist, activist and bureaucratic imaginations: the first brought them recognition within feminist circles and their employers, the state of Rajasthan. The second propelled them into making an indelible mark on national consciousness. In 1990, 40 *sathin*s belonging to Kekri *panchayat* in rural Rajasthan travelled nearly 1,400 miles to participate in the National Women's Conference in Calicut, Kerala. At the Calicut conference, however, they represented themselves not as development workers, but congregated under a banner which read 'Mahila Samooh Kekri' (Women's Group of Kekri). Upon their return from Calicut, they were sacked from the *sathin* programme on the pretext that they were 'government workers' and could not attend events as an independent women's group. The irony, of course, was that the *sathin*s had not only been explicitly denied the status of 'state worker or employee' by the state as they only received an 'honorarium' and not an employee's wage, but also that they were embodying and enacting the 'empowerment' that the state and its feminist partners had 'trained' them to adopt. But in doing so, the *sathin*s had clearly exceeded the state mandated remit of what women's empowerment means and looks like.

Within two years of the *sathin*s registering their presence at Kekri, one event above all brought the *sathin*s into direct confrontation with the state and installed them into national imagination. The gangrape of *sathin* Bhanwari Devi took place on 22 September 1992. The sexual assault of Bhanwari Devi, a Dalit *sathin*, attracted the attention of national media as well as of metropolitan women's organisations based outside of Rajasthan. However, the sexual assault itself constituted only the first in a long list of humiliations heaped on Bhanwari Devi, most of them institutional in nature. The local police station refused to file a FIR (first information report) of the incident and when they did so after coming under considerable pressure from the higher ups in the development programme, Bhanwari Devi was denied a medical examination for nearly 52 hours after the assault. Throughout the ordeal, Bhanwari Devi was humiliated by the police and the medical professionals. She was locked up in a cell and her clothes were taken away from her.[41] A month later on 22 October 1992, a women's rally was organised with thousands of women activists from other states joining rural women who came out of their villages to march through the streets of the state capital, Jaipur, in protest against the state for its spectacular failure to uphold justice. The legal travesty attached to Bhanwari Devi's case led a local NGO called Vishakha to file a PIL case in the Supreme Court of India, demanding safety for women in the workplace. In response, the court, invoking the UN Convention on the Elimination of All Forms of Discrimination against Women, expanded the meaning of 'fundamental rights' and held that gender equality included protection from sexual harassment at work and the right to work with dignity. In passing a landmark judgment in the Vishakha case, the court laid down guidelines to be followed by establishments dealing with complaints about sexual harassment with the proviso that these guidelines were to be in place until legislation was passed to deal with the issue.[42] The court's judgment was taken up for action by The National Commission for Women who took the lead in drafting a bill called Sexual Harassment of Women at the Workplace (Prevention and Redressal) Bill (2006).[43]

As things stand today, justice continues to elude Bhanwari Devi. Her legal fight continues in the Supreme Court of India, more than a quarter of a century from her sexual assault. In the length of time it has taken for the wheels of justice to turn, one of her rapists has escaped indictment through death. Bhanwari Devi continues to wait for justice in penury. She has received a number of awards but no meaningful financial support. As Kavita Srivastava, a prominent civil liberties activist, points out, 'Bhanwari's case was a pioneering one for the anti-rape movement. It brought about a change even in the system of accountability of the police. While many women have gained from Bhanwari Devi's struggle, however, justice has continued to elude Bhanwari Devi.'[44]

A Feminist Historical Ontology of Rights as Truth

A feminist historical ontology is invested in tracking the 'making up' of gendered subjects in the vernacular. The vernacular in vernacular rights cultures flags the specific languages of claiming rights but also that this language of rights is gendered, generative and makes up people. The justificatory premise of *haq* as citizenship that I was documenting in the earlier parts of the chapter was not only claiming *haq* as a citizenship right but also claiming a particular relation to the self as a citizen. Citizenship has historically been a masculinist, racist, colonialist project but it has also been central to the anticolonialist movement. The postcolonial Indian state gave itself a constitution in 1950 where it guaranteed fundamental rights for all citizens. However, it would take another 35 years after the adoption of the Indian constitution before the news of these constitutional guarantees would reach rural heartlands of Rajasthan and gain entry into the moral and political imaginary of Dalit and Adivasi women living in its impoverished tiny hamlets and villages.

The political imaginary of individual rights began making inroads into rural hamlets through the women's development programme. Nearly all the *sathin*s identified their participation in the WDP as their first point of contact with the idea of individual rights. The feminist trainers in the WDP held training workshops on the legal constitutional basis and protections afforded to rights, which stressed that the state or *sarkar* was duty bound to uphold these rights and that rights belonged to all citizens. The language of constitutionally guaranteed rights presented a novelty. The *sathin*s had never heard about women's rights or that these were owned by and belonged to Dalit and Adivasi women before. And, there was no evidence or example of their presence or working that could help them visualise or describe the concept. The novelty of this idea of rights, however, did not reach them via translation. There was no need for literal or conceptual neologisms in order to have a conversation about individual and citizenship rights. The *sathin*s deployed the existing and familiar Arabic and Urdu term *haq* to speak of their rights. The complexity of their deployments of rights lay not in that they needed to translate rights from a 'foreign' language but that the language of entitlement and of rights that they knew was attached to privileged upper caste subjects, was hierarchial and exclusionary and, if and when deployed by Dalit and Adivasi women, resulted in severe and violent reprisals and retribution. As a moral term, *haq* was put to use to maintain social hierarchies in everyday transactions. For instance, upper caste men and women exerted their *haq* to claim entitled and exclusive of public utilities such as water handpumps and water wells. And, when used in private spaces, *haq* was the preserve of male household members, and used mostly to demand rightful shares in familial property and landholdings. Therefore, what confronted the *sathin*s was not only a problem of the chasm between formal and substantive rights but of a language of rights that was firmly attached to gender and caste privilege, and which worked to protect and uphold these. Their narratives of their early days in the WDP are replete with the moral and cognitive dissonance together with a real sense of fear, conflict and trepidation that rights talk sets off. How to claim this language of rights that had never belonged to them, and of which they had no experience? Many admitted never even using the word *haq* before. Also, how to embody this rights bearing self in interactions with others together with an expectation that those others would also recognise them as rights bearing persons? Their feminist training had made them aware of both the formal existence of constitutional rights but also of the feminist demands and interpretations of rights, which encouraged them to relate to their body outside of patriarchal claims and outside of discourses of shame, disgust and impurity and to critically rethink popular norms governing women's modesty, behaviour, comportment and 'good conduct'. These are powerful rights lessons and in keeping with the democratic and liberatory potential of rights, the deployment of *haq* in this new mode and imaginary set off complex processes of political subjectivation. The heady mix of feminist visions of empowerment in the WDP training manuals together with the forms of discipline directed by the state at the *sathin*s led them to undertake self-fashioning exercises where in order to perform their duties as the public face of women's rights also meant becoming that subject of rights. Articulating *haq* in public view and also becoming the subject warranted by *haq* meant a complex undertaking that was somewhat easier to justify when the injustice or breach of rights was either in full public view or unambiguously backed by full legal sanction of the law. For instance, rights for women in marital and natal property, often referred to as *dakin haq*, could be defended by invoking equal rights to property, or the removal of girls from schools could be opposed on the basis of legal equality of girls and boys, or the denial of welfare entitlements to widows could be backed by existing state laws on the same. It is striking of course, that 'dakin' in hindi translates as a 'witch'. And, therefore, it's quite telling how neatly the phrase *dakin haq* captures both the enormity of the social pressure but also the vilification that ensues when rural women decide to ask for rights in the familial property. But it was the painstaking, careful building of a public and private profile of an intersectional subject of rights who embodied *haq* and invoked it freely and without fear and favour, which was the hardest part. How does one justify the existence and the experience of being a Dalit, Muslim and Adivasi woman with full legal rights when they could not conjure up any real life examples of such a woman living among their midst? How does a Dalit *sathin* whose lived experience is structured and informed by oppressive, threatening and violent caste relations, and who lives in fear of the Rajputs in the village, referring to them by the honorific title of *annadata* (provider of food), and who till recently, was not allowed to walk with shoes near the *hatai*[45] (designated meeting place in the village where upper caste men conduct their business) concretely and meaningfully exercise her *haq*, a word and an idea that was long accepted as attached and belonging to the powerful and privileged?

For the *sathin*s, it was the WDP with its strands of multiple rights discourses that provided the intellectual and moral justification of *haq*, and in the absence of any other competing discourse on rights, the *sathin*s came to regard the state as the source of all rights and thereby, rely on a state-centric discourse of rights. As I have detailed elsewhere, the association with the state was not without risks, even if in the short run, it gave the *sathin*s some semblance of security in the midst of the social hostility that engulfed them. The sexual assault of Bhanwari Devi proved the associational security from the state to be illusory and fragile and even counterproductive. The flagrant failings of the state in the wake of the sexual assault, perhaps more than any other, led to a radical revision in their generally positive assessment of the state in the face of serious failings of the state. The moral regression of the state and in particular, its collusion with the upper castes and classes, came into a sharp relief after the gang rape of Bhanwari Devi and the failure of the state to stand up for the rights of Dalit women. In her interviews with me (Madhok 2013), Bhanwari Devi characterised the Indian state as classist, casteist and masculinist, and radically estranged from any real commitment to social justice. The immediate aftermath of the sexual assault of Bhanwari Devi led the *sathin*s into a crisis of reflection over the nature of their relationship with the state, and subsequently, into open conflict with it over the question of rights, which they had thus far identified with the state.

The sexual assault of Bhanwari Devi tore open the wounds and injuries the *sathin*s had experienced and accumulated in becoming and working as *sathin*s in the WDP. Their relationship with and public commitment to rights had evolved through immense personal risk, cost, injury, courage and even social ostracism and the crucial question and moral conundrum staring at them was whether they could continue justifying their rights politics and work in a language that was intimately connected to the state, which they associated with moral corruption and intrinsically prejudicial to women's rights? It soon became clear to them that the moral collapse of the state over its failure to protect Dalit women's rights meant that they needed to wrest *haq* away from its problematic association with the state. Given the deep betrayal of women's rights, particularly the rights of Dalit women, the *sathin*s were left with little choice but to weave their own independent theoretical and practical defence of the idea of rights independent of constitutional citizenship supported by the state and to consequently espouse a different normative basis for defending rights.

The new and different justificatory premise of *haq* was no longer derived from the state but was now grounded in the idea of Truth. It is not surprising that *sathin*s would turn to Truth as the justificatory premise for rights. In their narratives, Truth had received a fatal blow when the state institutions and the courts chose to believe Bhanwari Devi's rapists and not her testimony; and, in upholding Bhanwari Devi's rapists' defence, the courts and the investigative agencies simply maintained and protected the widely held popular view that Dalit women are not capable of the truth and are not to be believed. Mobilising Truth as a justificatory premise of *haq* enables an existential and structural critique of the life of marginalised gendered subjects while also shoring up an ideal of justice in social and political life. In the narratives of the *sathin*s, Truth is an expansive and non-cognitive term.[46] It is informed by ideas of rightness and justice and certain 'ideal' and uncorrupted aspects of politics and political life. This is not a human rights politics of minimalism or despair but one that is strongly committed to a politics of justice. Here, Truth occurs both as an ideal order of justice in the form of a pack of principles and as an order of facts in the form of concrete practices. But Truth also invokes moral rectitude and morally correct and fearless political agency. Let me illustrate this through the following narrative:

> We *sathin*s exist so that we can assist the depressed and deprived women and become their voice ... we speak the Truth and walk the path of Truth ... The *sarpanch and patwari* [official responsible for lands records] are partners in corruption; why should they speak the Truth? They benefit by not walking the path of Truth. Whereas the *sathin* always speaks the Truth and is not party to their corrupt schemes.[47]

The narratives of the *sathin*s are replete with *haq* as embodying ideals of Truth in political life. They invoke images of this Truth, or of *haq*, in public life by linking it to their own moral example and by contrasting their own work and moral rectitude with the actually existing corrupt practices of the *sarpanche*s and the various officials of drought relief programmes and other state development schemes. For instance, during the famine that ravaged Rajasthan from 1985 to 1988, the *sathin*s joined women's groups in raising awareness and demanding justice against the widespread forced sterilisation of women by state department officials as a precondition for receiving state assistance and employment under the famine relief works set up by the government of Rajasthan. They were also at the forefront of demanding equal wages for women and for equality in distribution of food grains to all affected in the 'food for work' programmes. However, before rushing to celebrate their various successful initiatives, we have to be extremely careful and ethical to foreground the inordinate gendered risk, injuries and social and institutional backlash that precarious gendered subjects experience while taking on the powerful. As the *sathin*s often said to me, it is one thing to make demands of the state and quite another to do so from the social community one lives amongst. And even though engaging both involves conflict, however, at least, in the case of the citizenship rights there is a possibility of some legal answerability and accountability. There are no such guarantees of answerability, they often stressed, that one can expect while exercising individual and bodily rights in interpersonal relationships. Paradoxically, however, even as citizenship and its associated rights provide the *sathin*s with a vocabulary to assert their constitutional rights but as Bhanwari Devi's case tragically highlighted, the assertion of these rights also makes them visible targets for injury and violence. Their association with the state is a complex and contradictory one; making them both the agents of the state and also its adversaries. This complex relationship of proximity as well as antagonism with the state was highlighted powerfully by *sathin* Batto Devi of Danganwada village when she spoke with me on how upholding the Truth means that *sathin*s are often seen as unelectable political representatives or indeed find it difficult to contest elections to local bodies.

> If *sathin*s were to be elected as *sarpanch* then we would not be able to oppose the many things we now oppose or fearlessly bring up the issues that we do. Also, we speak the Truth openly and on becoming a *sarpanch* our voices will get muted. For example, if there is a child marriage taking place somewhere in the *panchayat*, the *sarpanch* will not oppose it. If he did, then he will end up anatagonising important interests. The politics of *sarpanch* is such that neither can he stop a child marriage from taking place, nor can he stop a *nukta* [death feast] from taking place, or indeed, can he stop people from giving or demanding dowry. He gets wrapped up in all sorts of obligations and relationships. Moreover, if the *sarpanch* spoke the Truth then who would vote for him next time? The *sathin* on the other hand, will always speak the Truth and therefore they [the people] will do everything to stop her from contesting elections or speaking up.[48]

I have written elsewhere that very few *sathin*s contest local government or *panchayat* elections. And when they have done so, nearly all of them have lost. Although much can be learnt from the experience of the *sathin*s with political institutions and the democratic processes of seeking political office (Madhok 2013), however, my aim here has been to offer a feminist historical ontology of the politics of rights and developmentalism. Central to this reading has been the critical role of concepts in 'making up people' and in laying bare gendered processes but also tracking the rights encounter and the forms of political subjectivation that rights discourses set off in development contexts. In effect, the *sathin*s' encounter with rights sets off two separate processes of political subjectivation, each of which have a bearing on the conceptual content of *haq* but also for a more expansive content for human rights discourses. The participation of the *sathins* in the WDP sets off the first phase of their political subjectivation, whereby they engage in self-fashioning exercises in alignment with the developmentalist goals of the state and of the WDP programme. Their particular contexts of coercion and precarity together with the utter novelty and alienness of women's rights leads them to ground their justification of rights in state discourses and legal constitutionalism. However, when the state fails them at crucial moments, the *sathins* seize *haq* away from the state to weave a justificatory premise independent of the state. The justification of rights as Truth present us with an expansive view of human rights, one that is not led by either a politics of minimalism or that of despair. An attention to the complex forms of moral engagement of the *sathins* with *haq*, allows us to track several transformations in their rights thinking and to identify the justificatory premise that underpins their rights talk. Their different and transformed thinking on rights is consequently reflected in their dynamic and singular deployments of *haq*. This distinctive and innovative engagements on *haq* is forged through their particular immersion in state developmentalism and from their struggles to fashion a different justification for rights independent of the state.

Conclusion

Through focusing on the forms of counter-conduct and the forms of political subjectivation that are produced in the context of developmentalism, this chapter draws attention to the productive and generative power of human rights, rights and developmentalism. The justificatory premises of citizenship and Truth occur within every day and sustained engagements with developmentalism. These justificatory premises provide insights into how subaltern subjects deploy rights but also produce political cultures of rights. Crucially, the encounters with human rights and developmentalism are epistemic as well as experiential encounters and give rise to not only new modes of relating to the self and becoming a subject of rights but also generate different ways of justifying and supporting a commitment to rights.

Notes

1. If anything, food scarcity and food consumption within this scarcity have been a conspicuous part of India's version of postcolonial citizenship. In newly postcolonial India, for instance, citizens were exhorted to demonstrate their

responsibility and stake in the new imaginary of citizenship and development by refashioning their 'diets' in very specific ways that would ease the import burden of the newly industrialising state (Siegel 2016).

2. For the PIL as a form of 'juridical democracy', see Baxi (1985). The PIL has a chequered history. While it is indeed the case that the PIL reinvented itself in the post-emergency era primarily as a tool for addressing pressing public issues, however, in recent decades, it has shown strong economic conservatism and 'betrayed a lack of sensitivity towards the rights of the poor and disadvantaged sections of society' (Bhushan 2004: 1770). And where courts have handed down pro-poor judgments, they have not only mostly refrained from penalising the government (Shankar and Mehta 2008: 147) but also mainly tinkered with 'temporary solutions' (Shankar and Mehta 2008: 178), preferring to rely on 'weak remedies such as setting up committees and negotiation channels' (Shankar and Mehta 2008: 147). Some note that there is a paradox in the PIL which has meant that: 'it has strengthened the rule of law by delivering justice to the poor and guaranteeing various social rights, but its development has an aspect of undermining the rule of law through the informalization of judicial proceedings' (Sato 2017: 67). Relatedly, Anuj Bhuwania writes (2014: 321) that the growth of PIL has contributed to a 'delegitimization of legal procedure', which has made it easier for courts to uphold draconian laws and statutes (2014: 321).

3. These laws include The Right to Information (RTI) Act of 2005, The Mahatma Gandhi National Rural Employment Guarantee Act (NREGA) of 2005, The Scheduled Tribes and Other Traditional Forest Dwellers (Recognition of Forest Rights) Act, 2006, The Right to Education Act of 2009, The Right to Food Act or The National Food Security Act (NFSA) of 2013 and The Land Acquisition, Rehabilitation and Resettlement (LARR) Act of 2013.

4. There now exists a growing and sophisticated scholarship analysing the functioning, shortfalls as well as the impact of these newly introduced acts and policy measures. See, among others, Drèze (2004), Shah (2007), Khera (2008, 2011), Banerjee and Saha (2010), A. Sharma (2013), Drèze and Khera (2017) and Nilsen (2018b).

5. I am grateful to Diane Perrons and Shirin M. Rai for clarifying this point. Personal communication, February 2018.

6. Neoliberal economic reforms have disproportionately negatively impacted the already vulnerable and precarious condition of Adivasis and Dalits. See, for instance, Kannan (2018).

7. See in particular Drèze and Khera (2017) for the benefits of these social security legislations on rural women's empowerment.

8. See Drèze and Khera (2017) for an excellent review of the expansion of rights-based social security programs in India.

9. Census of India 2011. See in particular: https://www.censusindia.gov.in/2011-prov-results/data_files/india/Final_PPT_2011_chapter5.pdf (accessed 13 October 2020).

10. Among females of the Scheduled Castes, the literacy rate was 44.6 per cent in 2011 and among the Scheduled tribes, it was 37.3 per cent (World Bank 2016). Also see S. Sharma (2013).

11. See GoI (2019b).

12. See *Times of India* (2018).

13. Field interviews, Jhadla, Phagi Block, Jaipur district (2004).

14. Field interviews, Jhadla, Phagi Block, Jaipur district (2004).

15. The website of the Right to Food Campaign (http://www.righttofoodcampaign. in/) provides detailed information and resources on court orders, research reports, briefing notes, posters, pamphlets and campaign updates.

16. For a detailed discussion of the 'backlash' against the organisation of the *jan sunwai*s, see Neelabh Mishra's excellent account (2003).

17. For an insightful account of how governments respond to demands by citizen groups for 'transparency' and accountability, see Alasdair Roberts (2006).

18. A District Collector is the senior most officer in-charge of the administration of a district.

19. This point was made by Aruna Roy and then repeated at several occasions during the course of the *jan sunwai* by the MKSS representatives.

20. The BDO informed the gathering that following the Janawad *jan sunwai* in 2001, the government had instituted *jan sunwai*s at the seven villages in Janawad *panchayat* and although new incidents of corruption came to light, none were of the magnitude that were exposed at Janawad. Furthermore, legal cases had been lodged against all the accused officials and elected representatives so they were legally required to return the money they had stolen. In addition, the anti-corruption bureau had launched an investigation into the fraudulent muster rolls with a view to identify the correct beneficiaries of the famine relief programmes undertaken in the village. The BDO concluded by saying that at present all those indicted in the Janawad report had taken their case to the High Court at Udaipur, which had put a legal stay on their arrests, and that things could only proceed further once the legal stay was removed from the courts.

21. With the passage of the National Food Security Act in 2013, aspects of the PDS such as the NFSA became reoriented towards a near universal coverage, with a stipulated coverage of 75 per cent in rural areas and 50 per cent in urban areas. See Drèze et al (2018).

22. See Madhok and Rai (2012).

23. Interview with Manohari Devi, field worker, Marudhar Ganga Society, village Baodi, *tehsil* Gopalgarh, *panchayat samiti* Osian, district Jodhpur, caste Meghwanshi, interviewed in Baodi, 2005.

24. Interview with *sarpanch* Tej Singh and *sarpanch* Narayan, Jawaja and Kelwara, 29–20 January 2004.
25. Cecoedecon's influential position in Rajasthan's NGO sector was brought to my notice by Sunny Sebastian, Rajasthan correspondent for *The Hindu*, interviewed, February 2004, Jaipur.
    Prem Bairwa interviewed in March 2004, Kotkhawada, Phagi Panchayat, Jaipur.
26. For conflation in philosophy, see, for instance, the *Stanford Encyclopaedia of Philosophy*; and within policy documents, see in particular UNRISD or its various background papers on migration, gender equality.
27. See Brett (2003). On *haq*'s particular quality of legal 'non-coincidence' as well as its moral authority, see Madhok (2013).
28. As is well known, Foucault (2000: 341; see also Gordon, 1991: 2) defined governmentality as the 'conduct of conduct' and government as 'governing the conduct of the self and others', and scholars note that the crucial feature of governmentality is that it signifies 'the irreducible connection between 'practices of governing and the modes of thought underpinning those practices' (Golder 2015: 52).
29. The organisers produced their own prototype titled 'Rajasthan, Bhagedaari Jawabdehi aur Saajedhari Ankekshan Bill 2016'.
30. Rajasthan was one of the first states to implement the NFSA, 2013. However, its implementation was rushed and chaotic and relied on 'old lists' replete with errors whilst including new and previously excluded beneficiary populations. All of this resulted in the state exceeding its mandated quota of covering 69 per cent of the total population (Khera 2017). The new BJP government elected to power in 2013 was quick to seize on the statistical chaos and swiftly went about 'pruning' the list of 'undeserving beneficiaries'.
31. The severity of the drought led the Government of Rajasthan's Disaster Management and Relief Department to extend the operation of drought measures in 14,487 villages uptil July 2017. Accordingly, it sought and consequently, received additional funds under MNREGA from the Union government in the form of 50 days of additional employment for the drought affected villages (Government of Rajasthan 2016).
32. During 2015–16 when I was interviewing the activists of the right to food movement, the Aadhaar Bill was under consideration by a five member constitution bench of the Supreme Court. On 29 September 2018, the Supreme Court passed its judgment on the constitutional validity of Aadhaar. In a split judgment (4:1), the court upheld the constitutional validity of Aadhaar while declaring some aspects of the bill unconstitutional. In particular, the Supreme Court opined that Aadhaar could not be used by private entities even as a voluntary scheme. And, that, furthermore, it could not apply to children and that an Aadhaar card was not a prerequisite for enrolment to schools. The judgment also put in a stipulation for the elderly and the infirm, stating that

Aadhaar authentication was not required for pensions. Finally, the judgment encouraged the federal government to legislate a 'data protection act' that would act as a deterrent and a protection against identity fraud, theft and official misuse of biometric data belonging to the citizens. It, however, upheld the most vigorously contested aspect of the Aadhaar hearing, which was to do with the welfare exclusions that had resulted as a consequence of state governments making Aadhaar compulsory for receiving welfare including access to the PDS (Khera 2018). The judgment makes a clear distinction in relation to fundamental rights in the constitution (such as the right to education for all children till the age of 14) and those which are legal rights, such as the National Food Security Act (NFSA) 2013 and the Mahatma Gandhi National Rural Employment Guarantee Act (MNREGA), 2005. These welfare rights are not fundamental rights and therefore, the court did not seek to remove them from the purview of Aadhaar authentication. However, it did move to protect the fundamental 'right to education' by making Aadhaar inapplicable to children's services including school admissions. Both sides claimed vindication on the Aadhaar judgment: those who opposed it on the grounds for the clear legislative directive towards providing a data protection law and for declaring as unconstitutional the use of Aadhaar by private stakeholders. The government on the other hand, lauded the Court for upholding the constitutional validity of Aadhaar. On 2 January 2019, the government introduced amendments to the Aadhaar Bill (2016) to the Parliament. Barely two days after its introduction in the Lok Sabha (lower house of India's Parliament) on 4 January 2019, the bill was passed without as much as an amendment being introduced to the government bill or indeed even the briefest debate.

33. In an interview, Shyam Lal Purohit, the State Coordinator of the right to food movement at the people's organisation Aastha Sanghathan, told me that it was important to log the complaints directly on the state web portal as it was the designated website for citizens' complaints, and in light of the fact that it was personally monitored by the District Collectors and also by the Chief Minister, complaints logged here were required to be disposed of within a fortnight at the latest. See also http://jawabdehiyatra.in/.

34. As Nilsen (2016: 272) notes, many studies 'both of the micropolitics of everyday development encounters ... and of large-scale social movements ... have established that subaltern groups do not oppose or reject development in its entirety, but rather seek to negotiate and change the direction and meaning of development.'

35. See interview with Shankar Singh of the MKSS where he highlights the end to inefficient and corrupt practices of state officials as the main demands of the *yatra* (Kumar 2016).

36. Judicial biopolitics (Biehl 2013) has a specific legal and political trajectory in India. Its high point occurred in 2001 when the Supreme Court, working on

an expanded interpretation of 'the right to life' under Article 21 of the Indian constitution, issued orders for the provision of mid-day meals to all children in government schools.

37. Anthropologists Bornstein and Sharma (2016) note that in the current global neoliberal context, a 'technomoral' (2016: 76) language of law and policy, which fuses moral pronouncements with technical details for implementing policy, and shared by not only state and nonstate organisations but also by transnational organisations has 'emerged as the key terrain of struggle where non-state actors express their distinctive identities and moral projects and negotiate their political relations with the state through judicialized activism' (2016: 77).

38. See http://rajasthan.gov.in/wp-content/uploads/2019/02/SA-Bill-Draft.pdf.

39. For an account of the governmentalised power of development in the Indian context, see Sanyal (2013) and Madhok (2013).

40. As I have written elsewhere (Madhok 2013), what soon became apparent to me was their polarised and binary representations. Driving these polarised representations of the *sathins* were two things: an attachment to a particular conception of agency that valourised a transgressive subject who performed overt acts of subversion in the face of power without fear; and second, the fluent articulation of rights by the *sathins*. However, it was when the discourse of rights deployed by the *sathins* was directed against the state that the institutional backlash against them began.

41. Author's interviews with Bhanwari Devi between 1999 and 2005. These took place in Jaipur and Bhateri.

42. *Vishakha and others v. State of Rajasthan and Others*, AIR 1997, SC 3011; see the text of the decision at http://www.iiap.res.in/files/VisakaVsRajasthan_1997.pdf. In Mihir Desai's (2003) words, the Vishakha decision found that 'if the Indian Government makes ... commitments in international fora it shall be binding on the Government even within the nation and it will be treated as part of the national law unless there is a law within the country which is in direct conflict with such a law'.

43. As defined in the 1997 Supreme Court guidelines in the Vishakha decision, sexual harassment includes such unwelcome behaviour as physical contact, a demand or request for sexual favours, sexually colored remarks, showing pornography, or any other unwelcome physical, verbal or non-verbal conduct of a sexual nature, for example, leering, telling dirty jokes, making sexual remarks about a person's body, and so on. A revised version of the sexual harassment legislation is available on the National Commission for Women's website at http://ncw.nic.in/sexualharassmentatworkplacebill2005.pdf.

44. Kavita Srivastava, personal communication, July 2016, Jaipur.

45. Interview with Kiran Dubey, 18 March 1999, Ajmer.

46. In ordinary social science writing, truth is often regarded as a cognitive concept, which is invoked in order to establish 'falsifibaility or 'verifiability; of a claim. In the discourse of the *sathins*, however, it is an expansive term encompassing morality and justice.

47. Interview with *sathin* Kalyani, village Mokumpura, *panchayat samiti* Dudu, Jaipur, 1998.

48. Interview with *sathin* Batto Devi, Village Danganwada, Jamwa Ramgarh, Jaipur, January 1999.

5   Resisting Developmentalism and the Military

Haq as a Cosmological Idea and an Islamic Ideal

In May 2012, Napi Bai, the Adivasi *sarpanch* of Medi *panchayat* in Kotra Block of Udaipur, organised a *gram sabha*[1] to pass a 'no-confidence' motion against a development project intent on expanding the boundaries of a wildlife sanctuary. Kotra is the Adivasi block of Udaipur district and nearly 96 per cent of its population (GOI 2011b) belongs to India's Indigenous or Adivasi communities. It nests in the Southern Aravalli hills where the Wakal river flows through. The Adivasi block is also part of southern Rajasthan's 'hunger belt'. Kotra is where India's pre-eminent news magazine *Frontline* reported 47 hunger deaths in 2001 (Mishra 2001). Hunger continues to haunt Kotra while bureaucratic apathy and death by starvation continue to be a persistent presence.

For nearly four decades, the Adivasi peoples of Kotra have been resisting the steady bureaucratic inroads that Phulwari Ki Naal, the wildlife sanctuary which was declared as such in 1983, has been making into their life-worlds by gradually swallowing up their ancestral lands, forests, streams and villages and forcing them to live under the uncertainty and terror of being dispossessed from their lands. Today, the Phulwari Ki Naal wildlife sanctuary covers a total area of 511.41 square kilometres out of which 365.92 square kilometres is designated as 'Reserved Forest' and encompasses 134 villages in the area (Forest Department Rajasthan 2014: 3). The event, however, that precipitated the passage of the 'no-confidence' motion in the *gram sabha* on that fateful day was the proposed extension of the wildlife sanctuary into two villages in the *panchayat*. If the extension plans for the sanctuary were to go ahead, then in effect, this would mean the displacement and relocation of these two villages along with its people, cattle and livestock elsewhere. But where was this elsewhere? No one quite knew to where the villages would be relocated.

The word going around in the *panchayat* was that this elsewhere would be somewhere in Jaisalmer. Those who are familiar with the topography of Rajasthan would know that Jaisalmer is the desert district of Rajasthan and it could not be more in contrast with the lush hills and forests of Kotra. This dread of displacement is hardly an abstract one. While official figures admit that between 1951 and 1990, 21.5 million people in India have been displaced from their lands as a result of development projects, scholars however, have put the figures of displaced populations at three times higher, at 60 million (Fernandes 2007). Recent figures published by the Internal Displacement Monitoring Centre in 2016 note that between 1950 and 2015, 65 million people have been displaced in India as a result of development projects (IDMC 2016). As many as 40 per cent of all those displaced and dispossessed of their lands have been Indigenous people,[2] which means that given the total population of Adivasis in the country, 'nearly one in four have experienced some kind of displacement' (Sundar 2016: 10).

The history of forest dispossessions is hardly new and predates the postcolonial state in India and is more than a century old (Guha 1989). These dispossessions became systematised with the enactment of the Indian Forest Act in 1865 by the colonial state and its subsequent amendments in 1878 and 1927, which reserved a fifth of land area as 'government forest' primarily for increasing revenue and for 'marketable timber' (Rangarajan and Shahabuddin 2006: 368), resulting in the removal of forest communities from designated 'government forests'. In postcolonial Rajasthan, the dispossession and eviction of Indigenous peoples from their land is a fallout of the passage of the Rajasthan Forest Act of 1953 that converted tribal forest rights into 'concessions' and required Adivasi dwellers to show 'proof' in the form of documentary evidence in support of their land or dwelling rights over the forest land. In the absence of official land certificates, the land belonging to the Adivasis was suddenly transferred to the state forest department and they became known in official speak as 'tribal tillers' and thereby 'encroachers' upon forest lands. Over the years, the state government has sought to address the conditions of 'tribal tillers' by the ensuing notifications in 1978 and 1991 to regularise forest land possession, yet these governmental circulars were not publicised among the beneficiary populations and even less implemented. The year 2002 became a watershed year in the postcolonial history of state violence against forest communities with arbitrary, violent and coercive evictions of the Indigenous forest communities and other non-tribal forest dwellers from their homes and lands carried out at a scale 'unprecedented in recent history'.[3]

In October 2006, India's Parliament passed a legislation decreeing a bill of rights protecting the forest land of Indigenous people known as the Scheduled Tribes and other Traditional Forest Dwellers (Recognition of Forest Rights) Act. India is not a signatory to the ILO Convention 169 on the rights of the Indigenous peoples but it does provide special constitutional safeguards for Indigenous people or the administrative category of Scheduled Tribes (ST) through which they are recognised in constitutionalist legal and policy discourses. The legislation itself was a direct outcome of a nationwide displaced forest dwellers campaign and the passage of the legislation was seen as a way to address the 'historical injustices' suffered by India's forest communities.

The Forest Rights Act 2006 provides for individual rights and also collective community governance over forest land. Importantly, it mandates explicit approval of development projects by the *gram sabha* in Indigenous villages. Napi Bai exercised this particular safeguard when she called a joint *gram sabha* of all eight villages in her *panchayat* to debate the planned extension of Phulwari Ki Naal. However, organising a *gram sabha* of all the eight villages is no mean feat and in the ordinary run of things takes a great deal of organisation, time and planning, all three of which as Napi Bai narrated to me over several interviews, were in limited supply at the time. Here is how Napi Bai explained the roll-out of events on that particular day in May 2012. She was on her way to the *panchayat* office in her village when she was told that a written 'notice' had arrived addressed to her from the State Forest Department. Not being able to read herself, Napi Bai took the letter to the village school teacher so that he could read out the contents to her. The letter was an official notice announcing the population survey of two villages in her *panchayat*. These two villages shared a boundary with Phulwari Ki Naal. As is well known in Kotra, the conduct of an official survey marks the first step in the preparation of state plans to relocate and rehabilitate populations who inhabit the land and forests that the sanctuary wants to 'conserve'. The contents of the letter left Napi Bai in no doubt about the seriousness of what was being proposed by the state forest officials. She immediately set off for Kotra to confer with the NGO, Adivasi Vikas Manch, and from there on to the state capital Udaipur, to seek advice from a well-known lawyer based in the city who has been associated with Indigenous rights. The lawyer advised her to call a 'joint special meeting' of the *gram sabha* of all the eight villages of the *panchayat*[4] and to make sure to record all the proceedings in writing. In her interviews with me, Napi Bai describes the events leading to the 'no-confidence' motion in the following way:

An official notice arrived at the *gram panchayat* office at Medi in May 2012 announcing that a relocation survey would be carried out the day after tomorrow in Bheem Talai and Bao Veeran; the two villages were to be relocated to another site so that the development of Phulwari Ki Naal could be carried out. The notice said that the *gram sarpanch* was required to assist the Block Development Officer, the Forest Ranger and the veterinary department officials in conducting a population survey in the two villages—to ascertain as to how many people resided in the two villages, how many animals were reared, and the number and varieties of crops grown in the villages and in the forest. I cannot read Hindi or Bagri but there was a school master who was walking by and I asked him to read the contents of the letter out to me. I immediately realised the serious implications for the *panchayat* villagers; there was no time to be lost and I took a taxi from Medi to Kotra, which is 25 kilometres away and first went to the NGO office (Adivasi Vikas Manch) and informed them of the impending survey. The next day, I took the bus to Udaipur around 2 hours away and met with Advocate Nandwana*ji* and showed him the letter; on my return, I hired a private taxi and went to all the 8 villages of the *panchayat* and told them about the plans to relocate two villages and urged them to come to a *gram sabha* meeting at 9 am the next day.

By 2 pm the next day, nearly 500–600 people had congregated at the *panchayat bhawan* for the *gram sabha* meeting, and not much time after that, the officials arrived. The forest ranger pulled me aside to ask me: '*Sarpanch sahib* how have you called these people?' I replied: 'They are the people of the whole *panchayat*; they are the public; you have sent a letter announcing relocation of two villages but you know that under Fifth Schedule [of the constitution] and under the PESA *kanoon* (PESA: Panchayat Extension to Scheduled Areas Act 40 of 1996)[5] and also the Forest Rights *kanoon* (2006)[6] you need to consult with and seek the approval of the village *gram sabha* for any acquisition of Adivasi village lands? And now, everyone is here because they have a *haq* to hear your proposal and also decide on it. Let me ask you all first and foremost: what are the *sarkar's* plans for the rehabilitation of all these people?' They remained quiet and had no answer—they had come unprepared and did not have any documents or plans with them. At this point, I asked the assembled villagers to consider passing a 'no-confidence' motion against the official proposal for the relocation and they agreed. I turned to the *gram sachiv* (village *panchayat* secretary) and asked him to make a formal note that in our village *gram sabha*, we have decided to pass a 'no-confidence' motion against the relocation survey. All the gathered people signed the note and we made a photocopy of the document and sent it off to the Forest department Office at Kotra. There has not been any talk of relocation ever since.[7]

The proceedings of 'no-confidence' that the villagers of Medi *panchayat* launched against state development project under the leadership of Napi Bai was organised under the provisions of the Forest Rights Act and the PESA Act. It is worth noting that this 'no-confidence' measure undertaken by the Adivasi villagers is hardly a commonplace occurrence and one led by an Adivasi woman *sarpanch*, is even rarer. In the last few years, there have been a few celebrated cases of Adivasi villages taking on the might of powerful transnational corporations and stopping them in their tracks. On the whole, however, these have been few and far between not least because the costs of opposition are inordinately high in a context where the developmentalist state is transparently aligned with the commercial interests of transnational capital.

And, while it is certainly the case that the Forest Rights Act has invigorated and encouraged democratic energies, however, the rights of the Indigenous and forest communities over the forests and its produce is by no means a settled question. In addition to bureaucratic indifference, implementation lethargy and a distinct lack of political and administrative will to implement the provisions of the act, forest communities are also seen as 'encroachers' by the conservation lobby, who sees the forest communities as obstacles to their conservation efforts. Recently, the Indian Supreme Court ruled in the latter's favour potentially placing 1.5 million Indigenous families at risk of eviction from their homes and lands.[8] Not unsurprisingly, the Court's judgment met with a great deal of criticism especially from Indigenous groups, and even though the court has suspended its original judgement, the threat to India's Indigenous communities remains ever present.

Overall, in terms of its implementation, the authorities have preferred to deal with individual claims over forest land and paid 'little attention to provisions to facilitate community control of state-owned forest areas' (Kumar and Kerr 2012: 758). The government's own figures reveal the extent of non-implementation of the act. In Rajasthan, till 31 March 2020, just over 50 per cent of the titles to individual claims to land were distributed and only 7.1 per cent of community titles to land approved. In sum, only 51 per cent of all submitted claims to land titles were upheld.[9] The figures behind the land titles distributed do not tell the whole story, though. For even where the claims for land rights have been upheld, these have not meant that the full extent of the claims have been recognised. Furthermore, serious questions have been raised over the propriety, transparency and accountability of the instituted process for deciding forest rights, especially community rights. Adivasi activists in Rajasthan point out that while the Forest Rights Act establishes a process to decide community rights over forest land, the state of Rajasthan has yet to establish a proper process for the same with the result that the state department of forest and environment continues to exert inordinate power over the process.[10]

At this point, I want to draw attention to the use of *haq* in Napi Bai's narratives and also those of her fellow Adivasi activists in Kotra. The first thing to note here is that Napi Bai and other Adivasi interlocutors in Kotra spoke to me in Bhili/Bhilodi language, which made the presence of *haq* in their vocabulary, a word whose intellectual provenance and trajectory is vastly different from Bhili/Bhilodi, appear quite arresting. Also, the justificatory premises of *haq* that the Adivasi activists articulated, encompassed both individual and collective claims that intersected in interesting ways with legal constitutionalism, albeit not entirely, and certainly not for all claims.

The Cosmological Justification of *Haq*

After coming to know the contents of the letter addressed to her by the forest officials, Napi Bai told me that she first called on the NGO Kotra Adivasi Vikas Manch (Kotra Adivasi Development Group), of which she is a member, and which has its main office in Kotra. The NGO is part of the large umbrella movement of Adivasi activists known as the Jungle Zameen Jan Andolan (JZJA), which is engaged in a struggle for rights to forest land in southern Rajasthan. JZJA came into existence in 1995 as a response to the forcible evictions and disposession of Rajasthan's Adivasis from their lands and homes deep in the forests. In southern Rajasthan, there are several locally based Adivasi organisations affiliated to the JZJA that mobilise on issues of collective governance over forest land and forest produce and also against state-led eviction and violence at development projects inside forest land, which they regard as ancient and sacred. One of these local groups is the Kotra Adivasi Vikas Manch which is specifically concerned with the fallout from the designation of Phulwari Ki Naal as a sanctuary.

The Adivasi activists of Kotra Adivasi Vikas Manch mostly allude to *haq* in ancestral and cosmological terms.[11] Here, the justificatory premise for *haq* is predominantly embedded in ideas of the 'ancestral', the 'historical', the 'prior' and the cosmological. Importantly, and as I emphasised earlier in Chapter 4, this justification of *haq* is not articulated in a discrete or an ahistorical way but as before, emerges in particular political, institutional and historical contexts of developmentalism, dispossession, citizen activism, state violence, and legal constitutionalism. In the interview I represent below, one of my interviewees, Harmi Bai, a former secretary of the Kotra Adivasi Vikas Manch, belonging to the Bhil tribe, describes the Adivasi peoples' resistance to the declaration of the Phulwari Ki Naal sanctuary and of the difficulties that this has caused. The designation of Phulwari Ki Naal as a sanctuary has led to a series of restrictions on people's access to the forest and on their collection and consumption of forest produce such as honey, firewood, fruits, medicinal herbs, tree bark and leaves, which the Adivasi villagers depend upon for their everyday survival. The ban also has a commercial sting: the villagers used to collect *tendu* leaves (leaves of Diospyros melonoxylon, which is classed as a forest produce) from the forest, made these into bundles and then sold them to contractors from the cities for manufacture as *beedi*s (roughly rolled cigarettes wrapped in *tendu* leaves). The sale of *tendu* leaves is a seasonal activity and even a two-week collection could earn a medium sized household cash in hand for the whole season.[12] The ban on forest produce has led to a substantial loss of earnings for Adivasi households with the result that a majority of these are now forced to undertake 'seasonal migration', mainly to work on the large landholdings in neighbouring states as agricultural sharecroppers or labourers. In an excerpted conversation, Harmi Bai reflects on some of these difficulties:

> Earlier, we used to take the produce openly from the jungles and without any restriction and then suddenly, we were told that there was a prohibition on the forest produce as this was now a sanctuary for wild animals. We were told that we could not build homes or rear our animals or sow the field inside the jungle. We were told that this was now protected land and a sanctuary and that they were now going to develop a park inside it and that tourists were going to come from abroad to visit the sanctuary.
>
> We continue to take the produce from the forests. We only take what we need. We are the owners of this jungle and the lands therein; we have a *haq* over these. Wherever there are Adivasis there are jungles, in the cities there are no jungles. We have protected the jungles. The *haq* over these forests and water comes from our ancestors. These are our sacred lands—our ancestral spirits reside here—we have ancestral rights over these lands. Our forefathers have used this land for centuries. We tell the state forest officials, you do your job and stay here and that together we can stop the jungle mafia who go into the jungles in their lorries illegally and for commercial purposes. But you cannot stop us from taking the produce for our own use from these jungles or force us off our land.[13]

In the above narrative and those of the Bhil activists I interviewed, *haq* has very specific applications: It is hardly ever used to claim gender rights and equality and where it does, it draws on legal constitutionalism and not on prior entitlements. It is more often than not deployed to claim *qudrati haq*, or those rights justified by and/or in alignment with what nature or the cosmos intended. It is also used to signify *nazar qabza* or community recognition, a possessive claim to untitled land and property not recognised in legal or state documents but one that is upheld by a council of community chiefs known as *bhanjgarhiya*.[14]

The deployments of *haq* articulated by Bhil activists encompass individual and collective claims but also legal, moral and cosmological ones. In demanding their *haq* to their forests, the Bhil activists are staking a 'valid or justified claim' (Feinberg 1970) over ancestral forests lands—these claims are recognised under the Forest Rights Act, 2006, which also identifies the state as the obligation bearer—even though their justification of these rights claims is independent of the state and its constitutional legalism framed primarily around liberty and welfare. In their narratives, *haq* signals a different source of power and authority and is a rights claim not linked with the political authority of the state. Audra Simpson in her important book *Mohawk Interruptus* (2014) argues that taking up the challenge of Indigeneity seriously requires an accounting which is able to locate Indigenous claims for sovereignty, nationhood and citizenship outside a different frame of reference and authority than that of the settler colonial state. Simpson's book narrates the 'awkwardness if not outright refusal' of settler colonial citizenship by the Mohawk of Kahnawà:ke to be 'enfolded' within settler colonial state logics, a 'refusal' (2014: 11) of its recognition, and a refusal to disappear. In place of citizenship deriving from the settler colonial state, the Mohawk of Kahnawà:ke speak of 'living' 'primary, feeling citizenships' that do not depend on institutional recognition 'but are socially and politically recognized in the everyday life of the community, and people get called out on them' (Simpson 2014: 175). In the case of the Bhil activists, the struggle for recognition does not involve an 'outright refusal' of the state but rather opens up something akin to a 'third space of sovereignty' (Bruyneel 2007); a political space where the political authority of *haq* derives from an altogether different political imaginary than that of the state while also demanding that this different political authority be recognised by the state. The Bhil activists open up a new 'supplemental' (Bruyneel 2007: xvii) discursive and political space, which 'exposes the practices and contingencies' of the state in respect of its principles, policies and practices of rights. They stretch and trouble administrative abstraction and bureaucratic dispossession. In seeking 'non-derivative' rights from the state, the Bhil activists underline their historicity and epistemic presence to point out that rights are not creations of the state or of the government but that they are 'dynamic' (Gewirth 2001: 332) and have independent justifications. Let me make two remarks about the distinctions between the discursive deployments of *haq* in the above narrative and the category of a positive legal right in Anglo-American rights theorising. Unlike the moral individualism espoused by several dominant rights theories, *haq* is not the moral property of self-regarding individuals and thereby, does not only engage in establishing jural 'correlatives' and 'opposites' (Hohfeld 1978) between 'pairs of individuals' (Simmonds 1998: 142), that is, in establishing what rights individuals have in relation to others and to which the latter are obligated. Propelling the analytical debate on rights is the existence of 'dichotomies', not least between abstract freedom and the material circumstances of choice or the one between individual autonomy and the public good (Simmonds 1998: 129). However, the deployment of *haq* by Bhil activists does not suggest or uphold dichotomous relationships between individuals and the public good, rather, it signifies a cosmic *inseparability* and *indivisibility* of individuals from the collective good. Moreover, even if rights theorists do not premise rights on a commitment to individualism or when they refuse a rights-based morality, they continue to insist that rights provide grounds 'for action in the interest of other beings'. In other words, rights are envisaged to serve the interests only of individuals as human beings whether as individuals or in collectives; rights whether individual or collective have to be 'consistent with humanism' (Raz 1986: 208). Therein lies the rub. Neither humanism nor moral sovereignty of the individual or their interests, whether collective or individual, provide the justification for the *haq* claimed by the Bhil activists over their ancestral forests and against their dispossession. In their narratives, *haq* operates to uphold a cosmological and a normative order with its prescribed set of ethical relations and responsibilities, which include duties to (protect) nature.[15] It has a normative, non-humanist, cosmic-ontological quality and its normative and ethical remit extends beyond self-regarding individuals and their acts of claim-making to invoke a social and political imaginary of living in the world alongside other beings.

Now, although Bhil activists at Kotra have been unsuccessful in their bid to get the sanctuary notification quashed in the courts, they were able to use the rights under the Forest Rights Act especially those empowering elected village councils to decide on the use of forest lands for 'non-forestry' purposes and for 'mega industrial projects' to stop the relocation of two villages to facilitate the progress of the Phulwari Ki Naal sanctuary.[16] The act clearly released democratic energies and strengthened *gram sabha*s, which have organised popular refusals of large capital takeover in the name of development such as by the global mining giant Vedanta Aluminum (Jena 2013) while also leading to increased coercion and state violence on the Adivasi communities withholding consent to these. In recent years, however, these democratic gains of the Forest Rights Act have been severely curtailed through executive orders and directives (Aggarwal 2014), and also by legislative acts of Parliament. In July 2016, India passed the 'Compensatory Afforestation Fund Act', 2016 (CAF Act), which formally takes away the requirement of seeking the consent of the *gram sabha*s prior to carrying out development or industrial projects affecting Indigenous lands (Amnesty International 2018; Shrivastava 2018), thus leaving the Adivasi communities even more exposed to dispossession and violence by transnational capital and state development.

The Fragile and Gendered Subject of *Haq*

Before I bring to close the discussion on *haq* as a cosmological idea, I want to revisit the actions of *sarpanch* Napi Bai. Similar to the case of counter-development exhibited by the *jawabdehi yatra,* the counter-conduct in the 'no-confidence' motion passed by Medi *panchayat* under Napi Bai's direction and leadership is evident in the collective action of the Adivasi villagers who deploy existing legal constitutionalism and legal rights to demand that the state properly uphold the laws and policies that it has itself promulgated. In this case, too, a 'critical counter-conduct' of rights—of very marginal groups acting in concert and holding the rulebook guaranteeing self-governance rights of Indigenous groups over natural resource management—is forged through activism and legal constitutionalism. But the staging of this counter-conduct by a collective assembling in a public space does beg the question as to who it is that is allowed to be the subject of rights in the terms of rights and recognitions set out by the state? Can the *homo juridicus* and the *homo politicus* only ever appear as an already recognised abstract and autonomous subject with full rights able to represent themselves either individually or as a unitary collective subject? What about intersectionally marked gendered subjects who are unable to inhabit this abstract autonomous personhood and who are only ever recognised through their concrete relational identities? How do these subjects stake a claim to rights in the absence of either an ability to appear as abstract autonomous subjects or to mobilise and represent the collective will? This question becomes crucial especially in contexts when concrete gendered subjects are unable to mobilise a critical collective mass to appear on their behalf. Let me illustrate my point by turning once again to the case of Napi Bai. As I have outlined above, Napi Bai emerged as a key figure in forging the collective will of the people of the *panchayat* against the state but paradoxically she is also a fragile, gendered and precarious subject of rights herself. Elected twice as *sarpanch* to a 'reserved'[17] seat for women in 1995 and in 2010, Napi Bai is very well regarded for her competence, wisdom and courage. Despite her various achievements and standing, in the recently conducted *panchayat* elections in Rajasthan in 2015 when she declared her intention to contest elections again, the constituents of her *panchayat* told her in no uncertain terms that they would never elect a woman to an unreserved or 'general post'. A 'general' post, Napi Bai told me is a 'man's post' and when voting for a general seat, most people will 'vote for a man'. Her decision to contest a 'general seat' was widely read as challenging the entitlement of Adivasi men to the 'general seat'. Consequently, a concerted effort was mounted against Napi Bai's election campaign, involving not only large sums of bribe money but also alcohol, both of which she says she was unable to compete against or indeed raise resources for. Undeterred and confident of her standing and experience in the *panchayat*, Napi Bai went ahead regardless and contested the 'general' *sarpanch* seat. Unsurprisingly though, she failed to be re-elected to the post of the *sarpanch* on a 'general seat', but her defeat was only by the narrowest of margins—in the end, she only received 130 votes less than her opponent, out of a *panchayat* constituency of nearly 3000 registered voters. Napi Bai's experience of contesting elections points to the paradox of quotas for women: of shoring up representation for women while also limiting it to what it delimits. For instance, Napi Bai's election as *sarpanch* in the first instance through winning a reserved seat for Adivasi women in the *gram panchayat* both underscores the importance of institutional correctives to secure substantive equality (in this case of the right to hold political office and to put oneself forward for political representation), and the significant loss of representation in the absence of these. However, institutional correctives also function to police and regulate gender representation and thereby limit and shackle women's rights to just those specific institutions. In this case, the representational quotas for women do the work of increasing representation of women only ever in the presence of quotas and thereby, also have the effect of obstructing the logic of gender representation from seeping into the broader politics. A critical focus on the work of institutional correctives in both addressing but also shoring up gender inequalities and conflicts is crucial in order to avoid political arguments that view the failure of gender equality as a problem of backward cultures who fail to modernise through the state. In the context of Napi Bai and other Bhil women, quotas or 'reserved seats' allows the political appearance of gendered Adivasi subjects but only in the terms of recognition set up by the state. And, the failure of Adivasi women to show up within these statist political frames often incites straightforward, binary and non-complex analysis quick to locate Adivasi groups within an ahistorical and depoliticised cultural framework untouched by modernity or development, while locating the state as civilisationally modern and progressive. Crucially, though, this analysis removes the state from responsibility with respect to the dispossession, forced displacement, violence, precarity and vulnerability it has unleashed on Adivasis in India and to zone in exclusively and discretely on the problem of gender inequality in Adivasi communities and to diagnose it as that which can be addressed through re-adjusting the terms of recognition and representation. This is not an argument to either remove these institutional quotas or indeed to downplay the very real nature of gendered political struggles for representation within Adivasi communities but only to strike caution against the easy slippage into ahistorical and non-intersectional thinking that keeps the intersectional struggles for gender equality outside of institutional power relations, political context, and the everyday violent and oppressive interactions with the state.[18]

An Islamic Justification of *Haq*

Tracking *haq* further northwest takes me from the foothills of the Aravalli mountain ranges into the plains of the Punjab in Pakistan where the nearly two decade long mobilisations of the Anjuman Mazarain or the AMP (Tenants Association of Punjab) in rural Punjab have been demanding the restoration of their ownership and sharecropping rights to the land taken over by the Pakistani military. The mobilisations of the AMP provide us with yet another insight into the specific political imaginaries which produce particular vernacular rights cultures. The peasant mobilisations for land rights in the military stronghold of the Punjab is the most significant working class movement in postcolonial Pakistan explicitly directed at challenging the institutional and financial power and privileges enjoyed by the military in Pakistan. Formed in 1999, the AMP represents one million tenant farming households (Rizvi 2019: 296). The enormity and significance of this mobilisation cannot be underestimated, not least because the military has been in direct rule in Pakistan over long periods, and of the magnitude of social, political and economic capital it wields in the country. In ostensibly democratic India, where the Adivasis have been invited to participate and cast their votes to elect representatives in regularly held elections, and where there are formal constitutional rights in place that guarantee entitlements, the actual exercise of rights has invoked severe state repression and there has been an active executive and legislative bid to dilute these rights by the state. In Pakistan, the stakes could not be higher: the peasants are locked in a direct battle with Pakistan's military, the state's strongest and most powerful institution. The state has not held back from using its military might against the Mazarain, deploying tanks, bullets, barricades and internal security laws against them. Predictably, the mobilisations of the peasant farmers have been brutally repressed and the repression against the Mazarain has been the strongest when the military has been in government in Pakistan. Over the last 20 years, the repressions of the Mazarain have resulted in 17 deaths and several thousand peasants have been arrested. Most notoriously, however, many of the Mazarain leaders have been placed under Section 7 of Pakistan's National Action Plan for Terrorism.[19] The poor landless peasants are now designated as terrorists by the Pakistani state for demanding ownership over the land they have been tilling for over a hundred years and for seeking to wrest it back from the control of the Pakistani military, which has illegally usurped it.

The struggles of the AMP must be understood in the context of the dominance of the military in Pakistan which is also among the largest landowners in Pakistan; a position it has achieved through organising 'land transfers' to itself and the wider 'military fraternity', not by illegal or extra-institutional means but through legal and institutional manipulations with some aid from systematic acts of state violence (Siddiqa 2007). Recent scholarship on Pakistan has documented the nature and extent of the military's 'economic predatoriness' (Siddiqa 2007: 5) and traced its roots to the 'unique colonial social contract' (Khan and Akhtar 2014: 23) that produced loyal colonial subjects through operating land distribution/transfers; a mode of patronage that the military in Pakistan has carried over into the postcolonial state with great effect. In fact, a striking commonality in the struggles of both the JZJA and the AMP is that they both bring into sharp relief the continuing coloniality of legal, social and economic arrangements. In the case of Pakistan, the carry-over of colonial legal arrangements has helped forge a postcolonial 'state-society consensus' based on the 'guardianship of the military' (Khan and Akhtar 2014: 36). For not only do these 'land transfers' to the Pakistani military owe their legal and institutional legitimacy to various colonial era laws such as the Land Acquisition Act of 1894 and The Colonization of Land Act 1912 (later updated by the Government of Pakistan in 1965), but also the management of these lands by the military in postcolonial Pakistan is based on the Cantonment Land Administration Rules, 1937, used by the colonial military (Siddiqa 2007: 177). Yet it is also the case that it is over the question of land that the 'state-society consensus' in Pakistan suffers its first 'public fracture' (Khan and Akhtar 2014: 28) with the struggles of the peasant sharecroppers at Okara and Khanewal mounting a 'resistance to the post-colonial state dominated by the army' (Akhtar 2006: 481).

Essentially, the AMP are demanding ownership over the 68,000 hectares of land they have been tilling ever since 1885. The historical antecedents of the peasant discontent at Okara and Khanewal can be traced directly to the vast population transfers that were undertaken by the British colonial State in order to populate its vast irrigation projects particularly in the Punjab. From 1885 onwards, nine population resettlement projects were set up at the sites of canal irrigated projects along the five rivers which drained the province of Punjab in undivided colonial India. New legislation was drafted to legitimize this 'unique historical experiment in imperial social engineering' (Akhtar 2006: 483). Consequently, The Punjab Tenancy Act of 1887 granted tenancy status to the transferred populations, and the Punjab Alienation of Land Act, 1900, allowed the colonial state to bequeath land to its 'loyal' subjects (Akhtar 2006; Saigol 2004; Siddiqa 2007). Through transferring whole communities of people from across India to these irrigated agricultural sites, the colonial state aimed both to create an independent class of proprietary peasants as well as to transfer ownership rights to those who would help secure its economic and political legitimacy (Akhtar 2006; Saigol 2004). The 'transferred' populations to the irrigated land settlements in the Punjab were given an undertaking by the colonial state that they would be given inalienable property rights to the land after a period of 10–15 years but that in the interim, they would have usufruct rights only and would cultivate the land as sharecroppers. However, this promise was never upheld, either in the colonial period or by the postcolonial state. As a result, these peasants continued cultivating only on the basis of usufruct rights over the land and as sharecroppers rather than as landowning peasants. Except for a short period between 1957 and 1960, when ownership of some of this land was transferred to the Mazarain, an order that was subsequently rescinded, the peasant populations on these lands have more or less continued to till the land according to the sharecropping and tenancy rights established under the 1887 Act. In the early half of 2000, the military administrators of these farms introduced changes to the original terms of the contract and revised the basis of the prevailing peasant sharecropping arrangement concluded over a century ago, which regulated the share of the agricultural produce and occupancy rights. The revised terms of the contract replaced sharecropping with its proportional division of crop yields to requiring cash rentals (Human Rights Watch 2004). Fearing economic destitution and eviction, the peasant sharecropper farmers organised themselves as the Anjuman Mazarain adopting the slogan *malki ya maut* ('ownership or death') in order to oppose the new terms of the contract and, in so doing, openly challenged the Pakistani military state.

On 7 October 2000, 5,000 peasant farmers organised a peaceful protest against the new tenancy laws proposed by the military. Two days later, armed police along with the Frontier Constabulary entered the Okara Farms and started a campaign of violence against the village sharecroppers. Thus, began four years of intimidation and siege of the Okara farms by the military leading to arbitrary imprisonments without trial, intimidations, beatings and fatalities. In the course of the agitation and in aftermath, various legal challenges were mounted by the AMP against the military in Pakistani courts which, in turn, placed the military ownership of the farmlands under legal scrutiny, thus making the very claim of ownership to these lands a legal and even a political question. The court proceedings established that the Pakistani military was, in fact, not in any legal position to introduce changes to the peasant contract and even less able to establish through documentary evidence, its proprietary status as the landowner.[20] As a consequence of the legal pronouncements, the tenants of Okara and Khanewal military farms have not surrendered any share of their crop yields to the military, Pakistan's most powerful institution, and have continued to retain control over the land.

On first reading, it might seem not altogether unsurprising that the activists of the AMP deploy the term *haq* to demand their land rights. After all they represent the predominant religious and national group most identified with Urdu in the subcontinent, that is, Pakistani Muslims. However, while it is the case that newly formed state of Pakistan adopted Urdu as Pakistan's lingua-franca in 1948, this neither establishes that all Pakistanis are either 'native' Urdu speakers nor that Urdu is widely spoken throughout the country. In fact, neither is Urdu the most popular language spoken in Pakistan, coming in after Punjabi, Sindhi and Pashto and only spoken by 8 per cent of the population (Government of Pakistan 2014), nor does it, and as we have seen already through the deployment of *haq* in Rajasthan, have any less presence and influence in India. If anything, the number of Urdu speakers in India total three and a half times those of Pakistan and even though the learning of Urdu script is declining in India, the spoken language is itself thriving. And, all this of course, establishes the widespread use of *haq* as the predominant word for a right in the subcontinent.

In the lush fields of the military farms in the Punjab in Pakistan, the justificatory premise underpinning the deployment of *haq* by the AMP is neither cosmological nor tied to demands for citizenship, instead, it is embedded in and derives its justification from Islamic jursiprudentialism and Qur'anic meanings and is consequently tied very strongly to the idea of 'right conduct'. However, not unlike the demands of the activist groups in Rajasthan that I described before, the Islamic premise deployed by the Mazarain also exceeds the legal category of rights, and in contrast to the Islamic accounts of *haq* presented by Rosen (1980), Hirsch (1998) and Geertz (1993), are claims against the state for the restitution of laws of ownership under secular legal arrangements and not against particular persons under Islamic personal law. The following narrative of an activist of the AMP at Khanewal allows us to document *haq* that derives its mainstay from a popular Islamic understanding, but one used outside of a strictly religious context and towards what might be seen as secular ends.

> This word (*haq*) comes from Islam because Islam clearly marks out a very clear definition of the practices and conduct that constitute right behaviour. Islam invokes *haq* in two separate ways: a) as *Haqooq ul Allah* which is to do with right conduct in the discharge of religious obligations such as offering prayers five times a day, fasting during Ramzan and fulfilling all those religious that make me a good Muslim and b) *Haqooq ul abad* which relates to right conduct in respect of other human beings including towards my government and my family ...
>
> The right to cultivate and possess ownership is prescribed in the Holy Qur'an. For instance, in the Qur'an on paragraph three, it says very clearly: if someone who cultivated the land for five years, he then becomes the owner of the land. Therefore, the Mazarain have a right over the land which is justified by Islam itself.[21]

I want to make clear that by documenting a particular justificatory premise of *haq* that explicitly derives from an Islamic imaginary, I am neither suggesting that the AMP is an Islamic movement or that an Islamic imaginary dominates understandings of *haq* among the AMP activists. Moreover, I am not arguing that this narrative reflects a definitive version of Islamic *haq* but only that it is a conception of *haq* that traces its normative underpinnings to Islamic texts and to mystical Islam (Schimmel 1975). And, therefore, in this particular narrative, I am less interested in questions of 'purity' or the faithful recalling of the Qu'ranic passage and more in the marshalling of Qur'anic texts by peasant activists in their struggle for land rights. As noted correctly by the above narrative, within Islamic scholarly heritage, the notion of *haq* is often evoked as right conduct. In Islamic texts for instance, *haq* or *haqq* is referred to as 'right things' and contrasted with *batil* or wrong things. '*Haq* is the doing of right things like the acts of obedience, the doing of which God has not forbidden' and *batil* or 'wrong things' is 'associated with injustice, *Kufr*, and the acts of disobedience. Both are equally God's creation. But the one is right and the other is wrong' (Isutzu 1965). This interpretation of something being morally right or 'morally upright' is quite distinct from having a right over something or possessing something. It is important for me to add here that *haq* as 'right conduct' must not be viewed as a gender-neutral term nor should its intellectual justification invoking Islamic heritage be regarded as 'nonpolitical' (Mernissi 1991; Ouedghiri 2002).

The fortunes of AMP have risen and fallen. At its peak, the membership of the movement rose to a million. Although it became a 'broad movement' for land rights, the leadership struggles within the movement and the brutal reprisals by the military took their toll. Consequently, the AMP movement has splintered over the years and religious and political divides have become more stubbornly entrenched. In an interesting twist to the predominantly binary narratives of social movements in Pakistan that are more often than not led by a focus on political Islam and Islamisation of Pakistan and which roughly cleave these into either as secular or religious (Khan and Kirmani 2018), many of the Mazarain's prominent members and leadership in the early years were Christian. It was spearheaded in its initial years by Dr Christopher John and Iqbal Younus, both Christians. However, over the years, and as Aasim Sajjad Akhtar (2019) writes, the movement 'subsequently slowed and eventually stopped moving with regards to *quam*, *biraderi*, and religious efforts' (Akhtar 2019), resulting in the locus of power shifting to the numerically stronger Muslim Arain groups and their leader Mehr Abdul Sattar. Even as the question of religion did emerge to become a site of leadership contest, however, there were other pressing reasons for the splintering in the AMP leadership. In particular, these arose over accepting donor funds from international NGOs such as Action Aid, and also over the question of joining formal politics. In effect, the first break within the AMP came about with the expulsion of Christopher John and Iqbal Younus for unilaterally accepting funding from Action Aid and without consulting with rest of the AMP leadership (Rizvi 2019). As for the question of AMP's association with party political groups, while the initial stand of the AMP was explicitly 'nonpolitical', to maintain no formal affiliation with formal political parties, however, under the leadership of Mehr Abdul Sattar, the AMP did become affiliated with the main opposition party, the Pakistan's People's Party (PPP). Mehr Abdul Sattar, who is the secretary general of the AMP contested the general elections twice: first in 2013 as an independent candidate supported by the left parties and the second time, as a candidate for the PPP; he lost both elections.

'In a Field of One's Own'? Gender and Questions of Land Ownership

The AMP protests have been marked by large mobilisations of women peasants. Mobilising as the '*Thappa* Brigade', women peasants were out in the 'frontlines', standing vigil during the military siege, often leaving their children behind at home in order to go to the police stations to get the men released from police custody (Saigol 2004).[22] The word *thappa* means a bat or a thick stick that women use to wash the dirt off clothes. The *thappa*s inscribed with the slogans of the Mazarain, *malki ya maut* ('ownership or death') and *thappa haq mangda ay* ('my *thappa* demands my rights') (Saigol 2004: 58) have become symbolic of the non-violent and unarmed struggle of the landless peasants against the military might of the Pakistani state, which lined up its heavy weaponry against the AMP. Being under military siege meant that not only were roads, telephones, electricity and water supplies cut off and contact with the world outside heavily surveilled if not altogether blocked but also that the visibility of women in the movement made them targets of state violence including sexual violence. There are reports of women being beaten mercilessly and threatened with sexual violence. The threats of sexual violence were directed both at the women Mazarain as they stood at the frontlines but also at their male kin who were in custody.[23] Furthermore, not only were the women threatened with sexual violence but also their children could no longer attend school. Rubina Saigol (2004) interviewed women peasants at Okara farms who spoke of soldiers kidnapping their children and subjecting them to all kinds of torture and abuse in a bid to pressurise their parents to sign the new contract.

The visibility and presence of women in large numbers in the peasant mobilisations was not ignored by the AMP and women were accommodated in the organisational structure of the AMP which also has a separate AMP women's wing. The mobilisation of women in political movements in large numbers inevitably begs the question of the actual effect, if any, that the large numbers of women mobilising have on gender politics both within those particular movements and also on the broader terrain of gender politics that exists independently of those movements. In short, what have the popular mobilisations of women in the AMP meant for feminist and gender politics in Pakistan? Scholars writing on the AMP have noted that it challenged established and entrenched social and political hierarchies including existing gender norms (Shaheed 2010; Saigol 2004; Mumtaz and Mumtaz 2010; Akhtar 2019; Khan and Kirmani 2018). They note that women's mobilisations in the AMP have increased women's political agency and empowerment and loosened some patriarchal controls, as evident in the noticeable increases in the mobility of women and education of girls among the Mazarain but also in the marked reduction in the incidents of domestic violence within the homes of the Mazarain (Mumtaz and Mumtaz 2010). However, some scholars also point out that this 'newfound' sense of empowerment has not resulted in a clear, strong and a separate demand for women's ownership to the land that they till alongside the men. In an early study of the AMP women, the feminist scholar Rubina Saigol (2004) raised important questions in relation to land ownership within the movement and noted that the question of land ownership for women was clearly a question that baffled and confounded her field respondents. In studies since, including interviews for this book with the AMP women activists, it is not that the question of women's land ownership rights is not acknowledged or outrightly dismissed but that it is considered secondary or a deferred one—deferred to a time after the ownership question of the land has been legally settled. Across South Asia, land and property ownership underpins and regulates patriarchal gender relations and women are systematically excluded from property rights (Agarwal 1994). It is worth noting in this regard, that the exclusion of women from property rights occurs in spite of the equal rights to own property within both Pakistani and Indian legal constitutionalism. Therefore, despite legal constitutionalist guarantees, in South Asia, no more than 10 per cent women own land in their own names, with women in India driving this figure towards the top end of the statistic. Across the border in Pakistan, the figure falls steeply to 4 per cent (UNDP 2016).[24] In the case of the AMP, Saigol (2004) notes that even if women

Mazarain were to demand their right to ownership of the land, under the terms of the 1887 Tenancy Act laid down by the colonial state, under which the demand for land ownership is being made by the AMP, there is no reference to ownership rights of women (Saigol 2004: 71).[25] In short, the law that is being appealed to reinstate the ownership rights of the Mazarain recognises only 'male tenants' as entitled to 'permanent occupancy'.

Yet again, we see that the gender question on land rights when it has been raised has had to be begged separately. The question of women's ownership of land has not come up organically within the AMP mobilisations. In 2008, the question of women's right to own the land was articulated by some AMP women members in Khanewal who set up the 'Peasant Women's Society' to demand land rights for landless peasant women from the state (Mumtaz and Mumtaz 2010). On the whole, however, the demand for land rights for women has not become a part of the demands raised by the AMP and neither has it emerged organically among the women members of the AMP or indeed shared across the movement, including by the women peasants in the AMP.

It is worth asking, however, if the political mobilisations of the AMP and the very large number of women participants within it has led to the articulation of the land question and indeed of land dispossession as the most pressing demand within the women's movement in Pakistan? Over the years, the Mazarain women have received support from a range of women's groups and activists in Pakistan but it would be safe to say that the cause of the Mazarain has not occurred as a central demand of the women's and feminist movement in Pakistan and neither has the question of land ownership been propelled to the top of the feminist agenda in Pakistan. Having said this, feminist scholars in Pakistan acknowledge that the fragmented and diffuse demands for women's land ownership that have arisen within the AMP have in fact, 'indicated a shift (even if only in symbolic terms) in the existing thinking predominantly focused on community rights to that of women's rights. This shift is not without significance, especially, when due share in inheritance and property were until very recently not subjects of public debate' (Mumtaz and Mumtaz 2010: 148). However, as they also point out, any consolidation of this 'shift' will require building up 'long term linkages' across the women's movement in Pakistan (Shaheed 2010), including alliances of solidarity between peasant women in rural Pakistan and urban women activists campaigning for women's rights in the cities of Lahore and Karachi.

The fissures in the Pakistani feminist movement that operate along urban and rural women's activism are not without resonances within the Indian feminist movement. As I noted in Chapter 4, in the aftermath of the rape of

Bhanwari Devi, women's activists and organisations from metropolitan India descended to offer support to Bhanwari Devi and to express their outrage at the shoddy criminal investigation and her humiliating treatment at the hands of state investigating agencies. Not unlike the case of the Mazarain women, the *sathin*s are rural women without the cultural and social capital of metropolitan feminists. Even though the public show of solidarity on the ground with the *sathin*s was important, it did not mean either that the representational capacity of the Indian feminist movement had either shifted radically, or that it has been able to demonstrate a strong commitment to intersectional oppressions across class, caste, regional and sexuality divides, or to a politics of solidarity that bridges the rural–urban divide, ever since.

In recent years, in addition to the rural–urban divide, the glaring intersectional deficit of feminist movements in India and Pakistan has been their inability to articulate a sufficiently transnational frame that would enable them to represent struggles in the region that call into question the category of the nation state itself. For instance, it is telling that the widely documented evidence of sexual violence, enforced disappearances, acts of torture and extrajudicial killings perpetrated by Indian military and para-military forces in India's 'states of exceptions' in Kashmir and Manipur have never been the top demand of India's feminist movement (Madhok 2018), and for that matter, neither have allegations of sexual violence committed by the Pakistani army against those it has deemed as terrorist sympathisers figured as the pre-eminent demand of the feminist movement in Pakistan. In Pakistan, the military operations launched in the name of the 'war against terror' have used the Anti-Terror Act (1997) to clamp down on democratic politics of dissent. In using the anti-terror laws against the Mazarain, the Pakistani state has decided not only that the Mazarain are 'terrorists' but also has put a siege on their lands and occupied them. As occupation is always corporeal, the fact that sexual violence has accompanied military siege is no surprise but only in keeping with the patterns of military siege and occupation. Therefore, the key point here is not the prevalence of sexual violence but rather the easy conversion of democratic dissent into an act of dissent against the nation state and the normalisation of sexual violence used to discipline dissent against the nation.

Meanwhile, The Last Few Years ...

The repression of the peasants' mobilisations at Okara, Khanewal and at other military farms have neither escaped critical scrutiny nor condemnation (Human

Rights Watch 2004). The Pakistan Senate's sub-committee on Human Rights has produced a set of recommendations to resolve the dispute.[26] On 27 June 2016, The National Commission for Human Rights Pakistan (NCHR), a statutory body[27] issued an interim report on the Okara Farms, in which it recommended that the cases under the 'Anti terrorism Act should not be proceeded with until the NCHR or the body constituted in collaboration with NCHR hands down its findings ...' (NCHR 2016: 17). In recent years, the imposition of terrorism charges against the peasant activists has been condemned by several Pakistani Senators (Butt 2017). However, this public censure by Pakistan's Senate has not detained the military from pursuing the Mazarain. Since 2001, scores of charges have piled up against the Mazarain leaders, with the most notorious among them being that they are now branded as the 'enemies of the state'. In March 2016, Okara's district coordination officer issued a 30-day detention order against Mehr Abdul Sattar ostensibly so that the authorities could proceed with the 26 cases pending against him since 2001. *The Herald* newspaper reported that a letter written by the Management of Military Farms Group Okara claimed that 'his arrest had absolutely nothing to do with the military farmlands' but rather to do with his 'anti-state activities' in association with 'foreign, Indian agency RAW'. Along with a few AMP activists, Sattar was 'detained in a newly set up high security jail in Sahiwal town meant for hardened criminals and feared terrorists' (Sheikh 2016). In 2017, Pakistan's pre-eminent Supreme Court lawyer, the late Asma Jahangir, brought a petition in front of Pakistan's Supreme Court against procedural violations in Mehr Abdul Sattar's imprisonment at Sahiwal. In 2018, the Supreme Court granted Mehr Abdul Sattar bail, but he was shortly sentenced to a 10 year imprisonment on charges of terrorism filed against him at a police station in Okara in 2015 (W. A. Khan 2018). On September 8, 2020, The Lahore High Court acquitted Mehr Abdul Sattar of terrorism (*The Dawn* 2020). While Abdul Sattar is by no means the only AMP member to be imprisoned—in that 2015 Okara case, for instance, 165 farmers were named in the FIR and 2 were eventually charged—nonetheless, by directly targeting the AMP leadership under anti-terrorism laws, the Pakistan military has registered its strong refusal to accede lands to the Mazarain.

The military repression of the Mazarain, however, is not the dominant story here; the political struggle for *haq* waged by the Mazarain is. The Mazarain have mobilised in their villages and in the streets; they have taken their fight to the courts and to Pakistan's Parliament. Recently, the National Commission for Human Rights in Pakistan, has taken the lead in trying to bring a settlement to the dispute. On March 29 2019, the Pakistani newspaper *The*

News carried a statement from the NCHR declaring that the Okara Military Farms case had been settled and that it has now 'disposed off the case'. The terms of the settlement were for the 'farmers to pay *batai* (share-cropping) as agreed during negotiations and for the Military Farms administration to refrain from harassment or psychological torture.' These settlement terms had emerged from an earlier meeting of 01 January 2019, convened by the NCHR between the representatives of the Mazarain, the Awami Worker's Party, Pakistan Government officials and a representative of the Military and the NCHR where it had been proposed that '... criminal cases registered against the tenants will be withdrawn. Batai (share from crop), which existed prior to the year 2000, will be restored and tenants would start giving 50 per cent of their production to the army or the government. Tenants would not get ownership rights, but no one will harass them in future and they will not be dislocated' (Junaidi 2019; Imran 2019). The Pakistani military acknowledged for the first time that it did not own the land, and that it was the legal property of the government of Punjab. And, even though, the proposed settlement does not recognise the Mazarain as the owners of the land, the astounding admission by the military changes the dynamic of the dispute considerably. It remains to be seen how this proposed settlement is received by the Mazarain and also by other stakeholders in Pakistan's military establishment.

Six Remarks on Human Rights, Political Subjectivation and Gendered Counter-Development

As I close the two empirical chapters, I want to make six remarks on the politics of *haq*, human rights, political subjectivation, counter-development and gendered counter-conduct that I have been discussing in Chapters 4 and 5.

First, the feminist historical ontologies of *haq* that I present in these two chapters draw attention to the gendered conceptual life and work of concepts. Tracking *haq* across political mobilisations in India and Pakistan shows that even while *haq* generates political possibilities and shifts normative horizons of rights talk, however, these normative possibilities are deeply gendered and marked by intersectional inequalities. It is worth noting that in each of the political mobilisations that I have been studying and documenting, I have not come across a single instance where the gender question came up organically within these or was raised as part of the collectively raised demands for rights. Furthermore, it is striking that despite the different justificatory premises for *haq* that are mobilised by these struggles and which in turn, enable us to envision an expanded landscape for rights and human rights, the question of gender equality and rights is almost always justified on the basis of existing legal constitutional guarantees and rights and rarely ever on religious and historical premises.

Second, as I have shown across the two chapters, developmentalism produces its own particular forms of governmentalised power, including modes of 'perpetual questioning' that sets off what I have called counter-development. Paying attention to counter-development enables us to foreground the centrality of developmentalism as the background context within which rights talk takes place in 'most of the world'. Not only does development provide a great deal of the intellectual mainstay for rights talk but through producing counter-development, it also shines a light on development's vast hinterland, which is generated and regulated through intricate networks of governmental and non-governmental technologies of power, engaged in manufacturing consent and mobilising legitimacy for developmentalism across different sites. Importantly, it shows the intertwined and shared nature of discourses, concerns and strategies of development and also of its critics.

Third, counter-development enables us to track more carefully the production of subjects and subjectivities under development contexts. The right to development with its coupling of human rights and development, and through its declaratory power, interpellates rights bearing subjects into existence by making them 'co-bearers' of development. The ideational energies released by human rights open up spaces for political subjectivation and for counter-development, which paradoxically, by instituting a 'perpetual questioning' of development, reproduce the object of their questioning, that is, development all over again. However, and as the case of Napi Bai illustrates, there are limits to counter-development. In other words, counter-development does not necessarily challenge or resist state policies and development interventions in order to only ever align these with emancipatory ends. It might, infact, use the letter of the law or policy to hold out against the broader spirit or implications of some laws and state policies. I have in mind here the resistance to the initiatives on gender equality which, as I have noted throughout the book, have needed to be begged separately.

Fourth, and this is important to note, counter-development emerges within specific institutional and policy contexts of development. The right to food movement, for instance, coincided with the neoliberalisation of the Indian economy in the mid 1990s. The growing official apathy to the farming distress as a result of successive years of drought and the resultant difficulties of access

to food, lead activists to develop legal and activist strategies and responses to
it. The decision of Napi Bai to contest *panchayat* elections too, is rendered
possible by two things: the passage of the 73rd Constitutional Amendment,
which provisioned that 'not less than one third seats be reserved for women'.[28]
The second aspect was the decision to include women as co-participants in the
development process as an explicit policy objective of India's sixth five-year
plan. Referencing the objectives outlined in the UN International Decade of
the Woman (1975), the announcement of inclusion of women in development
in India's national and state-led policy making laid the groundwork for the
setting up a series of innovative state sponsored programmes for women's
development explicitly directed at inaugurating rural women as subjects of
development (Madhok 2013).

Fifth, the temporality of these rights mobilisations places a mild question
mark on some of the contemporary scholarship on neoliberalism that ascribes
to it, among other global effects, the imminent death of the *homo politicus*.
These citizen mobilisations crystallise and activate in a time identified by
many scholars as one characterised by the ascendance and intensification of
neoliberalism and one marked by the commercialisation of social relations and
the evacuation of citizenship and politics. However, far from neoliberalism
ringing in the impending death of the *homo politicus* (Brown 2015), or indeed
all of feminist activism joining hands with neoliberalism, in South Asia, the
mid 1980s to the present has witnessed the subaltern mobilisation of radical
views on citizenship aimed at both countering the truncating of their rights
and citizenship by the neoliberal state and also towards pressing for the
conversion of welfare entitlements promised through development, into legal
rights. These mobilisations have not only engendered novel activist strategies to
demand innovative public policies but have also been successful, as the right to
food movement shows, at expanding existing sets of rights and entitlements. In
short, in light of these subaltern mobilisations in South Asia, we would still be
able to say that a great success of neoliberalism and neoliberal market rationality
has been the devastating blow these have dealt to global redistributive politics.
However, we would be less able to say that it is universally the case that the
ascendance of neoliberalism has entirely vanquished movements for economic
justice, rights and redistribution around the globe.

Sixth and finally, it is certainly the case that rights and human rights talk
sets off processes of subjectification. However, this subjectification does
not result in the production of a homogenous sovereign and free subject of
global human rights but a subject of rights in the vernacular—one inflected,

constrained and enabled by existing intersectional, material and power hierarchies. Consequently, the politics of human rights in 'most of the world' is not one only of simply enacting or reproducing the global subject of human rights or indeed of translating global human rights. It is a politics of struggle for justice that is materially, intersectionally, geopolitically located, and arises from historically specific encounters with rights and human rights in 'most of the world'.

Notes

1. *Gram sabha* is a village assembly, comprising all persons whose names are included in the electoral rolls for the *panchayat* at the village level.
2. The Tenth Five Year Plan document 2002–07 states:

   As per the information readily available, a population of 21.3 million have been displaced between 1951 and 1990 in the states of Andhra Pradesh, Bihar, Gujarat, Maharashtra, Madhya Pradesh, Rajasthan and Orissa. Of whom, 8.54 million (40 per cent) are tribals and of those only 2.12 million (24.8 per cent) tribals could be resettled, so far.

   See also Fernandes (2009) and Mosse et al. (2002).
3. See Campaign for Survival and Dignity (2003).
4. Joint meetings of *gram sabha*s in a *panchayat* can be called on matters where 'co-ordination with other Gram Sabhas is required,' and these joint meetings are to be chaired by the *gram sarpanch*. See Department of Rural Development and Panchayati Raj (Department of Rural Development and Panchayati Raj), Notification No.F.4(6)PESA Rules/Legal/PR/2010/ 1938 Jaipur, November 01 2011, http://www.rajpanchayat.rajasthan.gov.in/Portals/_default/PESARules2011.pdf.
5. Department of Rural Development and Panchayati Raj (Department of Rural Development and Panchayati Raj), Notification No.F.4(6)PESA Rules/Legal/PR/2010/ 1938 Jaipur, November 01 2011, http://www.rajpanchayat.rajasthan.gov.in/Portals/_default/PESARules2011.pdf.
6. See in particular Chapter III (4.2e) of the Forest Rights Act, 2006. See also Chapter V, Department of Rural Development and Panchayati Raj, Notification No.F.4(6) PESA Rules/Legal/PR/2010/ 1938 Jaipur, 1 November 2011, http://www.rajpanchayat.rajasthan.gov.in/Portals/_default/PESARules2011.pdf.
7. Interviews with Napi Bai also known as Rapli Bai, July 2015, August 2016 and December 2017, in Kotra and Medi, Kotra Block, Udaipur.
8. The news reportage of the judgment was carried in the national and international press. See also Chandra (2019).

9. The actual figures behind the dismal percentages are: a total of 74, 414 individual claims and 1,414 collective ones were made to land titles out of which 38,007 individual claims were accepted and 103 collective claims recognised. For India wide reports published by the Ministry of Tribal Affairs,Government of India, see https://tribal.nic.in/FRA/data/MPRMar2020.pdf.

10. This power of forest department officials over the process and decision making on Adivasi claims was emphasised by Dharam Chand Kher, who is the state coordinator of Rajasthan Adivasi Vikas Manch, which is a collective of 27 organisations working in the area of Adivasi issues across 12 districts in Rajasthan. In his interviews with me, Kher said:

> In Kotra, Mawla Ghata, in Jhuda, there is a jungle of Junapader, there are about 40 people who live in that village, they put in a collective claim for ownership over their land, but their claim was rejected. Now there is a process to reject these claims. If the *qabza* (habitation) is a recent one, then the *van adhikaar* committee or the *gram sabha* can reject the claim. Also, during the process of an ongoing verification, the Patwari and the Forest department or indeed the collector can verify/reject the claims. But these claims that were rejected were done at the *upkhand* committee, which has seven members, including the SDM (Sub-Divisional Magistrate), the BDO (Block Development Officer), officials of the Ministry of Tribal Affairs, the Forest Department, and three members of the public. In this committee meetings, there is a verification of claims and where the claims are seen as lacking verifiable evidence or enough information, they can be sent back to the *gram sabha* to be revised or fixed. However, these claims were rejected on the basis of one official of the Forest Department directing the others to reject these claims. There was no meeting held, not even notes or minutes were prepared for this decision, however, the committee endorsed the view of the forest official that the claims were invalid. Now the people of Junapader have been living there for centuries, we resubmitted their case as 'appeal' and put it in the 'appeal process', but nothing has come out of it yet, however, the Forest Department has swung into action and begun evicting Adivasis from their ancestral homes and lands. (Interviews with Dharam Chand Kher, Udaipur and Kotra, 2015–2016)

11. For accounts of cosmic tales and traditions detailing aboriginal originating myths and status, see Elwin (1937).

12. Interview with Napi Bai, *panchayat*, Kotra, 6 August 2015.

13. Interview with Harmi Bai, Kotra, Udaipur, Rajasthan, 2005.

14. Interview with Dharam Chand Kher, Rajasthan Adivasi Rights Organisation, Udaipur, 9 August 2015.

15. Interview with Rapli Bai (also known as Napi Bai), Medi *panchayat*, Kotra, Udaipur, 6 August 2015.
16. Interview with Rapli Bai, 2015.
17. Under the 73rd Amendment to the Constitution, one-third reserved seats or quotas for women were instituted in local government institutions. The Constitutional Amendment also instituted a three-tier structure for local governance in India, or the *panchayats*. The *panchayat* is a democratically elected system of local governance with elected councils at the village level (*gram panchayat*), block level (*panchayat samiti*) and district level (*zilla parishad*). Both the PESA Act and the Forest Rights Act, 2006, have formally empowered the village council or the *gram sabha* with important develpement related functions and powers. For the specific rules laid down by the Government of Rajathan to implement the PESA Act, see Department of Rural Development and Panchayati Raj (Department of Rural Development and Panchayati Raj), Notification No.F.4(6) PESA Rules/Legal/PR/2010/ 1938 Jaipur, 1 November 2011, http://www.rajpanchayat.rajasthan.gov.in/ Portals/_default/ PESARules2011.pdf.
18. See also Simpson (2014).
19. See Tariq (2016). See also Human Rights Watch (2016) and Mehlab (2016).
20. It has since emerged that the Pakistani military at the time of gaining independence in 1947 had the lands transferred from the British military to them, but had in effect, paid no rent to the Punjab Revenue Department, which was the lessee of the land, and, hence, as a result of reneging on its contractual agreement with the revenue department, had very little legal authority to administer these agricultural farms in the first place.
21. Interview with Mustafa, Khanewal, Pakistan, 2008.
22. Rubina Saigol (2004) conducted interviews with the women at Okara farms and in particular, this description of the Thappa Brigade is evocative:

> They had fifteen police cars that they used in the blockades. They constantly used abusive and sexual language to intimidate us. In front there were Rangers, and at the back there was the police. They kidnapped one of our boys and left him unconscious on a stack of hay. We thought, all right, if you have arms and ammunition, we have *thappas*. The whole village reached the spot. The Rangers escaped as we emerged with our *thappas*. We don't have any arms. We don't have even food let alone guns. We have small tracts of land, barely enough to feed our children. We hit the police with our *thappas*. They will never forget how we fought back. If need be, we will fight again and use our *thappas* again. (2014: 55)

23. In an interview, the chairman of AMP, Liaquat Ali, said: 'The army and the rangers would take away our women to private detention centres and torture

them. Soldiers would ask us to sign contracts, and if we refused they threatened to rape our daughters and sisters' (Saigol 2004: 3; Shehzad 2004).

24. According to UNDP (2016) women in Pakistan own less than 3 percent of land but comprise 72.7 per cent of the agricultural labour force. UNDP (2016f). This abysmal statistic reflects the very high levels of gender inequality in the country. Pakistan has a Gender Inequality Index value of 0.547 which ranks it 123 out of 148 countries. Its Human Development Index rank is 148 out of 188 countries. This ranking accounts for the low education and literacy rates among women and of the high infant and maternal mortality rates and a low number of women serving in Parliament (http://hdr.undp.org/sites/all/themes/ hdr_theme/country-notes). See Agarwal (1994) for an extensive overview of the questions at stake in women's ownership of land in South Asia

25. According to clause 5 (1) A of the 1887 Tenancy Act, 'male tenants and their direct descendants who had cultivated the land for more than two generations (twenty years) were entitled to permanent occupancy.'

26. A three-member sub-committee of the Senate on Human Rights visited Okara on 12 August 2004 and tabled its report in the Senate on 7 December 2004 (*The Dawn* 2005).

27. Pakistan established a National Commission for Human Rights (NCHR) in 2012. On its web page, the NCHR defines its role as providing ' ... a broad and overarching mandate for the promotion, protection and fulfilment of human rights, as provided for in Pakistan's Constitution and international treaties'. Furthermore, it states that 'as an impartial state body, the NCHR works independently of the Government and is directly accountable to the Parliament of Pakistan'. For the Interim Report of the NCHR on the Okara Farms, see National Commission for Human Rights Pakistan, 'Annual Report (2015–16)', which is available online at https://nchr.gov.pk/wp-content/uploads/ 2019/01/Annual-Report-2015-16.pdf.

28. 'Not less than one-third (including the number of seats reserved for women belonging to the Scheduled Castes and the Scheduled Tribes) of the total number of seats to be filled by direct election in every Panchayat shall be reserved for women and such seats may be allotted by rotation to different constituencies in a Panchayat' (The Constitution Seventy-third Amendment Act, 1992). See http://indiacode.nic.in/coiweb/amend/amend73.htm.

6 Conceptual Diversity, Feminist Historical Ontology and a Critical Reflexive Politics of Location

How to tell different stories of rights and human rights? How to tell stories of rights and human rights that are not only ever those of their origins, or of the powerful efforts by the powerful including by nation states to institutionalise global human rights, or of their unidirectional travel, translation and vernacularisation into 'other worlds', or indeed those about the humanitarian and military interventions by global powers. How to not tell stories of 'different' human rights where 'difference' is enacted through categorising difference as "cultural", "custom", "local" or as "case studies" of global human rights talk? How to refuse standardly narrated stories of human rights that speak of 'difference' while keeping the epistemic frameworks of global human rights talk intact and impervious to serious consideration of the 'difference' that historical difference makes to global rights talk? In short, how to tell 'other' stories of world-making and meaning-making on rights without either reproducing the vast epistemic power and the time–space provincialism of the global human rights discourse or compromising the complexity, dynamism, difference and epistemic and political struggles of human rights mobilisations in 'most of the world'? These are the questions that constitute the burden of this book.

The stories of vernacular rights cultures that appear in this book aim at disrupting the originary, statist, institutional and Eurocentric stories that global human rights likes to tell about itself. Specifically, the stories of vernacular rights cultures make theoretical, conceptual and methodological claims to shine a light on different possibilities for engaging, imagining and expanding rights and human rights. Significantly, the stories of vernacular rights cultures signal that a theoretical and philosophical critique of global human rights alone cannot account for the life-worlds of subaltern struggles for rights and entitlements, or indeed for the critical vocabulary and political grammar within which these struggles and demands are articulated. For, quite simply, the terms of the critique of global human rights have been such that these end up resurrecting and reproducing the object of their critiques, that is, the West as the subject of human rights discourses albeit, this time via critique, while also simultaneously reproducing the global inequalities of knowledge production by investing epistemic agency in the West. Critiques of global human rights, though hugely useful and significant in demystifying the constellations of power and their entanglements must only be the starting point for the production of new intellectual and conceptual histories, geographies and epistemologies of rights from different locations, including subaltern locations around the globe.

Theory

The *Oxford Dictionary* defines 'vernacular' as 'a language or dialect ... naturally spoken by the people of a particular country or district....' (*OED* 1989). Both place and language are key to meanings of vernacular rights cultures, which are site specific, and historically and politically specific epistemological, ontological and political encounters with rights and human rights. Vernacular rights cultures shift the site of epistemic enquiry of rights and human rights by curating, assembling and documenting different registers, imaginaries and possibilities of and for rights encounters in the world. These alternative rights registers allow different subaltern politics of human rights in 'most of the world' to appear as an epistemic presence. The appearance of these subaltern politics of rights as an epistemic presence is crucial for shifting the epistemic centre of knowledge production on global human rights. The epistemic presence of vernacular rights cultures eschew stories of origins and global telos to think instead of geopolitically located and historically particular politics of subaltern struggles for justice.

Theoretically, the stories of vernacular rights cultures refuse the politics of origins. The politics of origins is a racial story that argues that human rights have particular origins, starting points, founding moments, which are all invariably in the West, or are assumed to be in the West from where they travel to the rest of the world. As I argued in Chapters 1 and 2, this politics of origins is shared by celebrators and detractors of human rights and is not without effects. In the hands of the detractors, it places a politically expedient argument to delegitimise modes of protest and questioning of excessive state power on the basis that human rights are illegitimate and foreign and therefore with little traction and locus standi. In celebratory and critical/progressive scholarship on human rights, this originary story shores up the West as the epistemic subject of human rights via celebration or via critique. This politics of origins is also a key framework for erasing and discounting epistemic authority and difference from elsewhere, and for assuming unidirectional, non-reciprocal simplistic translation and commensurability on the one hand, or a human rights void and a *tabula rasa* that needs to be filled with global human rights institutions and practices, on the other.

In place of originary stories of global human rights, vernacular rights cultures document and curate the languages and forms of world-making that inform, sustain and underwrite the politics of struggles for rights. It insists on attending to the 'other' struggles and worlds of rights that escape theoretical and conceptual capture through either failing to 'fit' the model of global human rights or are actively erased by the workings of the politics of origins. The epistemic presence of vernacular rights cultures crucially disrupts two assumptions of the global human rights discourse: universal and unidirectional translatability and radical commensurability. The politics of origins insists on the unidirectional travel of global human rights from a specified location but also that these become localised or vernacularised through translation into local contexts and into different local languages. However, vernacular rights cultures refuse this demand and also insistence on straightforward and simple translational global human rights practice to speak instead of different politics, meanings, epistemic authority, subjectivities and political cultures of rights and human rights. The refusal here is to appear only in terms of recognition already set in place (Povinelli 2011) and against the logic of 'deadly sameness of abstraction' (Rich 1984) while also insisting on the epistemic presence of vernacular rights cultures. This insistence on appearing as an epistemic presence interrupts the global and local binary which locates global human rights in a position of epistemic authority and as the originary site of human rights politics and scholarship, and the local as a passive receptacle of these global human rights through global projects of translation. The stories of vernacular rights cultures are invested in asking questions that query the context for and meanings of rights in different parts of the globe and about the forms of rights politics, subjectivities these engender including the political cultures, imaginaries, contestations and struggles that take place over rights. They insist on asking the following: Where do rights come from? Who do they belong to? Where do they derive authority from? Furthermore, what forms of politics and kinds of subjectivities do rights produce and uphold? I must hasten to add here that this is not a critique of translation or of the travel of theories and ideas but rather of the automatic and straightforward 'assumption of translatability' (Apter 2013) and of the conceptual symmetry and politics of epistemic inequality that inform global human rights. The trouble with the unidirectional travel and translation projects of global human rights is their epistemic refusal of relationality together with a weak recognition of global human rights as 'travelling theories' that might go beyond 'borrowing and adapting' (Said 2002: 421) to take on a wholly, radically new and invigorated intellectual life in different places and among different peoples. Crucially, the practices and projects of this simplistic unidirectional translation categorise and manage difference in terms of binary epistemic frames of those who are 'universal knowers' and those who are known through translation but even then only ever so, if they if they can fit or are made to fit the terms of that universal knowing. Writing in the context of comparative literature, Emily Apter (2013) argues that an 'assumption of translatability' can lead to a 'reflexive endorsement of cultural equivalence and substitutability, or toward the celebration of nationally and ethically branded "differences"... niche marketed as commercialized "identities"' (2013: 2). In the place of this 'assumption of translatability', Apter calls for 'untranslatability as a theoretical fulcrum' that would 'recognise the importance of non-translation, mistranslation, incomparability and untranslatability' (2013: 4). What Apter calls the 'untranslatable' and at times, incommensurable, constitutes a different meaning, politics and ethics in critical Indigenous theory. Here, incommensurability is not a critique of the 'embedded epistemologies of cultural equivalence and substitutability' but rather, institutes a 'refusal' (Simpson 2014) of the epistemological frameworks that have as their object the elimination of Indigenous peoples. Whereas Apter turns to elements of postcolonial scholarship as exemplars that challenge this assumption of translation, for Indigenous scholars, postcolonial scholarship is itself implicated in the logic of elimination of the Indigenous. The incommensurability that Indigenous scholarship demands is the incommensurability of Indigenous life-worlds with the epistemic frameworks of the settler colonial state and its projects of self, subjectivity, citizenship, nation, territory and sovereignty, which are led by the genocidal logics of dispossession and elimination (Woolfe 2006; Byrd 2011; Simpson 2014). Consequently, Indigeneity troubles and disrupts the 'logics of colonialism' that inform the 'settled nature of settler colonialism' (Simpson 2014). Even though it might appear, at least on the surface, that decolonial, postcolonial and critical Indigenous studies scholars are engaging on a common platform of anticolonial, anti-imperial and decolonisation talk, however, the stakes and struggles and epistemic terms of critical Indigenous studies are very different (Byrd 2011; Byrd and Rothberg 2011; Tuck and Yang 2012; Simpson 2014). As is well known, for critical Indigenous studies scholarship, the question of decolonisation is not a 'metaphor' for social justice projects or indeed of 'epistemic disobedience' (Mignolo 2018) but requires repatriation of Indigenous land. And therefore, theirs is not only a question of settlement of land and the formal end of decolonisation and its afterlife, but, crucially, also of the continuing erasure and extinction of Indigenous peoples who live on that land. And, even though the decolonisation projects of postcolonial and critical Indigenous scholarship are in a large measure incommensurable, perhaps, it is also the question of incommensurability itself that may possibly open up a space for potentially productive dialogues between subalternity and Indigeneity (Byrd and Rothberg 2011).

Conceptual Diversity

Conceptual diversity is a key intellectual project of vernacular rights cultures. The conceptual intervention of vernacular rights cultures is to generate conceptual work from 'non-standard' locations and contexts, that is, contexts outside those in which concepts are standardly produced, described and visualised but also through demanding that theorists locate their subjects and themselves in the transnational 'political economy of knowledge production', at particular places and in different languages. The thinkability of this conceptual diversity becomes possible in a large part because of the crucial intervention that a critical reflexive feminist politics of location makes.

As an epistemic project and intervention, location renders the very thinkability and intellectual possibility of producing knowledge from different locations. However, what in effect, is the epistemic difference that a critical reflexive politics of location makes to knowledge production? Or, if you prefer, what particular stipulations and enablements does a critical reflexive politics of location put in place for doing social and political theory? Now, to centre location is to already establish two things right away: it is to flag the 'provincial' location of all theory and also to signal the specific context of unremitting power relations that inform theoretical and representational endeavours (Said 1978)—the imperial, colonial entanglements of epistemologies with contemporary global geographies, prevailing political economies (Cusicanqui 2012) and the transnational circuits of power through which knowledges travel and assume authority (Grewal and Kaplan 1994; Mohanty 1995; Alexander and Mohanty 2010). To put it in specific terms, location signifies the role of place in knowledge production as a generative site (McKittrick 2011) in which concepts and persons come into being (Hacking 2002) and, declares it as a productive site for methodological interventions while insisting on a critical reflexive ethics. The central work of the book, which is to think of rights and human rights politics from the standpoint of subaltern groups at the frontline of rights struggles, is enabled by the epistemic interventions that a critical reflexive politics of location makes. These epistemic interventions institute certain demands and constraints and are simultaneously both limitations but also enablements for engendering particular kinds of knowledge production (see Chapter 3). In effect, a critical reflexive politics of location requires asking different questions, naming the epistemic ground that one speaks and writes from, of refusing a technical application of theory while insisting on 'speaking back to it' and of working to and for justice: that is, to work towards demystifying and shifting the epistemic hierarchies and power relations that underpin knowledge production. Fundamentally, however, a critical reflexive politics of location demands an answer to the question: from where are you looking, and whom or what are you seeing?

It bears worth repeating that the production of concepts from 'most of the world' is a matter of urgency. We simply do not have the concepts we need in order to produce theorised accounts of our different and historically specific encounters with the world. But how do we study concepts in 'most of the world' without either falling into the trap of violent commensurability (Tuck and Yang 2012) or radical unintelligibility? The first trap of forced and violent commensurability leads to theoretical and conceptual misdescriptions and the latter, down the poisonous hole of cultural relativism. Both traps refuse meaningful and open theoretical engagement and shut down conversations.

Vernacular rights cultures is a key intervention for enabling and encouraging scholarship on conceptual diversity around the globe. The vernacular in vernacular rights cultures signifies the epistemic presence and authority of different literal and conceptual languages of rights deployed by subaltern groups in different parts of the globe. In refusing to assemble unquestioningly under the umbrella of global human rights, vernacular rights cultures signal their dynamism and difference but also their epistemic presence. Vernacular rights cultures intervene to disrupt the cycle of despair and exhaustion brought on by critique upon critique of human rights. In this book, I have been tracking and documenting the critical vocabularies, political imaginaries, conceptual and political presence in the gendered politics of *haq* in the subcontinent.

Urdu is often referred to as the 'pan Indian language', which is spoken across India and is also one of its officially recognised languages. In India the number of Urdu speakers is falling with only 4.2 per cent of the population declaring it as their mother tongue, however, in terms of actual numbers, the number of speakers is not insubstantial. In neighbouring Pakistan, Urdu is the national lingua franca but like across the border in India, the percentage of Urdu speakers is quite low registering at only 8 per cent of the population. Those who follow language politics in the subcontinent often note that despite the percentage of speakers of the language being recorded in single digit figures in both countries, Urdu extends an important influence on the cultural and literary landscapes in both countries. This symbolic cultural weight and influence of Urdu extends to the domain of social struggles and movements where Urdu revolutionary poetry has emerged in recent times to affectively bind the people of the subcontinent in solidarity against their authoritarian ruling dispensations (Kuchay 2019). The influence of Urdu on different spoken languages in India is also evident in the ways in which the word *haq* is the principal word used to denote a 'right' in all the five different languages that make an appearance in this book: Rajasthani, Hindi, Urdu, Punjabi and Bhili Bhilodi. In addition, I have also documented *haq* as far as northeast India in the frontier state of Manipur where activists also use *haq* (Madhok 2018). The striking thing about the conceptual presence of *haq* in India and Pakistan is that nowhere is Urdu the dominant language spoken by the majority of population groups And yet, *haq* pushes through to the surface to emerge as the foremost and most recognisable word for a right within subaltern struggles in the subcontinent.

Haq is, of course, principally an Arabic word. In contemporary times, Arabic is spoken by over 300 million people around the globe and therefore, scholarly work on the presence of the word *haq* in different locations and its deployments in different political contexts has an extraordinary potential to offer unique, productive and generative perspectives on the operation of rights and human rights. In this book, however, I document the conceptual life-worlds of *haq* in the Indian subcontinent through documenting the different political imaginaries of *haq* to shine a light on the complex, capacious and shifting meanings of *haq* that come into being when gendered subjects seize it. In attending to the justificatory premises of *haq* that animate and activate rights in the region, I insist not only on a scrupulous politics of location but also a refusal of originary discourses that dominate human rights politics thinking and politics. Anthropological scholarship on *haq* has drawn attention to its Arabic and Persian linguistic lineage and to its conceptual meanings steeped in Islamic jurisprudentialism (see Chapter 3 and, in particular, Rosen 1980, Geertz 1983, Hirsch 1998). However, as this book shows, the conceptual deployment of *haq* in India and Pakistan is not confined to Islamic jurisprudentialism alone, but has a wider presence that includes claim-making and seeking expanded citizenship entitlements from the state and its secular legal framework not always in alignment with Islamic juristic settlements of *haq*. It is, however, through paying attention to how gendered subjects both seize *haq* and reorient it in ways that make it 'speak to' and 'for them' that the normative orientations of *haq* become visible. These normative orientations reveal the ways in which *haq* orients proper ordering of relations among persons, maintains an image of a gendered moral order and mediates citizenship, political discourse and political struggles. The seizing of *haq* by intersectionally gendered subjects shows, for instance, that *haq* denotes masculine and caste relations of property ownership or due share in familial property; that it operates as a non-elite conceptual term with a predominant take up by relatively formally non-literate and marginalised people in 'rural areas', while its Hindi counterpart, *adhikaar* is often associated with 'educated' people living in urban areas. This popular impression of *adhikaar* as the term associated with legal speak, officialdom and the powerful is borne out by the fact that in the official Hindi language version of the Indian constitution, it is *adhikaar* that appears as the official word for right, whereas in the Urdu (GoI 2013) and Manipuri (GoI 2019a) versions, it is the word *haq* that stands in for and translates as a right. As opposed to *adhikaar* which is almost always invoked as a legal right, *haq* is something which belongs to one; and one is justified in 'snatching it back' if taken away. Finally, *haq* does not only signify minimalist negative rights of individuals, that is to be free from interference by others but also extends to include collective rights of sentient and non-sentient beings and posesses a maximalist imaginary that embraces ideas of justice and equality.

Feminist Historical Ontology

How to study vernacular rights cultures? In this book, I propose a feminist historical ontology as a methodological device for studying vernacular rights cultures. A feminist historical ontology is an unapologetically interdisciplinary methodological intervention that brings together an eclectic set of conceptual and theoretical investigations, and methodological tools, irrespective of their disciplinary habitations. Academic disciplines are notorious for policing boundaries and setting up disciplinary borders, leading to both the depoliticisation of academic scholarship (Said 1994) and a lack of accountability and reflexivity (Spivak 1999). My academic training as a political theorist made me acutely aware of the constraints of discipline bound conceptual and methodological tools that simply did not allow, encourage or facilitate the complexity required for theorising 'other worlds'. The power of Eurocentric frameworks is such that they convert these 'other places' into 'case studies' or into the 'local' and as devoid of epistemic authority, or as having something to say that matters epistemically. Two decades ago, as I set out to study the philosophical and theoretical investigations of the relationship between agency and coercion, I found myself turning to ethnography and to 'fieldwork' to make sense of but also to query the spatial geographies and intellectual contexts that formed the standard background contexts for theorising autonomy and agency. Soon enough, through attending to location as a generative site for theoretical work on agency and coercion, it became clear to me that the unquestioned, unlocated and therefore unnamed standard background context for theorising of agency and autonomy was one of negative freedom and that the governing measure of autonomy and agency was (and is) free action. The former institutes the latter by shoring up the heroic unbounded white onto-epistemic subject able to reproduce without exception this governing action bias. However, even a cursory regard for the grounded realties of my ethnographies showed that lives and living are constrained in all manner of ways, and that agency thinking could not continue to regard conditions of negative freedom as 'standard', and a necessary given, while also insisting that persons display their agentic selves through their ability to commit maximal free action in all circumstances. Therefore, reconceiving agency would involve refusing a technical application of theory but also challenging and speaking back to mainstream theories of autonomy and agency. In sum, it would mean shifting the standard background location of theory production of agency and autonomy—from negative freedom to one of ever present threat of coercion and subordination—and to a site specific historical, political and ideational context to enable a different theoretical perspective on agency (Madhok 2013).

The work on vernacular rights cultures reflects a continued commitment to combine philosophical and theoretical investigations alongside ethnographic undertakings but it is also a recognition that the conceptual, theoretical and empirical maps of vernacular rights cultures require more diverse and complex methodological tools. In particular, they require a multihued set of methodological tools that would enable scholarly explorations of the following: of the productive and generative work that rights and human rights do in 'most of the world'; of site specific historical and theoretical investigations of the ways in which concepts come into being at particular locations and to document and theorise the political imaginaries these are imbricated in, the political cultures of rights they engender, the intersectionally gendered subjects of rights they bring into being, support but also refuse; and of an accounting of the political stakes, and struggles over rights and human rights in 'most of the world'. Moreover, they require a methodological toolbox that facilitates an analysis of how concepts attach themselves to specific subjects but also how these concepts are seized by those who are not their intended attachments, together with an account of the gendered forms of political subjectivation that these concepts are implicated in but also enable. Finally, the study of vernacular rights cultures requires a methodological toolbox that enables an epistemic accounting of the world-making exercises of subaltern groups.

As a methodological device, a feminist historical ontology directs attention to not only how concepts come into being and are gendered but following Ian Hacking, also how concepts make up people. Consequently, a feminist historical ontology unequivocally locates itself firmly in the imbrication of epistemology and ontology (see Chapter 3) as it works to make explicit the ways in which concepts come into being in different locations and within particular knowledge systems. It tracks their political imaginaries and justificatory premises, the political cultures they enable, the kinds of people they make up, and the politics in which they are invoked and sustained. The work of a feminist historical ontology begins with an insistence that concepts are gendered and that 'making up people' is a gendered exercise, as 'people' are intersectional subjects. By drawing attention to the different and historically specific and located languages of rights/human rights—both literal and conceptual in different parts of the globe, a feminist historical ontology attends to the political imaginaries these languages make available, and to the subjectivities, forms of political subjectivation, conceptions of personhood and the claims for subject status and gender orders they render possible. A feminist historical ontology enables site specific investigations attentive to historical and political specificity of rights politics in 'most of the world' while refusing assumptions of universal translatability or of unidirectional translational practices. Importantly, it tracks the path of power that informs rights politics to shine a light on the intersecting axes of oppressions that characterise the attachment of rights politics to specific gendered subjects.

Practising ethical vigilance (Chapter 3), a feminist historical ontology of *haq* attends to the gendered saturated sites of grassroots political struggles to document the different meanings of *haq* that are mobilised, towards what and by whom? Alongside tracking the forms of subjectification *haq* engenders and the political imaginaries it engages, a feminist historical ontology is attentive to the forms of rights politics and the erasures/silences it puts in place. It seeks to illuminate what *haq* allows, articulates, renders intelligible, refuses, and to highlight how the gendered articulation of concepts/rights exceeds both the purpose and nature of their mobilisation. In other words, a feminist historical ontology of *haq* is explicitly concerned with the processes and discourses of subjectivation and how gendered subjects of rights come into being in the vernacular. The political subjectivation that rights discourses set off are circumscribed by intersectional gender relations. The justificatory premises of *haq* draw attention to the conceptual dynamism of *haq*. But *haq* is neither a neologism for a right and nor is it empty of normative content. It is a conceptual term that upholds particular subjectivities and political and moral imaginaries that bring into being particular subjects of rights and entitlements. These imaginaries of *haq* jostle alongside the rights discourse mandated by the state, which it seeks to revise and expand. The four different political imaginaries of *haq* that I document in this book demonstrate the limitations, narrowness and prejudicial nature of statist rights, not least for intersectionally marked non-normative subjects. I use the term 'jostle' and not 'refusal' (Simpson 2014) to characterise the deployments of *haq* and engagement with the statist discourse because the subaltern subjects in my ethnographies direct their energies at demanding the rights that they feel they are entitled to from the state. As I show in Chapters 4 and 5, the relationship of the state with respect to their rights is complex.

The justificatory premises of *haq* demonstrate that that even though the state is invoked to justify citizenship rights, these rights are in the final instance, non-derivative from the state. What is at stake in these negotiations with the state is to hold the latter accountable for these rights. In short, the state is the assigned and designated duty bearer of these rights but is not the origin of these. In the final instance, therefore, *haq* is non-derivative of the state. Assigning the state as the duty bearer of rights does not make for an outright epistemic refusal of the liberal democratic state and its institutions but for a trenchant critique of the moral and practical failings of the state; for failing to live up to its professed ideals and constitutional duties, and in particular, its failure to uphold women's rights and gender equality. The *sathin*s as well as the Bhil activists (Chapters 4 and 5) draw attention to the intersectional nature of the violence, terror, dispossession and lack of recognition as political subjects and citizens that characterise their life-worlds. What is evident in their narratives is how omnipresent the state is in their personal and as well as public lives, which makes the encounters with the state intimate, coercive but also potentially agential. The encounters with the state leave the *sathin*s to describe the state plainly as gendered, casteist and classist; the Bhil women activists are equally scathing of the state in their recounting of the violence, terror and dispossession from their sacred and ancestral lands. However, like the *sathin*s, the moral regression of the state does not turn them away from exercising their democratic and citizenship rights to representation and to stand for elections under the constitutionally sanctioned quotas and reserved seats in local governing councils. The difficulties, obstructions and coercion they face in exercising their citizenship rights must not fall into an analytical trap of seeing this as a problem of gender and women's rights in 'backward communities'. As I noted in Chapter 5, a failure to recognise the ways in which the state delegitimises and erases Indigenous lives and livelihoods cannot be separated from the overriding nature of conflictual gender relations that the state is actively involved in orchestrating and participating, but also intimately implicated in.

The political imaginaries, critical conceptual vocabularies and political struggles for *haq* are struggles for different possibilities and futures for rights and human rights. They call into being a different sense of justice and citizenship. They refuse the politics of origins while insisting on a politics of democratic accountability that holds the nation state to account. In centring questions of intersectionally experienced oppressions and inequalities, these struggles for *haq* insist on squaring the circle between inequality, justice and human rights but also insist on the epistemic presence of subaltern struggles for rights and human rights.

References

Abu-Lughod, L. (2013). *Do Muslim Women Need Saving?* Cambridge, MA: Harvard University Press.

——— (2010). 'The Active Social Life of "Muslim Women's Rights": A Plea for Ethnography, Not Polemic, with Cases from Egypt and Palestine'. *Journal of Middle East Women's Studies* **6**(1), 1–45.

Ackerly B. A. (2008). *Universal Human Rights in a World of Difference.* Cambridge: Cambridge University Press.

Agamben, G. (1998). *Homo Sacer: Sovereign Power and Bare Life.* Stanford: Stanford University Press.

Agarwal, B. A. (1994). *A Field of One's Own: Gender and Land Rights in South Asia* (Vol. 58). Cambridge: Cambridge University Press.

Aggarwal, M. (2014). 'Activists Up Against FRA Act Dilution'. *DnaIndia.com*, 31 October. Available at https://www.dnaindia.com/india/report-activist-up-against-fra-act-dilution-2030760 (accessed 15 March 2019).

Akhtar A. S. (2006). 'The State as a Landlord in Pakistani Punjab; Peasant Struggles on The Okara Military Farms'. *Journal of Peasant Studies* **333**(3), 479–501.

——— (2019). 'When a Movement Stops Moving: The Okara Peasant Struggle Twenty Years on Critical Asian Studies'. *Commentary* 23. Available at https://criticalasianstudies.org/commentary/2019/11/19/201923-aasim-sajjad-ahktar-when-a-movement-stops-moving-the-okara-peasant-struggle-twenty-years-on.

Alcoff, L. (1991). 'The Problem of Speaking for Others'. *Cultural Critique* **20**, 5–32.

——— (1993). 'How Is Epistemology Political?' In Roger S. Gottlieb (ed.), *Radical Philosophy: Tradition, Counter-Tradition, Politics.* Philadelphia: Temple University Press, 65–85.

All India Reporter of the Supreme Court (1997). SC: 3011. Available at http://ncwapps.nic.in/pdfReports/Sexual%20Harassment%20at%20Workplace%20(English).pdf (accessed on 20 October 2020).

Alexander M. J. and C. T. Mohanty (2010). 'Cartographies of Knowledge and Power: Transnational Feminism as Radical Praxis'. In A. L. Swarr and R. Nagar (eds), *Critical Transnational Feminist Practice.* Albany, NY: SUNY Press, 23–45.

Amin, Samir (1989). *Eurocentrism.* Translated by Russell Moore. London: Zed Books.

Anghie, A. (2019). 'Inequality, Human Rights, and the New International Economic Order'. *Humanity: An International Journal of Human Rights, Humanitarianism, and Development* **10**(3), 429–42.

Anzaldua, G. (1987). *Borderlands/la frontera*. San Francisco, CA: Aunt Lute Books.

Apter, E. (2013). *Against World Literature: On the Politics of Untranslatability*. London and New York: Verso.

Arendt, Hannah (1958). *The Origins of Totalitarianism*. New York: Meridian Books.

——— (1979). *The Origins of Totalitarianism*. San Diego: Harvest Books.

Arya, S. and A.S. Rathore (eds) (2019). *Dalit Feminist Theory: A Reader*. London: Taylor & Francis.

Asad, Talal (2000). 'What Do Human Rights Do? An Anthropological Enquiry'. *Theory and Event* **4**(4). Available at https://muse.jhu.edu/article/32601 (accessed 21 October 2020).

Badiou, A. (2012). *The Rebirth of History: Times of Riots and Uprisings*. London: Verso.

Balakrishnan, R. (2007). 'Pro-human Rights but Anti-poor? A Critical Evaluation of the Indian Supreme Court from a Social Movement Perspective'. *Human Rights Review* **18**(3), 157–86.

Balakrishnan, R. and J. Heintz (2019). 'Human Rights in an Unequal World: Structural Inequalities and the Imperative for Global Cooperation'. *Humanity: An International Journal of Human Rights, Humanitarianism, and Development* **10**(3), 395–403.

Balibar, Étienne (2013 [1994]). *Masses, Classes, Ideas: Studies on Politics and Philosophy Before and After Marx*. New York and London: Routledge.

——— (2002). *Politics and the Other Scene*. London: Verso.

——— (2016). *Citizen Subject: Foundations for Philosophical Anthropology*. Oxford: Oxford University Press.

Banerjee, Kaustav and Partha Saha (2010). 'The NREGA, the Maoists and the Developmental Woes of the Indian State'. *Economic and Political Weekly* **45**(28), 42–7.

Banik, Dan (2010). 'Governing a Giant: The Limits of Judicial Activism on Hunger in India'. *Journal of Asian Public Policy* **3**(3), 263–80.

Bansal, Priyanka (2018). 'Twitter Reacts to Imran Khan's Comment on Feminism & Motherhood'. *TheQuint.com*, 19 June. Available at https://www.thequint.com/neon/social-buzz/imran-khan-feminism-motherhood-social-media (accessed 6 March 2019).

Barkawi, T. (2018). 'From Law to History: The Politics of War And Empire'. *Global Constitutionalism* **7**(3), 315–29.

Barreto, J. M. (ed.) (2014). *Human Rights from a Third World Perspective: Critique, History and International Law*. England: Cambridge Scholars Publishers.

Basu, A. (2005). 'Women, Political Parties and Social Movements in South Asia'. No. 5, UNRISD Occasional Paper.

Bat-Ami Bar On (1993). 'Marginality and Epistemic Privilege'. In L. M. Alcoff and E. Potter (eds), *Feminist Epistemologies*. New York: Routledge, 83–100.

Baxi, U. (2007). *The Future of Human Rights*. Oxford: Oxford University Press.

———. (1985). 'Taking Suffering Seriously: Social Action Litigation in the Supreme Court of India'. *Third World Legal Studies* 4(6), 107–32. Available at: http://scholar.valpo.edu/twls/vol4/iss1/6 (accessed 17 September 2020).

Benhabib, S. (1994). 'Democracy and Difference: Reflections on the Metapolitics of Lyotard and Derrida'. *Journal of Political Philosophy* **2**(1), 1–23.

Bhabha, H. (1994). *The Location of Culture*. London: Routledge.

Bhandari, Vrinda (2019). 'Why Amend the Aadhaar Act without First Passing a Data Protection Bill?' *TheWire.in*, 4 January. Available at https://thewire.in/law/aadhaar-act-amendment-data-protection (accessed 17 September 2020).

Bhargava, R. (2006). 'Indian Democracy and Well Being: Employment as a Right', *Public Culture* **18**(3), 445–51.

Bhavnani, K. K. (1993). 'Tracing the Contours: Feminist Research And Feminist Objectivity'. *Women's Studies International Forum* **16**(2), 95–104.

Bhushan, Prashant (2004). 'Supreme Court and PIL: Changing Perspectives under Liberalisation'. *Economic and Political Weekly* **39**(18), 1770–4.

Bhuwania A. (2014). 'Courting the People: The Rise of Public Interest Litigation in Post-Emergency India'. *Comparative Studies of South Asia, Africa and the Middle East* **34**(2), 314–35.

Biehl, J. (2013). 'The Judicialization of Biopolitics: Claiming the Right to Pharmaceuticals in Brazilian Courts'. *American Ethnologist* **40**(3), 419–36.

Blaser, M. (2013). 'Ontological Conflicts and the Stories of Peoples in Spite of Europe: Toward a Conversation on Political Ontology'. *Current Anthropology* **54**(5), 547–68.

Bokil, Milind (2000). 'Drought in Rajasthan: In Search of a Perspective'. *Economic and Political Weekly* **35**(48), 4171–5.

Bornstein, E. and A. Sharma (2016). 'The Righteous and the Rightful: The Technomoral Politics of NGOs, Social Movements, and the State in India'. *American Ethnologist* **43**(1), 76–90.

Bradley, A. S. (2019). 'Human Rights Racism'. *Harvard Human Rights Journal* **32**(1), 1–58.

Brett, Annabel S. (2003). 'The Development of the Idea of Citizen's Rights'. In Quentin Skinner and Bo Strath (eds), *States and Citizens*. Cambridge: Cambridge University Press, 97–112.

Briggs, Laura (2008). 'Activisms and Epistemologies: Problems for Transnationalisms'. *Social Text* **26**(4), 79–95.

Brown, W. (1995). *States of Injury: Power and Freedom in Late Modernity.* Princeton, NJ: Princeton University Press.

———— (2000). 'Suffering Rights as Paradoxes'. *Constellations* **7**(2), 230–41.

———— (2004). '"The Most We Can Hope For ..."': Human Rights and the Politics of Fatalism.' *The South Atlantic Quarterly* **103**(2), 451–63.

———— (2015). *Undoing the Demos: Neoliberalism's Stealth Revolution.* Cambridge, MA: MIT Press.

Bruce-Jones, E. (2015). 'Death Zones, Comfort Zones: Queering the Refugee Question'. *International Journal on Minority and Group Rights* **22**(1), 101–127.

Bruyneel, K. (2007). *The Third Space of Sovereignty: The Postcolonial Politics of Indigenous relations.* Minneapolis: University of Minnesota Press.

Burchill, G. (1996). 'Liberal Government and the Techniques of the Self'. In A. Barry, T. Osborne and N. Rose (eds), *Foucault and Political Reason.* London: Routledge.

Burke, R. (2010). *Decolonization and the Evolution of International Human Rights.* Philadelphia, PA: University of Pennsylvania Press.

Butler, J. and Athanasiou, A. (2013). *Dispossession: The Performative in the Political.* John Wiley & Sons.

Butler, J. (1997). *Excitable Speech: A Politics of the Performative.* London.

———— (2015). *Notes toward a Performative Theory of Assembly.* Cambridge, MA: Harvard University Press.

Butt, Shafiq (2017). 'Bilawal Says PPP Will Support Tenants of Okara Military Farms'. *Dawn.com*, 21 September. Available at https://www.dawn.com/news/1359071 (accessed 24 November 2020).

Byrd, J. A. and M. Rothberg (2011). 'Between Subalternity and Indigeneity: Critical Categories for Postcolonial Studies'. *Interventions* **13**(1), 1–12.

Byrd, Jodi A. (2011). 'Been to the Nation, Lord, But I Couldn't Stay There'. *Interventions* **13**(1), 31–52.

Campaign for Survival and Dignity (2003). 'Endangered Symbiosis: Evictions and India's Forest Communities: Report of the Jan Sunwai'. Public Hearing July 19–20, 2003. Dahanu: Campaign for Survival and Dignity.

Carby, H. (2015). 'Foreword'. In M. R. Trouillot, *Silencing the Past: Power and The Production of History.* Boston: Beacon Press, xi–xiii.

Census of India (2011a). Provisional Tables, Registrar General of India. Available at http://www.censusindia.gov.in/2011-prov-results/prov_results_paper1_india.html.

———— (2011b). District Census Handbook, Udaipur Village and Town wise Primary Census Abstract (PCA) SERIES-09 PART XII – B, Government of India. Available at https://censusindia.gov.in/2011census/dchb/0832_PART_B_DCHB_UDAIPUR.pdf (accessed 06 October 2020).

Chakrabarty, D. (2002). *Habitations of Modernity: Essays in the Wake of Subaltern Studies*. Chicago: University of Chicago Press.

—— (2000). *Provincializing Europe: Postcolonial Thought and Historical Difference-New Edition*. Princeton, NJ: Princeton University Press.

Chandra, Rajshree (2019). 'How the FRA Is Being Cut Down to Size, and Tribals With It'. *TheWire.in*, 23 February. Available at https://thewire.in/rights/how-the-fra-is-being-cut-down-to-size-and-tribals-with-it.

—— (2016). *The Cunning of Rights*. Delhi: Oxford University Press.

Chandra, U. and D. Taghioff (eds) (2016). *Staking Claims: The Politics of Social Movements in Contemporary Rural India*. New Delhi: Oxford University Press.

Charlotte, Bunch (1990). 'Women's Rights as Human Rights: Toward a Re-Vision of Human Rights'. *Human Rights Quarterly* **12**(48), 486–98.

Chatterjee, P. (ed.) (1996). *State and Politics in India*. Oxford: Oxford University Press.

—— (2004). *The Politics of the Governed*. Chichester: Columbia University Press.

Cheah, P. (2006). *Inhuman Conditions: On Cosmopolitanism and Human Rights*. Cambridge, MA: Harvard University Press.

—— (2014). 'Second Generation Rights as Biopolitical Rights'. In C. Douzinas and C. Gearty (eds), *The Meanings Rights: The Philosophy and Social Theory of Rights*. Cambridge, UK: Cambridge University Press, 215–32.

Chow, Rey (2006). *The Age of the World Target: Self Referentiality in War, Theory and Comparative Work*. Durham and London: Duke University Press.

—— (2003). 'Where Have All the Natives Gone'. In R. Lewis and S. Milles (eds), *Feminist Postcolonial Theory: A Reader*. Edinburgh: Edinburgh University Press, 324–49.

Code L. (2012). 'Taking Subjectivity into Account'. In C. W. Ruitenberg and D. C. Phillips (eds), *Education, Culture and Epistemological Diversity*. Dordrecht: Springer, 85–100.

Comaroff, J. and J. L. Comaroff (2012). *Theory from the South: Or How Euro America is Evolving Toward Africa*. London: Paradigm.

Connell R. (2014). 'Using Southern Theory: Decolonizing Social Thought in Theory, Research and Application'. *Planning Theory* **13**(2), 210–23. doi:10.1177/1473095213499216.

Cornwall, A. and M. Molyneux (2006). 'The Politics of Rights: Dilemmas for a Feminist Praxis'. *Third World Quarterly* **27**(7), 1175–91.

Cornwall, A. and C. Nyamu-Musembi (2004). 'Putting the "Rights-Based Approach" to Development into Perspective'. *Third World Quarterly* **25**(8), 1415–37.

Cowan, Jane K. and Richard A. Wilson (eds) (2001). *Culture and Rights: Anthropological Perspectives*. Cambridge: Cambridge University Press.

Crenshaw K. (1989). 'Demarginalizing the Intersection of Race and Sex: A Black Feminist Critique of Antidiscrimination Doctrine, Feminist Theory, and Antiracist Politics'. *University of Chicago Legal Forum*, 139–67.

———— (2000). 'Were the Critics Right about Rights? Reassessing the American Debate about Rights in Post-Reform Era'. In Mahmood Mamdani (ed), *Beyond Rights Talk and Culture Talk*. Cape Town: David Phillip Publishers, 61–74.

Cruikshank, B. (1999). *The Will to Empower: Democratic Citizens and Other Subjects.* Ithaca, NY: Cornell University Press.

Cusicanqui, S. R. (2012). 'Ch'ixinakax utxiwa: A Reflection on the Practices and Discourses of Decolonization'. *South Atlantic Quarterly* **111**(1), 95–109.

Datar, C. (1999). 'Non-Brahmin Renderings of Feminism in Maharashtra: Is it a More Emancipatory Force?' *Economic and Political Weekly* **34**(41), 2964–68.

Daily Times (2016). 'PPP Senator Lambasts Mistreatment of Okara Farmers, Issue Referred to HR Committee'. *DailyTimes.com.pk*, 19 May. Available at https://dailytimes.com.pk/81273/ppp-senator-lambasts-mistreatment-of-okara-farmers-issue-referred-to-hr-committee/.

Darwall, S. L. (1977). 'Two Kinds of Respect'. *Ethics* **88**(1), 36–49.

Davidson, A. I. (2011). 'In Praise of Counter-Conduct'. *History of the Human Sciences* **24**(4), 25–41.

De la Cadena, M. (2010). 'Indigenous Cosmopolitics in the Andes: Conceptual Reflections Beyond "Politics"'. *Cultural Anthropology* **25**(2), 334–70.

De Sousa Santos, B. (2015). *Epistemologies of the South: Justice Against Epistemicide.* Routledge.

De Waal A. (1997). *Famine Crimes: Politics and the Disaster Relief Industry in Africa.* London: Afr. Rights.

Desai, M. (2003). 'Starting the Battle'. *Combat Law* **3**(5).

Dirlik, A. (1999). 'Place-Based Iimagination: Globalism and the Politics of Place. Review.' *Historical Systems and Civilizations* **22**(2), 151–87.

Douzinas, C. (2000). *The End of Human Rights: Critical Thought at the Turn of the Century.* Bloomsbury Publishing.

Drèze, Jean. (2004). 'Democracy and the Right to Food'. *Economic and Political Weekly* **39**(17), 1723–31.

Drèze, J. and R. Khera. (2017). 'Recent Social Security Initiatives in India'. *World Development* **98**, 555–72.

Drèze, J. and A. Sen. (2013). *An Uncertain Glory: India and Its Contradictions.* Princeton, NJ: Princeton University Press.

Drèze, Jean, Prankur Gupta, Reetika Khera and Isabel Pimenta (2018). 'Casting the Net: India's Public See Distribution System after the Food Security Act'. 13 May. Available at https://ssrn.com/abstract=3177691 or http://dx.doi.org/10.2139/ssrn.3177691 (accessed 21 April 2020).

Dunford, R. (2016). *The Politics of Transnational Peasant Struggle: Resistance, Rights and Democracy.* London: Rowman & Littlefield.

———— (2017). 'Peasant Activism and the Rise of Food Sovereignty: Decolonising and Democratising Norm Diffusion?' *European Journal of International Relations* **23**(1), 145–67.

Dunford, R. and S. Madhok (2015). 'On Vernacular Rights Cultures and the "Right to Have Rights"'. *Citizenship Studies* **19**(6–7), 605–19.

Eaton, R. M. (2019). *India in the Persianate Age: 1000–1765*. Oakland, CA: University of California Press.

Elwin, Verrier (1937). 'Myths and Dreams of the Baigas of Central India'. *Man* 37, 13-13.

Escobar A. (2017). *Designs for the Pluriverse: Radical Interdependence, Autonomy, and the Making of Worlds*. Durham, NC: Duke University Press.

———— (2005). *Encountering Development: The Making and Unmaking of the Third World* (Vol. 1). Princeton, NJ: Princeton University Press.

———— (2018). *Designs for the Pluriverse: Radical Interdependence, Autonomy, and the Making of Worlds*. Durham, NC: Duke University Press.

Fanon, F. (1963). *The Wretched of the Earth*. New York: Grove Inc.

Faruqi, S. R. (2003). 'A Long History of Urdu Literary Culture, Part 1: Naming and Placing a Literary Culture'. In Sheldon Pollock (ed.), *Literary Cultures in History: Reconstructions from South Asia*. Berkeley, California: University of California Press, 805–63.

Fassin, D. (2011). *Humanitarian Reason: A Moral History of the Present*. Berkeley, California: University of California Press.

Feinberg, J. (1970). 'The Nature and Value of Rights'. *Journal of Value Inquiry* **4**(4), 243–60.

Feldman I. (2012). 'The Humanitarian Condition: Palestinian Refugees and the Politics of Living'. *Humanity: An International Journal of Human Rights, Humanitarianism, and Development* **3**(2), 155–72.

Fergusson, J. (1773). *A Dictionary of the Hindostan Language in Two Parts: i. English and Hindostan, ii. Hindostan and English. The Latter Containing a Great Variety of Phrases, to Point out the Idiom, and Facilitate to Which is Prefixed a Grammar of the Hindostan Language*. London: T. Cadell.

Fernandes, Walter (2009). 'Displacement and Alienation from Common Property Resources'. In Lyla Mehta (ed.), *Displaced by Development*. New Delhi, Thousand Oaks, London, Singapore: Sage, 105–32.

Forest Department Rajasthan (2014). 'Management Plan of Phulwari Ki Naal-2013-2022-23'. Udaipur, Rajasthan.

Foucault, M. (1994). In Paul Rabinow (eds), *Ethics: Subjectivity and Truth*. London: Penguin.

———— (2004). *Security, Territory, and Population: Lectures at the Collège de France 1977–1988*. London: Palgrave MacMillan.

———— (2000). 'The Subject and Power'. In James D. Faubion (eds), *Essential Works of Foucault, 1954–84*, Vol. 3, *Power*, Robert Hurley et al. (trans.), 326-48. New York: New Press.

Frankenberg, R. and L. Mani (1993). 'Crosscurrents, Crosstalk: Race, "Postcoloniality" and the Politics of Location'. *Cultural Studies* 7(2), 292–310.

Fraser, N. (2005). 'Mapping the Feminist Imagination: From Redistribution to Recognition to Representation'. *Constellations: An International Journal of Critical and Democratic Theory* 12(3), 295–307.

Fricker, Miranda (2007). *Epistemic Injustice: Power and the Ethics of Knowing*. Oxford: Oxford University Press.

Fukuda-Parr, S. (2012). 'The Right to Development: Reframing a New Discourse for the Twenty-First Century'. *Social Research* 79(4), 839–64.

Gandhi, L. (2011). 'The Pauper's Gift: Postcolonial Theory and the New Democratic Dispensation'. *Public Culture* 23(1), 27–38.

Gandhi, N. and N. Shah (1992). *The Issues at Stake: Theory and Practice in the Contemporary Women's Movement in India*. New Delhi: Kali for Women.

Geertz, C. (1983). *Local Knowledge*. London: Fontana Press.

Gewirth, Alan (2001). 'Are All Rights Positive?'. *Philosophy & Public Affairs* 30(3), 332.

Gibb, H. A. R. (1960). In Hamilton Alexander Rosskeen (eds), *Encyclopedia of Islam*, Volume III. Leiden: Brill.

Gilchrist, John Borthwick (1790). *A Dictionary of English and Hindostanee*. Calcutta: Cooper and Upjohn.

Gilroy, P. (2010). *Darker Than Blue: On the Moral Economies of Black Atlantic Culture*. Harvard University Press.

Glasse, Cyril (ed.) (2001). *The New Encyclopaedia of Islam*. Walnut Creek, CA: Altamira.

Global Hunger Index. 2019. 'India'. GlobalHungerIndex.org. Available at https://www.globalhungerindex.org/india.html (accessed 20 October 2020).

GoI (Government of India) (2011a). 'Linguistic Survey of India, Rajasthan (Part 1)'. Ministry of Home Affairs, Government of India. Available at http://www.censusindia.gov.in/2011-documents/lsi/lsi_Rajasthan/4_introduction.pdf (accessed 3 September 2015).

———— (2011b). The Indian Census. Office of the Registrar General & Census Commissioner, India, Ministry of Home Affairs. http://www.censusindia.gov.in/2011census/C-01.html (accessed 6 March 2019).

———— (2013). 'The Constitution of India (As Amended Upto First July, 2013)'. Ministry of Law and Justice, Government of India. Available at http://legislative.gov.in/sites/default/files/urdu_constitution_complete091216.pdf.

———— (2015). 'Press Report from the Information Bureau'. Available at http://pib.nic.in/newsite/PrintRelease.aspx?relid=117218 (last accessed 7 May 2018).

———— (2018). 'Status Report on Implementation of the Scheduled Tribes and Other Traditional Forest Dwellers (Recognition of Forest Rights) Act, 2006 [for the period ending 31.05.2018]'. Ministry of Tribal Affairs, Government of India. Available at https://www.tribal.nic.in/FRA/data/MPRMay2018.pdf.

———— (2019a). 'The Constitution of India (English-Manipuri)'. Ministry of Law and Justice, Government of India. Available at http://legislative.gov.in/coi-regional-language/manipuri.

———— (2019b). 'Women and Men in India: A Statistical Compilation of Gender Related Indicators in India'. Social Statistics Division, Ministry of Statistics and Programme Implementation. Available at http://www.mospi. gov.in/sites/default/files/publication_reports/Women_and_Men_31_%20 Mar_2020.pdf.

———— (2013). Statistical Profile of Scheduled Tribes in India, Ministry of Tribal Affairs. Available at https://tribal.nic.in/ST/StatisticalProfileofSTs2013.pdf (last accessed 04 November 2020).

———— (2018). Ministry of Social Justice and Empowerment. *Handbook on Social Welfare Statistics.* Available at http://socialjustice.nic.in/writereaddata/UploadFile/HANDBOOKSocialWelfareStatistice2018.pdf (last accessed 04 November 2020).

———— (2017). Ministry of Statistics and Programme Implementation. 'Chapter 5: Participation in Decision Making'. Available at http://mospi.nic.in/sites/default/files/reports_and_publication/statistical_publication/social_statistics/WM17Chapter5.pdf (accessed 23 November 2020).

———— (2002). Planning Commission. *Tenth Five Year Plan 2002–07*, 11. Available at: http://planningcommission.nic.in/plans/planrel/fiveyr/10th/volume2/v2_ch4_2.pdf (accessed 12 September 2020).

GoI and UNDP (2014). 'Forest Rights Act, 2006: Act, Rules and Guidelines'. Ministry of Tribal Affairs, Government of India and United Nations Development Programme, India. Available at https://tribal.nic.in/FRA/data/FRARulesBook.pdf.

Golder, B. (2015). *Foucault and the Politics of Rights.* Stanford: Stanford University Press.

Goodale, M. (2006). 'Introduction to "Anthropology and Human Rights in a New Key"'. *American Anthropologist* **108**(1), 1–8.

Goodale, M. and S. E. Merry (eds) (2007). *The Practice of Human Rights: Tracking Law between the Global and the Local.* Cambridge University Press.

Goodale, M. and N. Postero (2013). *Neoliberalism Interrupted: Social Change and Contested Governance in Contemporary Latin America.* Stanford: Stanford University Press.

GoP (Government of Pakistan) (2016). 'The Interim Report on Okara Military Farms'. National Commission For Human Rights, Government of Pakistan, 27 June. Available at http://csjpak.org/wp-content/uploads/2017/11/Okara_Interim_report_3.pdf.

———— (1998). Pakistan Bureau of Statistics. 'The World Factbook: South Asia: Pakistan'. Available at https://www.cia.gov/library/publications/the-world-factbook/geos/pk.html (accessed 15 March 2015).

Gordon, Colin (1991). 'Governmental Rationality: An Introduction'. In Graham Burchill, Colin Gordon and Peter Miller (eds.), *The Foucault Effect: Studies in Governmentality*. Chicago: University of Chicago Press.

Government of Rajasthan (2011). 'Department of Rural Development and Panchayati Raj, Rajasthan Panchayati Raj: Modification of Provisions in Their Application to the Scheduled Areas Rules, 2011'. Available at http://www.rajpanchayat. rajasthan.gov.in/Portals/_default/PESARules2011.pdf (accessed 7 May 2018).

———— (2016). 'Letter Written to Union Ministry of Rural Development. No. F 1 (8) RD/NREGA?Misc?56074/2014'. Available at http://nrega.nic.in/netnrega/ writereaddata/Circulars/1671Rajasthan.pdf (accessed 7 May 2018).

———— (2018). 'Rajasthan Social Accountability Bill, 2018'. Available at http:// rajasthan.gov.in/wp-content/uploads/2019/02/SA-Bill-Draft.pdf.

Graeber, D. (2015). 'Radical Alterity Is Just Another Way of Saying "Reality": A Reply to Eduardo Viveiros de Castro'. *HAU: Journal of Ethnographic Theory* **5**(2), 1–41.

Grebmer, K. von, J. Bernstein, R. Mukerji, F. Patterson, M. Wiemers, R. Ní Chéilleachair, C. Foley, S. Gitter, K. Ekstrom and H. Fritschel (2019). *2019 Global Hunger Index: The Challenge of Hunger and Climate Change*. Bonn: Welthungerhilfe; Dublin: Concern Worldwide.

Grewal, I. (2005) *Transnational America: Feminisms, Diasporas, Neoliberalisms*. Durham, NC: Duke University Press.

Grewal I. and C. Kaplan (1994). 'Introduction: Transnational Feminist Practices and Questions of Postmodernity'. In Inderpal Grewal and Caren Kaplan (eds), *Scattered Hegemonies: Postmodernity and Transnational Feminist Practices*. Minneapolis: University of Minnesota Press, 1–33.

Guha, R. (1983). *Elementary Aspects of Peasant Insurgency in Colonial India*. Delhi: Oxford University Press.

———— (1983). *The Prose of Counter Insurgency, Subaltern Studies Volume II*. Delhi, Oxford, New York: Oxford University Press.

———— (1989). *The Unquiet Woods: Ecological Change and Peasant Resistance in the Himalaya*. Berkeley: University of California Press.

Guha, R. and G. C. Spivak (eds) (1989). *Selected Subaltern Studies*. New York: Oxford University Press.

Gündoğdu, A. (2014). 'A Revolution in Rights: Reflections on the Democratic Invention of the Rights of Man'. *Law, Culture and the Humanities* **10**(3), 367–79.

Guru, G. (1995). 'Dalit Women Talk Differently'. *Economic and Political Weekly* **30**(41–42), 2548–50.

Hacking, I. (2002). *Historical Ontology*. Cambridge, MA: Harvard University Press.

Haraway, Donna (1988). 'Situated Knowledges; the Science Question in Feminism and the Privilege of Partial Perspective'. *Feminist Studies* **14**(3), 581–607.

Harding S. (1993). 'Rethinking Standpoint Epistemology: What Is "Strong Objectivity?"' In L. Alcoff and E. Potter (eds), *Feminist Epistemologies*. New York: Routledge, 49–82.

Hartsock, N. C. (1983). 'The Feminist Standpoint: Developing the Ground for a Specifically Feminist Historical Materialism'. In Sandra Harding and Merrill B. P. Hintikka (eds), *Discovering Reality*. Dordrecht: Springer, 283–310.

Hemmings, C. (2005). 'Invoking Affect: Cultural Theory and the Ontological Turn'. *Cultural Studies* **19**(5), 548–67.

———— (2011). *Why Stories Matter: The Political Grammar of Feminist Theory*. Durham, NC: Duke University Press.

Hill Collins, Patricia (2000). 'Black Feminist Epistemology'. In *Black Feminist Thought: Knowledge, Consciousness and the Politics of Empowerment*. New York: Routledge, 251–71.

Hirsch, Susan F. (1998). *Pronouncing and Persevering: Gender and the Discourses of Disputing in an African Islamic Court*. Chicago: University of Chicago Press.

Hirschl, Ran (2000). '"Negative" Rights vs. "Positive" Entitlements: A Comparative Study of Judicial Interpretations of Rights in an Emerging Neo-Liberal Economic Order'. *Human Rights Quarterly* **22**(4), 1060–98.

Hodžić, S. (2017). *The Twilight of Cutting: African Activism and Life after NGOs*. California: University of California Press.

Hohfeld, W. (1978). *Fundamental Legal Conceptions*. Westport: Greenwood Press.

Holbraad, Martin and Morten Axel Pederson (2017). *The Ontological Turn: An Anthropolgical Exposition*. Cambridge, Cambridge University Press.

Holzberg, B. (2018). The Multiple Lives of Affect: A Case Study of Commercial Surrogacy'. *Body & Society* **24**(4), 32–57.

Hooks, Bell (2000). *Feminist Theory: From Margin to Center*. London: Pluto Press.

Htun, M. and L. Weldon (2018). *The Logics of Gender Justice*. Cambridge, UK: Cambridge University Press.

Human Rights Watch (2004). 'Soiled Hands: The Pakistan Army's Repression of the Punjab Farmers' Movement'. Available at https://www.hrw.org/ report/2004/07/ 20/soiled-hands-pakistan-armys-repression-punjab-farmers-movement.

Hunt, Lynn (2007). *Inventing Human Rights: A History*. New York: WW Norton & Company.

Hussain, F. (2011). *The Judicial System of Pakistan*. Islamabad: Supreme Court of Pakistan. Available at https://www.supremecourt.gov.pk/ downloads_judgements/all_downloads/Judicial_System_of_Pakistan/ thejudicialsystemofPakistan.pdf (accessed 20 October 2020).

Ignatieff, M. (2001). *Human Rights as Politics and Idolatry*. Princeton, NJ: Princeton University Press.

Ilumoka, A. (2006). 'Beyond Human Rights Fundamentalism: The Challenges of Consensus Building in the 21st Century'. Draft Thematic Paper, *What Next?* Dag Hammerskjold Foundation, Uppsala.

Imran, Myra (2019). 'The Okara Dispute Has Been Settled'. *The News*. 29 March. Available at https://www.thenews.com.pk/print/450163 (accessed 10 October 2020).

Indian Express (2016). 'New Surrogacy Bill Bars Married Couples with Kids, NRIs, Gays, Live-Ins, Foreigners'. 25 August. Available at http:// indianexpress. com/article/india/india-news-india/surrogacy-bill-sushma-swaraj-married-couples-can-now-opt-homosexuals/ (accessed 6 March 2019).

Irudayam, Aloysius, Jayshree P. Mangubhai and Joel G. Lee. 2012. *Dalit Women Speak Out: Caste, Class and Gender Violence in India*. New Delhi: Zubaan.

Isin, E. F. (2002). *Being Political: Genealogies of Citizenship*. Minnesota: University of Minnesota Press.

Isin, E.F. and G. M. Nielsen (eds) (2008). *Acts of Citizenship*. Zed Books Ltd..

Isutzu, T. (1965). *The Concept of Belief in Islamic Theology*. Yokohma: Yurindo Publishing.

Jaffrelot, C. (2015). *The Pakistan Paradox: Instability and Resilience*. London: Hurst & Co Publishers.

James, C. L. R. (2001). *The Black Jacobins: Toussaint L'Ouverture and the San Domingo Revolution*. London: Penguin.

———. (1989). *The Black Jacobins: Toussaint L'Ouverture and the San Domingo Revolution*. New York: Vintage Books.

Jayal N. G. (1999). *Democracy and the State: Welfare, Secularism, Development*. Oxford/ New Delhi: Oxford University Press.

——— (2013). *Citizenship and Its Discontents: An Indian History*. Cambridge, MA: Harvard University Press.

Jena, M. (2013). 'Voices from Niyamgiri'. *Economic and Political Weekly* **48**(35). https://www.epw.in/journal/2013/35/web-exclusives/voices-niyamgiri.html (accessed 20 October 2020).

Jenkins, R. and A. M. Goetz (1999). 'Accounts and accountability: Theoretical Implications of the Right-To-Information Movement in India'. *Third World Quarterly* **20**(3), 603–22.

Jensen, S. (2016). *The Making of International Human Rights: The 1960s, Decolonization, and the Reconstruction of Global Values*. Cambridge: Cambridge University Press.

John, Mary E. (1996). 'Gender and Development in India, 1970s–1990s: Some Reflections on the Constitutive Role of Contexts'. *Economic and Political Weekly* **31**(47), 3071–77.

Junaidi, Ikram (2019). 'Dispute over Okara Military Farms May Be Settled Soon'. *Dawn.com*, 1 January. Available at https://www.dawn.com/news/1454767(.

Jones, P. (2000). 'Human Rights and Diverse Cultures: Continuity or Discontinuity?'. *Review of International Social and Political Philosophy* **3**, 27–50.

Kalpagam, U. (2000). 'The Women's Movement in India, Today: New Agendas and Old Problems'. *Feminist Studies* **26**(3), 645–60.

Kannan, K. P. (2018). 'Macro-Economic Aspects of Inequality and Poverty in India'. In Alpa Shah, J. Lerche, R. Axelby, D. Benbabaali, B. Donegan, J. Raj and V. Thakur (eds), *Ground Down by Growth: Tribe, Caste, Class, and Inequality in Twenty-First Century India*. London: Pluto Press, 32–48.

Kaplan, C. (1994). 'The Politics of Location as Transnational Feminist Critical Practice'. In Inderpal Grewal and Caren Kaplan (eds), *Scattered Hegemonies: Postmodernity and Transnational Feminist Practices*. Minneapolis and London: University of Minnesota Press, 137–52.

Kapur, R. and C. Cossman. (1996). *Subversive Sites: Feminist Engagements with Law in India*. New Delhi: Sage Publications.

Kapur, R. (2006). 'Human Rights in the 21st century: Take a Walk on the Dark Side'. *Sydney Law Review* **28**(4), 665–87.

——— (2013, 2005). *Erotic Justice: Law and the New Politics of Postcolonialism*. London: Taylor and Francis; New Delhi: Permanent Black.

——— (2018). *Gender, Alterity and Human Rights: Freedom in a Fishbowl*. Cheltenham: Edward Elgar Publishing.

Karlsson, B. G. (2003). 'Anthropology and the "Indigenous Slot" Claims to and Debates about Indigenous Peoples' Status in India'. *Critique of Anthropology* **23**(4), 403–23.

Katzenstein, M., S. Kothari and U. Mehta. (2001). 'Social Movement Politics in India: Institutions, Interests and Identities'. In A. Kohli (ed.), *The Success of India's Democracy*. Cambridge, UK: Cambridge University Press, 242–69.

Kaviraj, S. (2010). *The Imaginary Institution of India*. New York: Columbia University Press.

Khan, A. (2018). *The Women's Movement in Pakistan: Activism, Islam and Democracy*. Bloomsbury Publishing.

Khan, A. and N. Kirmani (2018). 'Moving Beyond the Binary: Gender-based Activism in Pakistan'. *Feminist Dissent* (3), 151–91.

Khan, S. R. and A. S. Akhtar (2014). *The Military and Denied Development in the Pakistani Punjab: An Eroding Social Consensus*. London: Anthem Press.

Khan, H. (2016). 'Rajasthan: Over 1.2 Crore Names Removed from Food Security Beneficiary List, Claim Officials'. *Indian Express*, updated 20 August 2018. Available at https://indianexpress.com/article/india/india-news-india/rajasthan-over-1-2-cr-names-removed-from-food-security-beneficiary-list-claim-officials/ (accessed 20 October 2020).

Khan, Waqas A. (2018). '"Left Without Support After Asma's Death", Peasant Movement Now Faces Its Leader's 10-Year Prison Term'. *Daily Times*, 29 June. Available at https://dailytimes.com.pk/259508/left-without-support-after-asmas-death-peasant-movement-now-faces-its-leaders-10-year-prison-term/.

Khera, R. and Nayak, N. (2009). 'Women Workers and Perceptions of the National Rural Employment Guarantee Act'. *Economic and Political Weekly* **44**(43), 49–57.

Khera, Reetika. (2008). 'Empowerment Guarantee Act'. *Economic and Political Weekly* **43**(35), 8–10.

——— (2017). 'Four Videos That Show Why Rajasthan Needs to Desperately Fix Its Public Distribution System'. *Scroll.in*, 9 March. Available at https://scroll.in/article/830785/four-videos-that-show-why-rajasthan-needs-to-desperately-fix-its-public-distribution-system (accessed 4 January 2018).

——— (2011). *The Battle for Employment Guarantee*. New Delhi: Oxford University Press.

——— (2013). Democratic Politics and Legal Rights: Employment guarantee and food security in India, IEG (Working Paper No. 327, 2–21). Available at http://web.iitd.ac.in/~reetika/WP326democraticpolitics.pdf.

Kishore, A. and S. Chakrabarti. (2015). 'Is More Inclusive More Effective?' The "New Style" Public Distribution System in India'. *Food Policy* 55: 117–30.

Kiss, Elizabeth. (1997). 'Alchemy or Fool's Gold: Assessing Feminist Doubts about Rights'. In Mary Lyndon Shanley and Uma Narayan (eds), *Reconstructing Political Theory: Feminist Perspectives*. University Park: The Pennsylvania State University Press. 1–24.

Koopman, C. and T. Matza. (2013). 'Putting Foucault to Work: Analytic and Concept in Foucaultian Inquiry'. *Critical Inquiry* **39**(4), 817–40.

Koopman, C. (2015). 'Two Uses of Michel Foucault in Political Theory: Concepts and Methods in Giorgio Agamben and Ian Hacking'. *Constellations* **22**(4), 571–85.

Kotwal, Asha and Thenmozhi Soundararajan. 2014 'Dalit Women, Sexual Violence and the Geography of Caste: A Journey towards Liberation—An Interview with Asha Kowtal and Thenmozhi Soundararajan'. *The Feminist Wire*, 1 May. Available at https://thefeministwire.com/2014/05/dalit-women-sexual-violence/ (accessed 9 June 2021).

Krishnaswamy, M. (2005). 'One Step Forward, Two Steps Back'. *Economic and Political Weekly* **40**(47), 4899–901.

Kuchay, Bilal (2019). 'Poets Celebrated in Pakistan Inspire India's Protesters'. *AlJazeera.com*, 28 December. Available at https://www.aljazeera.com/news/2019/12/poets-celebrated-pakistan-inspire-india-protesters-191227121952494.html.

Kumar, K. and J. M. Kerr (2012). 'Democratic Assertions: The Making of India's Recognition of Forest Rights Act'. *Development and Change* **43**(3), 751–71.

Kumar, Rajat (2016). 'Rajasthan's Citizens Are on a Unique Journey to Demand Govt. Action on Pressing Issues'. YouthKiAwaaz.com, 24 February. Available at https://www.youthkiawaaz.com/2016/02/jawabdehi-yatra-rajasthan-accountability-law/ (accessed 3 January 2018).

Kurup, Saira (2006). 'Four Women India Forgot'. *Times of India*, 7 May. Available at https://timesofindia.indiatimes.com/home/sunday-times/deep-focus/Four-women-India-forgot/articleshow/1519056.cms (accessed 21 October 2020).

Lata, P.M. (2015). 'Silenced by Manu and "Mainstream" Feminism: Dalit-Bahujan Women and their History.' Available at https://roundtableindia.co.in/index. php?ption=com_content&view=article&id=8177:silenced-by-manu-and-mainstream-feminism-dalit-bahujan-women-andtheir-history&catid=120:ge nder&Itemid=133 (accessed 20 October 2020).

Lawrence Rosen (1980). 'Equity and Discretion in a Modern Islamic Legal System' *Law and Society Review* **15**(2): 217–45.

Lefebvre, A. (2018). *Human Rights and the Care of the Self.* Durham, NC: Duke University Press.

Levitt, P. and S. Merry (2009). 'Vernacularization on the Ground: Local Uses of Global Women's Rights in Peru, China, India and the United States'. *Global Networks* **9**(4), 441–61.

Li, T. M. (2007). *The Will to Improve: Governmentality, Development, and the Practice of Politics.* Durham, NC: Duke University Press.

Lowe, L. (2015). *The Intimacies of Four Continents.* Durham, NC: Duke University Press.

Lorde, Audre (2001). 'The Masters Tools Will Never Dismantle the Master's House'. In Cherríe Moraga and Gloria Anzaldua (eds), *This Bridge Called My Back: Writings by Radical Women of Color.* Massachusetts: Perspehone Press, 98–101.

Lugones, M. (2007). 'Heterosexualism and the Colonial/Modern Gender System'. *Hypatia* **22**(1), 186–219.

——— (2010). 'Toward a Decolonial Feminism'. *Hypatia* **25**(4), 742–59.

Madhok, S. (2010). '"Rights Talk" and the Feminist Movement in India'. In M. Roces and L. Edwards (eds), *Women's Movements in Asia: Feminisms and Transnational Activism.* London: Routledge, 224–42.

——— (2009). 'Five Notions of Haq: Exploring Vernacular Rights Cultures in South Asia'. LSE Gender Institute. New Working Paper Series (25), 1–52.

——— (2013). *Rethinking Agency: Developmentalism, Gender and Rights.* New Delhi: Routledge India.

——— (2015). *Developmentalism, Gender and Rights: From a Politics of Origins to a Politics of Meanings.* In J. Drydyk and A. Peetush (eds), *Human Rights: India and the West.* New Delhi: Oxford University Press, 95–119.

———— (2017). 'On Vernacular Rights Cultures and the Political Imaginaries of Haq'. *Humanity: An International Journal of Human Rights, Humanitarianism, and Development* 8(3), 485–509.

Madhok, S. and Rai, Shirin M. (2012). 'Agency, Injury and Transgressive Politics in Neoliberal Times'. *Signs: Journal of Women and Culture in Society* 37(3), 645–69.

Mahmood, Saba (2005). *The Politics of Piety*. Princeton: Princeton University Press.

Maldonado-Torres, N. (2007). 'On the Coloniality of Being: Contributions to the Development of a Concept'. *Cultural Studies* 21(2–3), 240–70.

———— (2017). 'On the Coloniality of Human Rights'. *Revista Crítica de Ciências Sociais* (114), 117–36.

Manfredi, Z. (2013). 'Recent Histories and Uncertain Futures: Contemporary Critiques of International Human Rights and Humanitarianism'. *Qui Parle: Critical Humanities and Social Sciences* 22(1), 3–32.

Mani, L. (1987). 'Contentious Traditions: The Debate on Sati in Colonial India'. *Cultural Critique* (7), 119–56.

———— (1990). 'Multiple Mediations: Feminist Scholarship in the Age of Multinational Reception'. *Feminist Review* (35), 24–41.

Marks, Stephen (2004). 'The Human Right to Development: Between Rhetoric and Reality'. *Harvard Human Rights Journal* 17: 137.

Marks, Susan (2013). 'Four Human Rights Myths'. In David Kinley, Wojciech Sadurski and Kevin Walton (eds), *Human Rights: Old Problems, New Possibilities*. Elgar, 217–35.

Mashkur, M. J. (1978). *A Comparative Dictionary of Arabic, Persian and the Semitic Languages*. Tehran: Bunyad-i-Farhang-i Iran.

Mbembe, A. (2016). 'Decolonizing the University: New Directions'. *Arts and Humanities in Higher Education* 15(1), 29–45.

McCall, L. (2005). 'The Complexity of Intersectionality'. *Signs: Journal of Women in Culture and Society* 30(3), 1771–800.

McCann, M. (2014). 'The Unbearable Lightness of Rights'. *Law & Society Review* 48(2), 245–73.

McClintock, A. (1995). *Imperial Leather: Race, Gender, and Sexuality in the Colonial Contest*. New York: Routledge.

McCloskey, H. J. (1976). 'Rights: Some Conceptual Issues'. *Australasian Journal of Philosophy* 54(2), 99.

———— (1965). 'Rights'. *Philosophical Quarterly* 15(59), 115–27.

McLoughlin, D. (2016). 'Post-Marxism and the Politics of Human Rights: Lefort, Badiou, Agamben, Rancière'. *Law and Critique* 27(3), 303–21.

McNay, L. (2014). *The Misguided Search for the Political*. Cambridge: Polity.

Mehlab, J. (2016). 'Badrunissa: Okara's "Terrorist" Peasant'. Available at https://www.tanqeed.org/2016/05/badr-okara-terrorist-peasant/.

Meister, R. (2002). 'Human Rights and the Politics of Victimhood'. *Ethics & International Affairs* **16**(2), 91–108.

Mendoza, B. (2015). *Coloniality of Gender and Power*. New York: Oxford University Press.

Menon, Nivedita (1999). 'Introduction'. In *Gender and Politics in India*. Delhi: Oxford University Press, 1–36

———— (2004). *Recovering Subversion: Feminist Politics Beyond the Law*. Urbana: University of Illinois Press.

Mernissi, F. (1991). *Women and Islam: An Historical and Theological Enquiry*. Oxford: Basil Blackwell.

Merry, S. E. (2006). *Human Rights and Gender Violence: Translating International Law into Local Justice*. Chicago: University of Chicago Press.

———— (2014). 'Inequality and Rights: A Commentary on Michael McCann's "The Unbearable Lightness of Rights"'. *Law & Society Review* 48(2), 285–95.

Mignolo, Walter D. (2012). *Local Histories/Global Designs: Coloniality, Subaltern Knowledges, and Border Thinking*. Princeton: Princeton University Press.

———— (2000). 'The Many Faces of Cosmo-Polis: Border Thinking and Critical Cosmopolitanism'. *Public Culture* **12**(3), 721–48.

———— (2014). 'From "Human Rights" to "Life Rights"'. In Costas Douzinas and Conor Gearty (eds), *The Meanings of Rights: The Philosophy and Social Theory of Rights*. Cambridge, UK: Cambridge University Press.

———— (2015). 'Sylvia Wynter: What Does It Mean to be Human?' In K. McKittrick (ed.), *Sylvia Wynter: On Being Human as Praxis*. Durham: Duke University Press, 106–23.

Mignolo, Walter, D. and C. E. Walsh (2018). *On Decoloniality: Concepts, Analytics, Praxis*. Duke University Press.

———— (2000). *Local Histories/Global Designs: Coloniality, Subaltern Knowledges, and Border Thinking*. Princeton, NJ: Princeton University Press.

Miller, D. (2012). 'Grounding Human Rights'. *Critical Review of International Social and Political Philosophy* 15(4), 407–27.

Mills, C. W. (2007). 'White Ignorance'. In S. Sullivan and N. Tuana (eds), *Race and Epistemologies of Ignorance*. Albany, NY: State University of New York Press, 13–38.

———— (2017). *Black Rights/White Wrongs: The Critique of Racial Liberalism*. New York: Oxford University Press.

Mir, F. (2010). *The Social Space of Language: Vernacular Culture in British Colonial Punjab*. University of California Press, 161–180.

Mishra, N. (2001). 'Drought and Deaths: A Tale of Persistent and Avoidable Human Misery in Rajasthan'. *Frontline* **18**(8). Available at https://frontline.thehindu.com/static/html/fl1808/18080710.htm (accessed 15 March 2019).

———— (2003). 'People's Right to Information Movement: Lessons from Rajasthan'. UNDP Discussion Paper Series–4: 1–74. New Delhi.

Mohanty, Chandra Talpade (1991). 'Under Western Eyes: Feminist Scholarship and Colonial Discourses'. In Chandra T. Mohanty, Ann Russo and Lourdes Torres (eds), *Third World Women and The Politics Of Feminism*. Bloomington: Indiana University Press, 51–80.

———— (1992) 'Feminist Encounters: Locating the Politics of Experience'. In A. Phillips and M. Barrett (eds), *Destabilising Theory: Contemporary Feminist Debates*. Cambridge: Polity Press, 74–92.

Morris, Madeline (1993). 'Structure of Entitlements'. *Cornell Law Review* **78**(5), 822.

Mosse, D., S. Gupta, M. Mehta, V. Shah, J. Rees and the KRIBP Project Team (2002). 'Brokered Livelihoods: Debt, Labour Migration and Development in Tribal Western India'. *Journal of Development Studies* **38**(5), 59–88.

Moyn, S. (2010). *The Last Utopia*. Cambridge, MA: Harvard University Press.

———— (2014a). *Human Rights and the Uses of History*. London and New York: Verso Books.

———— (2014b). 'A Powerless Companion: Human Rights in the Age of Neoliberalism'. *Law and Contemporary Problems* 77(4), 147–169.

———— (2018). *Not Enough: Human Rights in an Unequal World*. Cambridge, MA: Harvard University Press.

Mumtaz, K. and S. K. Mumtaz (2010). 'Women's Rights and the Punjab Peasant Movement'. *South Asian Journal* **35**, 138–50.

Narayanan, S. and N. Gerber (2017). 'Social Safety Nets for Food and Nutrition Security in India'. *Global Food Security* **15**, 65–76.

Natera, MÁC (2013). 'Postscript: Insurgent Imaginaries and Post-neoliberalism'. In M. Goodale and N. Postero (eds), *Neoliberalism, Interrupted: Social Change and Contested Governance in Contemporary Latin America*. Stanford, CA: Stanford University Press, 249–68.

NDTV (2019). 'Time To Redefine Human Rights Violations In Indian Context: Amit Shah'. Ndtv.com, 13 October. Available at https://www.ndtv.com/india-news/time-to-redefine-human-rights-violations-in-indian-context-home-minister-amit-shah-2115927.

Newberg, P. (2012). 'The Court Rules in Pakistan'. Available at http://yaleglobal.yale.edu/content/court-rules-pakistan (accessed 6 March 2019).

Nickel, James W. (1987). *Making Sense of Human Rights: Philosophical Reflections on the Universal Declaration of Human Rights*. Berkeley: University of California Press.

Nilsen, A. G. and S. Roy (2015). *New Subaltern Politics: Reconceptualizing Hegemony and Resistance in Contemporary India*. Oxford University Press.

Nilsen, A. G. (2016). 'Power, Resistance and Development in the Global South: Notes Towards a Critical Research Agenda. *International Journal Politcs Culture and Society* **29**, 269–87. Available at https://doi.org/10.1007/s10767-016-9224-8.

———— (2018a). *Adivasis and the State: Subalternity and Citizenship in India's Bhil Heartland*. Cambridge: Cambridge University Press.

———— (2018b). 'India's Turn to Rights-Based Legislation (2004–2014): A Critical Review of the Literature'. *Social Change* **48**(4), 653–65.

———— (Forthcoming). 'From Inclusive Neoliberalism to Authoritarian Populism: Trajectories of Change in the World's Largest Democracy'. In M. Ray (ed.), *State of Democracy: Essays on the Life and Politics of Contemporary India*. Delhi: Primus Books.

Nielsen, K. B. and A. G. Nilsen (eds) (2016). *Social Movements and the State in India: Deepening Democracy?* Springer.

Nussbaum, M. (2007). 'Human Rights and Human Capabilities'. *Harvard Human Rights Journal* **20**, 21–24.

Odysseos, L. (2015). 'The Question Concerning Human Rights and Human Rightlessness: Disposability and Struggle in the Bhopal Gas Disaster'. *Third World Quarterly* **36**(6), 1041–59.

Odysseos, L., C. Death and H. Malmvig (2016). 'Interrogating Michel Foucault's Counter-Conduct: Theorising the Subjects and Practices of Resistance in Global Politics'. *Global Society* **30**(2), 151–6.

OHCHR (2016). 'The Minnesota Protocol on the Investigation of Potentially Unlawful Death'. OHCHR, 2017 [1991].

Oldenburg, P. (2010). *India, Pakistan, and Democracy: Solving the Puzzle of Divergent Paths*. London: Routledge.

Ouedghiri M. (2002). 'Writing Women's Bodies on the Palimpsest of Islamic History'. *Cultural Dynamics* **14**(1), 41–64.

Oxford English Dictionary (OED), 2nd ed. (1989). 'Vernacular'. Available at https://www.oed.com/oed2/00276524 (accessed 22 April 2021).

Oxford Poverty and Human Development Initiative (OPHI) (2018). *Global MPI Country Briefing 2018: India (South Asia)*. Oxford. Available at https://ophi.org.uk/wp-content/uploads/CB_IND_2018.pdf (accessed 20 October 2020).

Palriwala, R. and N. Neetha (2009). 'The Care Diamond: State Social Policy and the Market'. UNRISD: 1–47. Geneva.

Pateman, Carole, P. (1988). *The Sexual Contract*. Stanford, CA: Stanford University Press.

Phadke, S. (2003), 'Thirty Years On: Women's Studies Reflects on the Women's Movement'. *Economic and Political Weekly* **8**(43), 4567–76.

Phillips A. (2015). *The Politics of the Human*. Cambridge, UK: Cambridge University Press.

Platts, Thompson John (1884). *A Dictionary of Urdū, Classical Hindī, and English*. Lincoln's Inn Fields, London: Cox and Baylis.

Pollock, S. (1998). 'The Cosmopolitan Vernacular'. *The Journal of Asian Studies* **57**(1), 6–37.

—— (2000). 'Cosmopolitan and Vernacular in History'. *Public Culture* **12**(3), 591-625.

Povinelli, Elizabeth A. (2011). 'Governance of the Prior'. *Interventions: Journal of Postcolonial Studies* **13**(1), 13–30.

Prakash, Gyan (1994). 'Subaltern Studies as Postcolonial Criticism'. *American Historical Review* **99**(5), 1475–90.

Probyn, E. (2003). *Sexing the Self: Gendered Positions in Cultural Studies*. Routledge.

Quijano, A. (2000). 'Coloniality of Power and Eurocentrism in Latin America'. *International Sociology* **15**(2), 215–32.

Rabinow, P. (2011). *The Accompaniment: Assembling the Contemporary*. Chicago: University of Chicago Press.

Rabinow, P. and N. Rose (2006). 'Biopower Today'. *BioSocieties* **1**(2), 195–217.

Raghavan, P. (2020). 'Resisting the Binary: Reconciling Victimhood and Agency in Discourses of Sexual Violence'. Unpublished PhD dissertation, London School of Economics.

Rai, S. M. (2002). *Gender and Political Economy of Development*. Oxford: Polity.

Rajan, R. S. (2003). *The Scandal of the State: Women, Law, and Citizenship in Postcolonial India*. Durham: Duke University Press.

Ramamurthy, P. (2003). 'Material Consumers, Fabricating Subjects: Perplexity, Global Connectivity Discourses, and Transnational Feminist Research'. *Cultural Anthropology* **18**(4), 524–50.

Ram, K., (2008). '"A New Consciousness Must Come": Affectivity and Movement in Tamil Dalit Women's Activist Engagement with Cosmopolitan Modernity'. In Pnina Werbner (ed.), *Anthropology and the New Cosmopolitanism: Rooted, Feminist and Vernacular Perspectives*. Oxford: Berg, 135–55.

—— (2000). The State and the Women's Movement: Instabilities in the Discourse of "Rights" in India'. In Ann-Marie Hildson, Vera Mackie, Martha Macintyre and Maila Stivens (eds), *Human Rights and Gender Politics*: *Asia-Pacific Perspectives*. New York and London: Routledge, 60–82.

Rancière. J. (1999). *Disagreement*. Minneapolis: University of Minnesota Press.

—— (2004). 'Who Is the Subject of the Rights of Man?' *The South Atlantic Quarterly* **103**(2), 297–310.

—— (2010). *Dissensus: On Politics and Aesthetics*. Bloomsbury Publishing.

Rangarajan, M. and Shahabuddin, G. (2006). 'Displacement and Relocation from Protected Areas: Towards a Biological and Historical Synthesis. *Conservation and Society* **4**(3), 359.

Rathore, M.S. (2004). 'State Level Analysis of Drought Policies and Impacts in Rajasthan, India'. International Water Management Institute (IWMI), Working paper 93: Drought Series Paper No. 6: 1–29, 40. Colombo.

Raz, J. (1986). *The Morality of Freedom*. Oxford: Clarendon Press.

—— (2010). 'Human Rights in the Emerging World Order'. *Transnational Legal Theory* **1**(1), 31–47.

Razack, S. H. (2000). 'Gendered Racial Violence and Spatialized Justice: The Murder of Pamela George'. *Canadian Journal of Law & Society/La Revue Canadienne Droit et Société* **15**(2), 91–130.

—— (2004). *Dark Threats and White Knights: The Somalia Affair, Peacekeeping, and the New Imperialism.* University of Toronto Press.

Rege, S. (1998). 'Dalit Women Talk Differently: A Critique of "Difference" and towards a Dalit Feminist Standpoint Position'. *Economic and Political Weekly*, WS39–WS46.

Rich, Adrienne (1984). 'Notes Towards a Politics of Location'. In *Blood, Bread and Poetry: Selected Prose 1979–1985.* London: Virago.

Rizvi, Mubbashir (2019). 'A Divided Movement: Urban Activists, NGOs, and the Fault-Lines of a Peasant Struggle'. *South Asian History and Culture* **10**(3), 295–308.

Robinson, Francis 1974. *Separatism Among Indian Muslims.* Cambridge: Cambridge University Press.

Roberts, A. (2006). *Blacked Out: Government Secrecy in the Information Age.* Cambridge: Cambridge University Press.

Rodríguez, Ileana and María Milagros López (eds) (2001). *The Latin American Subaltern Studies Reader.* Durham, NC: Duke University Press.

Rojas, Cristina (2013). 'Acts of Indigenship: Historical Struggles for Equality and Colonial Difference in Bolivia'. *Citizenship Studies* **17**(5), 581–95.

Rose, N. (1999). *Powers of Freedom: Reframing Political Thought.* Cambridge University Press.

Rosen L. (1980). 'Equity and Discretion in a Modern Islamic Legal System'. *Law and Society Review* **15**(2), 217–45.

Rosenberg, J. (2014). 'The Molecularization of Sexuality: On Some Primitivisms of the Present'. *Theory and Event* **16**(2). Available at: https://muse.jhu.edu/article/546470.

Rowena, Jenny. 2013. 'The Protests in Delhi and the Nationalist Paradigm'. Savari (blog). Available at http://www.dalitweb.org/?p=1510 (accessed 9 June 2021).

Roy, Aruna and Nikhil Dey (2012). 'Much More Than a Survival Scheme'. *The Hindu*, 31 August. Available at https://www.thehindu.com/opinion/lead/much-more-than-a-survival-scheme/article3840977.ece.

Roy, Srila (2015). 'The Indian Women's Movement: Within and Beyond NGOization'. *Journal of South Asian Development* **10**(1), 96–117.

—— (2017). 'Enacting/Disrupting the Will to Empower: Feminist Governance of "Child Marriage" in Eastern India'. *Signs: Journal of Women in Culture and Society* **42**(4), 867–91.

Sabsay, L. (2016). *The Political Imaginary of Sexual Freedom: Subjectivity and Power in the New Sexual Democratic Turn*. London: Palgrave.

Said, E. W. (2002). 'Traveling Theory Reconsidered'. In *Reflections on Exile and Other Essays*. Cambridge, MA: Harvard University Press.

——— (1979). *Orientalism*. New York: Vintage.

——— (1994). *Representations of the Intellectual*. New York: Vintage.

Saigol, Rubina (2004). 'Ownership or Death: Peasant Farmer's Struggle in the Punjab'. WISCOMP Project on Non-Traditional Security, New Delhi.

Salomon, M. E. (2013). 'From NIEO to Now and the Unfinishable Story of Economic Justice'. *International & Comparative Law Quarterly* **62**(1), 31–54.

Sanyal, K. (2014). *Rethinking Capitalist Development: Primitive Accumulation, Governmentality and Post-Colonial Capitalism*. Routledge India.

Sardar Ali, Shaheen (2012). *Overlapping Discursive Terrains of Culture, Law and Women's Rights: An Exploratory Study on Legal Pluralism at Play in Pakistan*. Legal Studies Research Paper no. 2012-09, University of Warwick Law School, University of Warwick.

Sato, H. (2017). 'The Universality, Peculiarity, and Sustainability of Indian Public Interest Litigation Reconsidered'. *World Development* **100**, 59–68.

Schimmel A. (1975). *Mystical Dimensions of Islam*. Chapel Hill: University of North Carolina Press.

Scott, J. W. (1997). *Only Paradoxes to Offer*. Harvard University Press.

Selmeczi, A. (2015). 'Who Is the Subject of Neoliberal Rights? Governmentality, Subjectification and rhe Letter of the Law'. *Third World Quarterly* **36**(6), 1076–91.

Sen, A. (2005). 'Human Rights and Capabilities'. *Journal of Human Development* **6**(2), 151–66.

——— (1986). *Food, Economics, and Entitlements*. Helsinki: World Institute for Development Economics Research, United Nations University.

Sengupta, A. (2002). 'On the Theory and Practice of the Right to Development'. *Human Rights Quarterly* **24**(4), 837–89.

Shah, Mihir (2007). 'Employment Guarantee, Civil Society and Indian Democracy'. *Economic and Political Weekly* **42**(45–46).

——— (2005). 'First You Push Them In, Then You Throw Them Out'. *Economic and Political Weekly* **40**(47).

Shaheed, Farida (2010). 'The Women's Movement in Pakistan: Challenges and Achievements'. In Amrita Basu (ed.), *Women's Movements in the Global Era: The Power of Local Feminisms*. Boulder, CO: Westview Press.

Shankar, Shylashri and Pratap Bhanu Mehta (2008). 'Courts and Socioeconomic Rights in India'. In Varun Gauri and Daniel M. Brinks (eds), *Courting Social Justice: Judicial Enforcement of Social and Economic Rights in the Developing World*. New York: Cambridge University Press, 146–82.

Sharma, Aradhana (2013). 'State Transparency After the Neoliberal Turn: The Politics, Limits, and Paradoxes of India's Right to Information Law'. *PoLAR: Political and Legal Anthropology Review* **36**(2), 308–25.

Sharma, Saurabh (2013). 'Rajasthan Among Bottom Five in Literacy Level for SC/STS: Survey'. *Times of India*, 2 November. Available at https://timesofindia. indiatimes.com/city/jaipur/Rajasthan-among-bottom-fivein-in-literacy-level-for-SC/STs-Survey/articleshow/25079442.cms?utm_source=contento-finterest&utm_medium=text&utm_campaign=cppst.

Shehzad, Mohammad (2004). 'Fighting the Army for Farmland'. In *Paid Enough and No More: The Great Peasant Revolt in Pakistan (2001–2003)*. Labour Party Pakistan Publications.

Sheikh, Saad Sarfraz (2016). 'How Okara Farmers Have Become the Latest "Enemies" of the State'. *The Herald*, 23 August. Available at http://herald. dawn.com/news/1153506 (accessed 24 November 2020).

Shrivastava, K.S. (2018). 'From Compulsory Consent to No Consultation: How the Government Diluted Adivasi Rights to Forestlands'. Available at https:// scroll.in/article/871191/from-compulsory-consent-to-no-consultation-how-the-government-diluted-adivasi-rights-to-forestlands (accessed on March 10).

Siddiqa, A. (2007). *Military Inc.* London: Pluto Press.

Sigel, B. (2016). '"Self-Help Which Ennobles a Nation": Development, Citizenship, and the Obligations of Eating in India's Austerity Years'. *Modern Asian Studies* **50**(3), 975–1018.

Sikkink, K. (2017). *Evidence for Hop: Making Human Rights Work in the 21st Century*. Princeton, NJ: Princeton University Press.

Simmonds, N. E. (1998). 'Rights at the Cutting Edge'. In M. H. Kramer (ed.), *A Debate over Rights*. Oxford: Oxford University Press, 142.

Simpson, Audra (2014). *Mohawk Interruptus: Political Life Across the Borders of Settler States*. Duke University Press.

——— (2016). 'The State is a Man: Theresa Spence, Loretta Saunders and the Gender of Settler Sovereignty'. *Theory & Event* **19**(4). Available at *Project MUSE*, muse.jhu.edu/article/633280.

Sinha, S. (2015). 'On the Edge of Civil Society in India'. In A. G. Nilsen and S. Roy (eds), *New Subaltern Politics*. Oxford: Oxford University Press.

Slaughter, J. (2007). *Human Rights, Inc.: The World Novel, Narrative Form, and International Law*. Fordham University Press.

Slobodian, Quinn (2018). *Globalists: The End of Empire and the Birth of Neoliberalism*. Harvard University Press.

Smith L. T. (1999). *Decolonizing Methodologies: Research and Indigenous Peoples*. London: Zed Books.

Spivak G. C. (2002). 'Righting Wrongs'. In N. Owen (ed.), *Human Rights, Human Wrongs: The Oxford Amnesty Lectures*. Oxford: Oxford University Press.

—— (1999). *A Critique of Postcolonial Reason*. Cambridge, MA: Harvard University Press.

—— (1988). 'Can the Subaltern Speak?' In C. Nelson and L. Grossberg (eds), *Marxism and the Interpretation of Culture*. Basingstoke: MacMillan Education, 271–306.

Suárez-Krabbe, J. (2016). *Race, Rights and Rebels: Alternatives to Human Rights and Development from the Global South*. Rowman & Littlefield.

Sundar, Nandini (2016). 'Introduction: Of the Scheduled Tribes, States and Sociology'. In *The Scheduled Tribes and Their India: Politics, Identities, Policies, and Work*. Oxford University Press, 1–46.

Tariq, Farooq (2016). 'Pakistan: Anti-Terror Laws Used against Peasants' Movement'. *GreenLeft.com*, 19 July. Available at https://www.greenleft.org.au/content/pakistan-anti-terror-laws-used-against-peasants-movement.

Taylor, C. (2002). 'Modern Social Imaginaries'. *Public Culture* **14**(1).

The Dawn (2005). 'Senate Seeks Report on Okara Farms'. *Dawn.com*, 15 January. Available at https://www.dawn.com/news/380383 (accessed 23 November 2020).

—— (2020). 'AMP Former Secretary Acquitted of Charges'. 9 September. Available at https://www.dawn.com/news/1578629 (accessed 20 February 2021).

The Hindu (2019a). 'Expand Definition of Human Rights: Amit Shah'. 13 October. Available at https://www.thehindu.com/news/national/other-states/expand-definition -of-human-rights-amit-shah/article29669758.ece (accessed 20 October 2020).

—— (2019b). 'Gehlot Government Gears Up for the Social Accountability Bill'. 19 February. Available at https://www.thehindu.com/news/national/other-states/gehlot-govt-gears-up-for-social-accountability-bill/article26307072.ece.

—— (2019c). 'Process to Bring Accountability Law to Start Soon In Rajasthan'. 28 January. Available at https://www.thehindu.com/news/national/other-states/process-to-bring-accountability-law-to-start-soon-in-rajasthan/article26114521.ece.

The Nation (2016). 'PPP Moves Senate on Okara Farms Issue'. 10 May. Available at https://nation.com.pk/10-May-2016/ppp-moves-senate-on-okara-farms-issue.

The Wire (2019). 'Western Standards on Human Rights Can't Be Blindly Applied to India: Amit Shah'. 13 October. Available at https://thewire.in/politics/western-standards-on-human-rights-cant-be-blindly-applied-to-india-amit-shah.

Ticktin, M. (2011). 'The Gendered Human of Humanitarianism: Medicalising and Politicising Sexual Violence'. *Gender & History* **23**(2), 250–65.

—— (2014). 'Transnational Humanitarianism'. *Annual Review of Anthropology* **43**, 273–89.

Times of India (2018). 'Rajasthan Assembly Elections 2018: Women Outshine Men in Voting Percentage Across Rajasthan'. 9 December. Available at https://timesofindia.indiatimes.com/city/jaipur/women-outshine-men-in-voting-percentage-across-raj/articleshow/67006922.cms.

Todd, Zoe (2016). 'An Indigenous Feminist's Take on the Ontological Turn: "Ontology" Is Just Another Word for Colonialism'. *Journal of Historical Sociology* **29**(1), 4–22.

Tola, M. (2018). 'Between Pachamama and Mother Earth: Gender, Political Ontology and the Rights of Nature in Contemporary Bolivia'. *Feminist Review* **118**(1), 25–40.

Trouillot, M. R. (1995). *Silencing the Past: Power and The Production of History.* Boston: Beacon Press.

Tuck, E. and K. W. Yang (2012). 'Decolonization Is Not a Metaphor'. *Decolonization: Indigeneity, Education & Society* **1**(1).

UNDP (2013). 'Rajasthan: Economic and Human Development Indicators'. 20 February. Available at http://www.in.undp.org/content/dam/india/docs/rajasthan_factsheet.pdf.

——— (2016a). 'Human Development Report'. Available at http://hdr.undp.org/sites/default/files/2016_human_development_report.pdf.

——— (2016b). 'About Pakistan'. Available at http://www.pk.undp.org/content/pakistan/en/home/countryinfo/.

——— (2016c). 'Inequality: Missing from the Public Agenda'. *Development Advocate Pakistan* **3**(2), 1–25. Available at http://www.pk.undp.org/content/pakistan/en/home/library/hiv_aids/development-advocatepakistan--volume-3--issue-2.html.

——— (2016d). 'Water Security in Pakistan: Issues and Challenges'. *Development Advocate Pakistan* **3**(4). Available at http://www.pk.undp.org/content/pakistan/en/home/library/hiv_aids/development-advocatepakistan--volume-3--issue-4.

——— (2016e). *Human Development 2016: Human Development for Everyone.* New York: UNDP.

——— (2016f). *Development Advocate Pakistan* **3**(2), 28 July. Available at https://www.pk.undp. org/content/pakistan/en/home/library/development_policy/development -advocate-pakistan--volume-3--issue-2.html.

Vimalassery, M., J. H. Pegues and A. Goldstein (2016). 'Introduction: On Colonial Unknowing'. *Theory & Event* **19**(4).

Visweswaran, Kamala (2010). *Un/common Cultures: Racism and the Rearticulation of Cultural Difference.* Durham, NC: Duke University Press.

Wallerstein, I. (1997). 'Eurocentrism and Its Avatars: The Dilemmas of Social Science'. *Sociological Bulletin* **46**(1), 21–39.

Waseem, M. (2012). 'Clash of Institutions in Pakistan'. *Economic and Political Weekly* **47**(28), 16–18.

Wasserstrom, Richard (1964). 'Rights, Human Rights and Racial Discrimination'. *Journal of Philosophy* **61**(20), 628–41.

Weeks, K. (2011). *The Problem with Work: Feminism, Marxism, Antiwork Politics, and Postwork Imaginaries*. Durham, NC: Duke University Press.

Weizman, E. (2011). *The Least of All Possible Evils: Humanitarian Violence from Arendt to Gaza*. Verso Books.

Whyte, J. (2017). 'Human Rights and the Collateral Damage of Neoliberalism'. *Theory & Event* **20**(1), 137–51.

——— (2018). 'Powerless Companions or Fellow Travellers? Human Rights and the Neoliberal Assault on Post-Colonial Economic Justice'. *Radical Philosophy*, 13–29.

Wiegman, R. and Elam, D. (1993). *Feminism Beside Itself*. Routledge.

Wilfred, Cantwell Smith (1971). 'A Human View of Truth Studies in Religion'. *Studies in Religion/Sciences Religieuses*, **1**(1), 6–24.

Wilson, K. (2012). *Race, Racism and Development: Interrogating History, Discourse and Practice*. London: Zed Books.

Wilson, R. A. (1997). 'Human Rights, Culture and Context: An Introduction'. In R. A. Wilson (ed.), *Human Rights, Culture and Context: Anthropological Perspectives*. London: Pluto Press.

Wolfe, P. (2006). 'Settler Colonialism and the Elimination of the Native'. *Journal of Genocide Research* **8**(4), 387–409.

World Bank. 'Rajasthan: Social Inclusion'. Available at http://documents1.worldbank.org/curated/en/255081468179096086/pdf/105876-BRI-P157572-ADD-SERIES-India-state-briefs-PUBLIC-Rajasthan-Social.pdf.

Wynter, S. (2003). 'Unsettling the Coloniality of Being/Power/Truth/Freedom: Towards the Human, After Man, Its Overrepresentation—An Argument'. *The New Centennial Review* **3**(3), 253–337.

Xaxa, V. (1999). 'Tribes as Indigenous People of India'. *Economic and Political Weekly* **34**(51), 3589–95.

Yamunan, Sruthisagar (2020). 'Kashmir: SC Beautifully Articulates Principle of Fundamental Rights–But Fails to Restore Them'. *Scroll.in*, 10 January. Available at https://scroll.in/article/949427/kashmir-sc-beautifully-articulates-principle-of-fundamental-rights-but-fails-to-restore-them.

Young, Iris Marion (1985). 'Impartiality and the Civic Public: Some Implications of Feminist Critiques of Moral and Political Theory'. *Praxis International* **5**(4), 381–401.

Index

For EU product safety concerns, contact us at Calle de José Abascal, 56–1°,
28003 Madrid, Spain or eugpsr@cambridge.org.